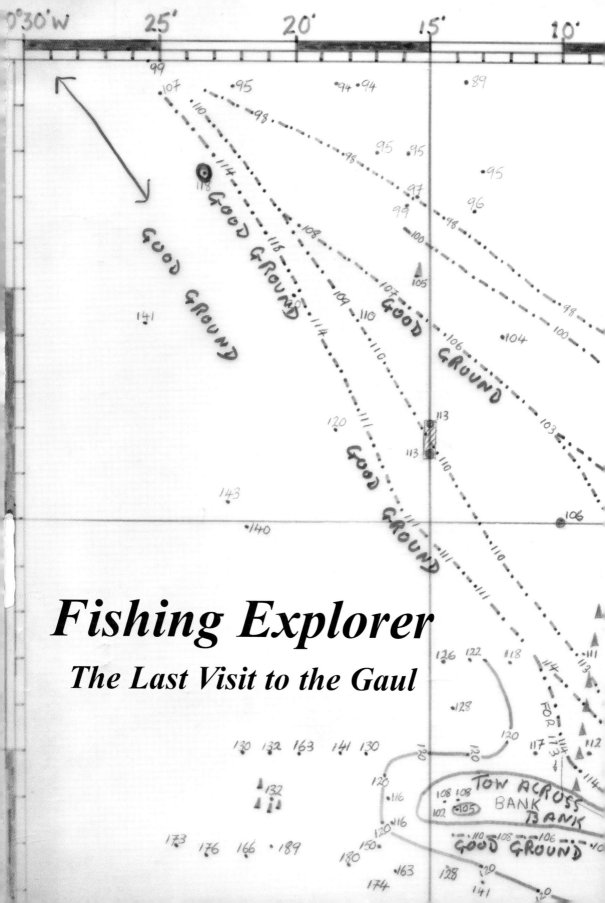

Fishing Explorer

The Last Visit to the Gaul

Ernest Suddaby

Fishing Explorer

The Last Visit to the Gaul

Printed by: Prinfo Unique, Larvik, Norway

Front Cover: This painting of the Gaul, seen here as the Ranger Castor in
                       her original Ranger Fishing Company colours, was painted
                       by Hull artist Eric Wedge.

Inside Covers   These are much-used handmade plotter charts of Falkland fishing
                       grounds that were used on board the Fishing Explorer

Back cover: The Author at Hull's St Andrew's Dock as it is today.
                       Photo: Quentin Bates

Design/layout: Krohn Johansen Forlag AS / Quentin Bates
Published by: Maritime Info UK Ltd, Hexham, UK

ISBN: 978-0-9557913-0-7

Maritime Info UK Ltd

2 Canon Savage Drive, Highford Park, Hexham NE46 2PE

Tel: +44 (0)7958 625 254
Email: admin@maritimeinfouk.com

Index

Introduction

by Alan Johnson,
MP for West Hull and Hessle

One of the most respected distant water trawler skippers of his generation, Ernie Suddaby grew up on Hull's Hessle Road and went to sea at a young age. My first introduction to him came shortly after my election as Member of Parliament for West Hull and Hessle, when I sought his personal views on the loss of the Gaul.

Throughout the thirty years since the disappearance of the Gaul in the Barents Sea, he had consistently stuck to his opinions on what he believed happened during that severe storm on Cape Bank.

The inquiry in 2004 supported his view. However, Ernie has not agreed with every conclusion that the inquiry reached. He has not been shy in saying so, but nothing less could be expected of a man who has always spoken his mind, although often with a wry sense of humour behind his plain speaking.

He is a remarkable character, and all the more remarkable for being the only Hull trawler skipper to have written a book of his experiences in both North and South Atlantic, spanning the heyday of the British fishing industry that Hull played such a large part in, to the decline of the distant water fleet that has now all but disappeared.

Ernie pulls no punches in his book - laying the blame for the loss of this once strong and vibrant industry firmly at the feet the European Union and successive British governments, as well as on those at the helm of the industry who preferred to leave than to seek new challenges.

Alan Johnson MP
Hull
December 2005

About the author

Ernest Suddaby grew up about as close as you could possibly get to the centre of Hull's fishing industry. The youngest of three brothers who also went to sea, he was born in Eton Street, just off Hessle Road, and only a stone's throw away from the fish docks themselves.

Apart from the fifteen months spent in the North Yorkshire village of Wrelton, where he was evacuated at the outbreak of the Second World War, he was educated at the famous West Dock Avenue Boys' School, which was situ-

Skipper Ernie Suddaby, now ashore and retired, with his wife Sylvia.

ated a few yards from the fish docks. A keen sportsman and rugby league supporter, he has followed the fortunes of Hull RFC since his schooldays, and has visited every rugby league ground in the north of England.

Not surprisingly, coming from a fishing family that moved north from Brixham in Devon as fishing in Hull began to flourish, he found himself contemplating a career at sea and after spending two years working on the fish docks, he sailed on his first trip to sea at sixteen on the old coal-burning trawler Tervani. Early years as a deckhand were spent with FT Ross and J Marr before moving on to Hellyer Brothers, where he spent most of his fishing career.

Having sailed in many of the old coal burning trawlers, he witnessed all of the major changes that took place in the fishing industry as the older type of trawlers made way for the newly built fleet of oil burners, the diesel-engined trawlers, and the emergence of a fine fleet of freezer stern trawlers.

On obtaining his mate's certificate in 1961, he served as mate of the Portia, a trawler that had the distinction of being the first Hull diesel-electric trawler. He also sailed in the Portia's sister ship, Falstaff, as well as in a number of other Hellyer Brothers trawlers.

On obtaining his skipper's certificate in 1963, his first command was the Loch Inver, and in later years as the trend towards freezing fish at sea became stronger, he went on to become skipper of the ill-fated factory trawler Gaul, which was lost with all hands off the North Cape of Norway in 1974 in severe weather conditions.

After leaving fishing in the UK, he spent several years fishing in the Falklands on Spanish owned trawlers and skippered several North Sea oil industry standby vessels before his retirement.

Since retiring, he has assisted the MAIB on a number of occasions since the wreck of the Gaul was located in 1997 and in 2002 sailed with the survey vessel Seisranger, which was chartered to carry out a full survey at the wreck site, returning with the remains of four of the crew of the Gaul almost thirty years after her loss.

Today he still lives in Hull. His saddest moment was seeing how the fishing industry came to an end and the greatest insult was to be classed a casual worker by people who would not know the stem of a trawler from the stern.

Acknowledgements

I would like to express my sincere thanks to those people who contributed so much in helping me put this book together and hopefully into making it an enjoyable read.

The pictures used in the book came from a variety of sources and in some cases the photographers are unknown in spite of efforts to track them down. I would like to thank Neil Murray and his team at Kingfisher Marine Services for their help and permission to charts that feature in the book, Eric Wedge for the use of part of his collection of photographs and his painting of the Gaul, Peter Horsley of Fleetwood for his photograph of Jacinta, Ted Lambert for the pictures of the Ross Orion and Phil Lockley of Fishing News for his photographs of Fishing Explorer.

Thanks are due to Quentin Bates, without whose advice and encouragement Fishing Explorer would not have got off the ground and to David Saltiel of the Royal National Mission to Deep Sea Fishermen for his encouragement.

Thanks are due in no small part to the inspectors of the Marine Accident Investigation Branch and especially to the captain and crew of the Seisranger for their hospitality and for a job well done during the survey of the wreck of the Gaul in the summer of 2002.

Finally, my wife Sylvia deserves my deepest thanks and appreciation for her years of patience.

Ernie Suddaby
Hull
December 2005

Returning To Fishing

After five years away from deep sea fishing, if anyone had asked me if I fancied returning to the job, my answer would have been a definite no.

I had completed what could be described as a lifetime at sea, doing what has been described as the most dangerous job in the world - deep sea fishing - a fact that few people would dispute, especially those connected in any way with the catching side of the fishing industry.

Deep sea trawling had been a way of life that brought much grief and sadness to the Humber ports of Hull and Grimsby, as well as to the fishing ports of Fleetwood and Aberdeen. This is a way of life that has over the years seen the tightly knit fishing communities of these four major deep sea fishing ports shattered time and again by the appalling losses of men and ships.

These losses had occurrd all over the northern hemisphere where fishermen had pursued shoals of fish in far flung waters, from Newfoundland, Greenland and Labrador in the west to the notorious water to be found off Iceland's North Cape. To the east, British fishermen found fishing grounds well beyond the Arctic Circle off the North of Norway, further east into the Barents Sea, along the Russian coast past Murmansk and eastwards to Cape Kanin. Places such as Spitzbergen and Bear Island has provided fishermen from Britain with some excellent rewards, yet for all this the costs in men and ships in these high northern latitudes had been high ever since British trawlers had opened up these distant water fishing grounds.

Since I had started going to sea I had fished these waters time and again, from a sixteen year old deckhand on the old coal-burning trawlers that were then coming to the end of their lives after returning from war service, and later as skipper of several sophisticated filleter factory trawlers, including the ill-fated Gaul, lost with all hands in February 1974 in severe weather conditions off the North Cape of Norway.

After all this, why go back to it at all?

The answer was simple. Instead of heading north beyond the Arctic Circle to familiar fishing grounds, this trip offered something of a different challenge. We would be heading south and crossing the equator to fish the waters around the Falkland Islands.

I had steady work delivering trawlers, mostly to Spain, and had just flown back from there in early 1985 after delivering the old trawler Boston Argosy to her new owners in the Spanish port of Vigo. As I walked through Millbay Docks in Plymouth towards the office of the company for whom I had completed the delivery, I could not help but notice a large stern trawler that was tied up on the opposite side of the dock.

It was not until I was directly opposite her that I stopped to take a closer look. Although unable to make out her name, it did not take me long to see that she was not an ex-Hull freezer, and I was just as sure that she was not from Grimsby. I was quite familiar with most of the freezer trawlers that had operated out of the two Humber ports, but could not recall having seen this particular ship before.

Not wanting to waste too much time, I carried on to the office, and after reporting on the smooth delivery, I was able to learn something about the freezer alongside in Millbay Docks. Her name was the Barreros Masso Dos, and she was in the process of being refitted. Built in Spain, she had spent most of her time fishing from Chile, which explained why I was not familiar with her lines

My stay in Plymouth turned out to be very brief. I was booked on the overnight sleeper from Plymouth to proceed from London to Lowestoft to deliver yet another British side trawler, the Suffolk Endeavour, to new Spanish owners in La Coruña.

Within two hours of arriving in Lowestoft, I was again at sea. After a brief word with the new owner, we cast off and made our way towards the English Channel.

The weather remained fine as we made our way through the Channel, and twice within the same January week I found myself crossing the Bay of Biscay in near perfect weather, delivering another British trawler to end her days fishing out of Spain.

The crossing was uneventful, and the weather remained perfect all the way across the Bay of Biscay, until we tied up alongside on a Sunday afternoon in La Coruña.

After going through the usual formalities of clearing the ship and having a few more words with the owner, who had chosen to fly home to Spain, it was decided that we would stay in a hotel for the weekend before flying back to England on Monday afternoon. This was my first visit to La Coruña, and after a meal with the chief engineer, we spent the night looking around and having a drink before returning to the hotel and a few hours' sleep.

A walk after breakfast in the hotel the following morning inevitably took us to the docks, where to our surprise, work had already started on the Suffolk Endeavour. The new owner greeted us and told us that he planned to fit a shelterdeck and one or two other modifications before the ship sailed. The chief engineer was asked if he was prepared to work for a few days on the ship before returning home, and after coming to an agreement, we continued our walk along the La Coruña docks, a walk that turned out to be a stroll down memory lane. Scattered all over were ex-British trawlers that had been sold to Spain. Ships that had been household names in our deep sea ports brought memories flooding back.

As I walked towards the former Hull freezer trawler Sir Fred Parkes, I cast my mind back to the number of times that I had fished alongside her. The last time had been at Newfoundland when things were already showing signs of going into decline for our deep sea fishing industry. I had known her skipper very well, yet here Sir Fred Parkes was preparing to go to sea once more for her new Spanish owners.

Our walk along the La Coruña dock was tinged with a little sadness at the number of former British trawlers that had been sold to Spain, and would now be fishing grounds around the coast of Britain.

Later in the day that I was informed that our plans had changed, and instead of flying home, I was to join the Spanish trawler Monte Maigmo to take her to Castletown in Ireland to hand her over to the skipper and men who would form the bulk of her crew, who would be arriving from Grimsby.

After a meal and a few drinks the following morning, I said goodbye to the chief engineer who had accompanied me on the Suffolk Endeavour, walked the short distance to the Monte Maigmo and introduced myself to the owner, who was also the skipper. He was a likable middle-aged man, who explained that he was not very familiar with the approaches to Castletown, and would leave everything to me until we arrived there.

After letting go, we steamed out of La Coruña, along with about five other Spanish trawlers, all heading towards the fishing grounds to the south-west of Ireland.

What wind there was came from the north, and although there was something of a swell, the conditions were reasonable for the time of year. Unfortunately, it was not forecast to last. When I left the bridge at midnight, the weather was no worse, and the lights of the ships that had sailed with us were still clearly visible as I handed over the watch.

The following morning the wind had increased to a northerly force five, but still presented no problems, and during the morning watch I had a chance to talk with the skipper-owner about the problems that were emerging in the fishing industry, both in Spain and in Britain. It was pleasant to listen to the opinions of the owner, who had found it very expensive to bring the Monte Maigmo up to the standards required by the DTI in Britain. One thing that we did agree on was that there would be plenty of problems in store for the fishing industry in the years ahead.

There were just seven of us on board the Monte Maigmo, with the rest of her full crew of fourteen due to join her as I left in Castletown. They would take her fishing for about twelve days before returning once again to land her fish in La Coruña.

During the next day the weather deteriorated even more, and with the heavy rain squalls throughout the morning, it was just as well that we expected to be arriving in Castletown at 20.00.

It was raining heavily when we approached Castletown, but after a heavy shower we picked out the leading lights and shortly after tied up alongside on what promised to be a wet and windy night for those still out at sea.

Within the hour I had handed over to my relief, and after wishing the owner good luck and good fishing, joined the ship's agent, who drove me to my hotel where I was to stay until a flight could be arranged for me direct from Cork to Plymouth.

At the hotel I once again chatted with the agent over a drink at the bar. He explained that it was possible that I could be in Castletown for up to three days, as it was not always easy getting a direct flight from Cork to Plymouth.

The following morning, I emerged from the hotel just in time to see the Monte Maigmo making her way out of Castletown, and although the weather did not appear to be very good, it was possible that he would not start fishing for some time. Most of the local boats remained tied up in the harbour, another indication that the weather outside was still too bad for fishing.

Most of my time in Castletown was spent around the local harbour, where I got to know a number of the local fishermen, and after being invited on board some of the local trawlers it was always the usual topic of conversation: fishing, fishing, and yet more fishing. Yet it is always interesting to hear new ideas and points of view.

On my third night in Castletown, I was informed that I would be on a flight for Plymouth the following afternoon, and would be leaving for Cork in the morning. It had been an enjoyable time in Castletown, and the hospitality had been first class. The following morning I was on my way to Cork, and after visiting an injured British fisherman in the hospital with the agent, I arrived at Cork airport just in time to hear the announcement that the flight had been delayed for two hours.

The weather was not good when we eventually took off from Cork, and by the time I arrived in Plymouth it was even worse with plenty of wind and heavy rain making it a very bad night indeed. After arriving at the hotel, it was a relief to hear there were no messages waiting for me.

At the office in Plymouth the next day, it came as no great surprise when I was asked if I was interested in a position as skipper of the freezer trawler that was tied up in Millbay Docks, now named Fishing Explorer. There was still a large amount of work to be done to the vessel, leaving me the weekend to think things over. But as there would be a large volume of paperwork that would need the skipper's signature the following week, I was asked to give my decision as soon as possible.

Later that morning, along with the ship's agent, I was taken aboard the Fishing Explorer to have a look around, and also to discuss what plans were being laid down for the ship, how long was she likely to be away, and where she would be fishing. Over a coffee in the lounge, everything was explained.

The plans were that the Fishing Explorer, after completing her DTI inspection to bring her up to British standards, would then return to La Coruña in Spain for a week and then proceed to the south Atlantic and fish the waters around the Falkland Islands.

There were a number of things to discuss. I had been away from this type of vessel for some years, and was not too sure that I was prepared to spend so much time at sea on what was obviously going to be a long trip.

By the middle of the afternoon, I had been given the full details, and left the Fishing Explorer with a weekend to think things over. I liked what I had seen of the 200 foot ship, a classic freezer stern trawler built in Spain, nicely laid out and very comfortable. She was a fine ship, not new, but had adequate power for fishing and to handle bad weather. Financially the terms were quite good, yet the only lingering doubts I had were over the length of time that we would be away.

I could not imagine conditions in the Falklands being any worse than the North Cape of Iceland or Bear Island in the wintertime, when ships had spent days on end dodging in heavy weather and freezing conditions, or running for shelter iced up. The Fishing

My first sight of the Fishing Explorer, during the frantic preparations in port in Plymouth to get the ship ready for sea.
Photos: Phil Lockley

Explorer looked like the type of vessel that could handle the weather we would obviously experience at some time down in the south Atlantic.

Eventually, the following day, and after listening to all kinds of reasons why I should accept the job, I accepted the position, and the following morning joined the Fishing Explorer, walking headlong into the vast and ever increasing sea of paperwork that seems to get bigger with every trip.

My first day on the Fishing Explorer was spent entirely dealing with floods of paperwork that had built up since the vessel's arrival in Plymouth, and which must have been responsible for the loss of at least one rainforest somewhere in the world.

Once I had installed myself on board the Fishing Explorer, I was able to make steady progress through my mountain of paperwork, and by 20.00 readily accepted the invitation to go ashore for a drink with a couple of friends who had been working all day on the vessel.

From these two I learned that the work on the Fishing Explorer was expected to continue throughout the next day, and would probably be finished about midday on the day after, so we would possibly sail later on that same day.

Returning to the Fishing Explorer around midnight, I soon found out that I had made a big mistake in moving on to the vessel from my hotel. In order to get the Fishing Explorer ready for sea the following day, work continued throughout the night, which made any sleep impossible.

The next day was just as hectic. Overnight a light covering of snow had fallen and it was still very cold, which did nothing to help the people still busy working on deck. As for myself, I made great inroads into most of the paperwork, and by midday had filed most of these documents away. After dispatching numerous packages and parcels to different parts of the ship, I was at last able to see the full extent of the living quarters where I would be spending the next few months.

My accommodation was quite spacious, with a separate dayroom containing a large desk which had already served its purpose well. New carpets had been fitted during the morning, and by midday my quarters bore no resemblance to what I had walked into just 36 hours before.

Throughout the day all kinds of items continued to arrive on board the Fishing Explorer - including inflatable liferafts and a number of fire extinguishers - mostly concerning the safety of the ship. Slowly but surely the Fishing Explorer once again began to resemble a fishing vessel.

Over the midday meal we were able to discuss what remaining work there was to do, and it seemed obvious that only some sort of delay in the arrival of more official papers would delay us from sailing the next day. Work continued, although most of the workforce had left the ship, leaving just a dozen men who would again be at work through the night completing more welding.

This would clearly be our last night ashore in Plymouth, and as can be expected, something by way of a small celebration was due. The hard bit had been done and it was time to unwind, and also to say goodbye to the number of friends I had made during the time that I had spent in Plymouth.

The Fishing Explorer had attracted a lot of interest in Plymouth during her stay. She had been featured in the press and a number of people had visited the ship when they had read or heard that she was bound for the Falkland Islands. The last night went well, and many people left the warmth of their homes to wish us well and join us for a farewell drink before we sailed.

On returning to the Fishing Explorer shortly after midnight, work on the vessel was still continuing, but not to the extent of the previous two nights, which allowed most of us something of a decent night's sleep.

Work on board was expected to continue throughout our final day, right up until we were due to sail at 1800, and all the time increasing amounts of paperwork continued to arrive at regular intervals. With the Fishing Explorer now officially registered as British, it was explained that we would have to carry a radio officer. After a desperate search at short notice, Sean Brooks, fresh out of college the previous day with his brand new radio officer's certificate, joined the Fishing Explorer for his first trip to sea, making up the other half of the British contingent.

This final day was typical of most sailing days, with people attending to all kinds of last minute instructions. But midway through the afternoon, people began to remove some of the equipment that had been used on board - a good sign that we would soon be sailing.

At 17.00, just before the evening meal, the engines were started and at last all that remained was to prepare the ship for sea and to see the remainder of the shore personnel safely off the ship. At last the Fishing Explorer was ready.

With her engines now running, the whole ship began to warm up as the workmen left. The crew had been busy laying carpets and various other jobs prior to sailing. However, at 18.30 all work was halted as the crew gathered on deck to take in the gangplank and prepare for sailing.

The author at the desk in Fishing Explorer's dayroom, making inroads into the mountain of paperwork that needed immediate attention.

Leaving Plymouth Behind

A small group of people gathered on Trinity Pier to give the Fishing Explorer an enthusiastic send-off as she slowly edged her way out of Millbay and into Plymouth Sound.

Apart from a couple of small inshore trawlers making their way back into Sutton Harbour after a day's fishing, there was nothing ahead of us as I steadily began to increase speed and we moved out into the English Channel. It was still bitterly cold and the northerly wind was forecast to continue for the rest of the week. However, in the warmth of the ship's bridge, all thoughts of weather disappeared at it seemed we would once again have a good passage across the Bay of Biscay.

With the lights of Plymouth astern, I increased our speed as we began what turned out to be a routine trip to La Coruña. The only thing to disturb us were frequent calls on Channel 16 concerning a coaster carrying explosives which had suffered a fire on board, but which had since been taken in tow. Things looked to be pretty much routine on our passage to La Coruña.

Before being relieved on the bridge at midnight, I remembered the number of times in recent weeks that I had crossed the Bay of Biscay, and on each occasion the weather had remained fine. After waiting up for the late shipping forecast, there was every indication that the weather would remain fine for this crossing as well.

On arrival, the plans were to give the crew who had accompanied the Fishing Explorer to Plymouth for the refit a week at home before rejoining the vessel to sail first to Las Palmas in the Canary Islands to take on fuel before heading south to the Falklands.

Most of the crew were busy cleaning and preparing for arrival at La Coruña. Through the night and the next day, everything went as well as possible. Even without going full speed, and with the wind astern, we made good time and expected to dock in La Coruña the following afternoon.

Fishing Explorer was one of what seemed an endless line of ships making their way down towards Cape Finisterre with the good fortune of good weather for the entire crossing of the Bay of Biscay, until we left the line of merchant ships and headed directly for La Coruña.

The run across from Plymouth had been quite uneventful, and after putting a call through to Plymouth as we neared the Spanish coast and reporting that everything had gone well, we tied up in La Coruña at 16.00.

The crossing had taken about 46 hours, and after the ship had been cleared by customs, a waiting taxi took me and my young radio officer companion to the hotel where we would spend the rest of our time in La Coruña.

We wanted for nothing during our stay in La Coruña. All our meals were provided, and we had only to ask for anything we required. After a quiet first night just walking around the town and having the occasional drink, we eventually returned to the hotel at two in the morning.

After breakfast we were taken to the office and brought up to date with the proceedings. The Fishing Explorer was now scheduled to remain only five days in La Coruña. Although this was good news for us, I doubted whether the crew members who had accompanied Fishing Explorer to Plymouth and back to

Spain would feel the same way.

Although seventeen of the crew had sailed with the vessel from Plymouth, the full complement when we sailed from La Coruña would be brought up to a total of 41.

The only thing of any importance required of me was to present myself on board the Fishing Explorer every day about noon to deal with anything requiring my signature. Once that had been carried out, we were free to spend the rest of the time doing exactly as we pleased. After being handed the money that we required to last us the rest of our stay in La Coruña, we made the first of our daily visits to the Fishing Explorer.

On most days we inevitably had a walk on the dockside, and usually met a number of British fishermen working out of La Coruña, and to a man they were disgusted at the way they had been treated by their own government. Each of them felt that the British government had left them to fend for themselves after serving an industry loyally, rewarding them by allowing them to be thrown on the scrapheap. Whenever we met any British fishermen this was always the main topic of conversation, and I could only agree wholeheartedly.

Every day we walked down to the Fishing Explorer, mainly to pass the time away, and with virtually nothing to do, it became a little boring. My own last delivery to La Coruña had begun to take on a whole new look as a new shelterdeck had been fitted and it was obvious that she would soon be ready for sea.

The new owner of the vessel I had recently delivered, the Suffolk Endeavour, was delighted with the ship, and always greeted us warmly when we visited to see the progress made in such a short time.

Visiting Fishing Explorer on the fourth day, things had at last started to happen. A large consignment of stores had been delivered and we were told that these were for another company vessel approaching the end of its trip around the Falklands. They would be eagerly awaiting our arrival in the South Atlantic with enough food and stores to see him back to Spain.

During the day it was explained that we would be having two short tows of about an hour's duration outside La Coruña and would be accompanied by a number of fitters who would check that everything was running smoothly. The intention was that they would then be taken off by a small boat and we would be on our way.

During our stay in La Coruña we had enjoyed some warm spring weather and had been able to discard our jackets. But this all changed on the fifth day. Wind and rain were forecast and we arrived at the Fishing Explorer in a taxi in a steady downpour and a freshening wind.

Fishing Explorer ready for the long voyage southwards.

The Ranger Fishing Company

North Shields was chosen to be the port from which the newly formed Ranger Fishing Company would operate its fleet of factory stern trawlers in 1970.

As filleting and freezing fish at sea became increasingly popular, the Ranger Fishing Company had three trawlers, Ranger Ajax, Ranger Apollo and Ranger Aurora, built at Brooke Marine's shipyard in Lowestoft, making the Ranger Fishing Company the UK's largest operator of filleter trawlers at the time.

Although not blessed with a great deal of engine power, these first three arrivals were exceptionally well laid out for vessels of their size, and offered plenty of shelter to the crew working on deck. Their main drawback was that due to the small size of their factory decks, these trawlers could only process eight to ten tonnes of fillets for a day's fishing.

But with comparatively little in the way of superstructure, these were exceptionally fine sea ships, and apart from a few initial setbacks, these class A ships, as they became known, began to fish successfully in the Barents Sea and at Bear Island.

As things improved, the company turned to Germany to purchase two much larger vessels, also filleter trawlers that were built to freeze catches at sea. The Ranger Boreas was soon shown to be the best addition to the fleet, and fished extremely well, while the Ranger Briseis was plagued with minor engine defects that lost the ship much fishing time.

It was at this time that the Ranger Fishing

The author – skipper of the Ranger Fishing Company's Ranger Ajax, before leaving for a trip to the Barents Sea in 1971.

Company had its first major setback. I had been skipper of the Ranger Ajax for some time, and for no reason that I could think of at the time, was told that I would be moved after a number of quick trips over to the Ranger Aurora.

As the ships were identical, I saw this as nothing in the way of a promotion, but I duly took command of the Ranger Aurora, and during our first trip to the Barents Sea was shocked to hear that the Ranger Ajax had suf-

The Ranger Apollo, one of the A class ships that the Ranger Fishing Company operated successfully. While not overblessed with engine power, these ships were built with relatively little superstructure and were excellent sea ships. They also offered plenty of cover to the men working on deck with much of the trawl deck under cover.
Photo: Hull Maritime Museum, Malcolm Fussey collection.

fered a serious fire on board while fishing at Greenland. The Ranger Ajax had eventually to be abandoned, and sank there, although there was no loss of life.

The loss of the Ranger Ajax was a severe blow to the company, which was going through its most successful period since it had taken the decision to base its fleet at North Shields. The popularity of sea frozen fish was such that straight away there was talk of replacing the Ranger Ajax.

Around North Shields, the Ranger Fishing Company provided jobs for a large number of local people, although the majority of the crews and almost all of the skippers were from Hull.

Rumours that additions to the fleet would be arriving from Germany proved to be just that, when it was announced that the company had placed an order to have four new factory stern trawlers built, again with Brooke Marine in Lowestoft. This would bring the Ranger fleet to eight, making it the biggest fleet of its kind operating in Britain.

The first of the new C class vessels to arrive was the Ranger Cadmus, which was skippered by John Dobson, a highly experienced and much respected Hull skipper, the ideal choice of skipper to take on a new ship and overcome all the accompanying teething problems that arise on a maiden voyage.

Within a short time the Ranger Cadmus was fishing well, and was shortly joined by new arrivals Ranger Caliope and Ranger Calisto. The last one to arrive, completing the programme of newbuildings, was the Ranger Castor.

By this time all of the ships were fishing well and it seemed that the Ranger Fishing Company was going through its best period since the company's formation.

I was informed that I would be taking command of the Ranger Castor and duly handed over the Ranger Aurora to George Petty, who had been mate with me and who was familiar with the ship, alongside at Honningsvåg in Norway, and flew home to take command of the new Ranger Castor in January 1973.

All four of these freezer factory ships were designed to process, fillet and freeze the entire

The Ranger Ajax alongside at North Shields. The Ranger Ajax was unfortunate enough to be lost after a fire on board during a trip to Greenland.

catch of fish as it came on board the ship. Any small fish or offal left over was processed into fishmeal on board, so nothing was wasted.

Unlike the older A class trawlers that the company owned, which could produce only eight tonnes of fillets in a day, the new trawlers could produce much more and on one occasion the Ranger Castor's factory deck produced 24 tonnes of fillets in a single day. These trawlers had excellent factories that were well thought out. They had adequate power, which was enough to tow a pelagic trawl, but had a steaming speed of only around 13 knots.

With the help of some good pelagic fishing around Maakur Bank and another spell of good fishing at Cape Bank, finishing around Malangen and Nordvest Bank, our first trip went very well.

The Ranger Castor's second trip was almost

The Kurd, which had been the Ranger Calisto, seen alongside at Hull in British United Trawlers colours.
Photo: Hull Maritime Museum, Malcolm Fussey collection.

the reverse of our first. Fishing started off the Norwegian coast, and after refuelling with half of the trip on board, we ended up fishing in the areas off Fruholmen and Yjelmsoy. The new trawler's first two trips had gone well, without incidents or serious problems.

At this time the were problems of another sort arising for the British trawler fleet. Trawlers fishing at Iceland had been harassed by Icelandic gunboats and the outlook was bleak for the fleet. With this uncertainty in mind, it was decided that our third trip would be to Newfoundland. Reports from other freezers fishing there were not encouraging, and after passing Cape Wrath with our course set for Flemish Cap, all of the trawlers there reported slack fishing. Overfishing on these grounds over many years had certainly taken its toll of the Grand Banks, and large fleets of trawlers had left the Labrador and Newfoundland fishing grounds in a depleted state.

Our first two trips had been short ones for a ship of this type at only seven weeks for each trip, but with very little cod to be found at Newfoundland, it was obvious that this trip would not be a replica of the previous ones.

After five slack days around Flemish Cap, a move inside to Cape Bonavista provided us

with a week's reasonable fishing, brought to an end as a number of trawlers descended on the area. Once again we moved to a position off Belle Isle, where hopes of good fishing were dashed when what looked to be a good haul of fish as it was hove up the ramp and released into the factory turned out to be almost entirely redfish with a small percentage of poor quality cod. After seeing no improvement, we moved on again, this time north to Hamilton Bank off Labrador, where the small amounts of poor quality fish there brought into focus all of the difficulties of finishing a trip in a ship equipped to land an entire trip's worth of frozen fillets.

During this trip we learned that the Ranger Fishing Company had been taken over by British United Trawlers and all eight ships would now operate from Hull.

Apart from another short spell of good fishing at Cape Bonavista, it was clear that it was going to be very difficult to land a reasonable trip of fillets unless there was a dramatic improvement in the fishing. Reports from ships scattered over a wide area suggested that this was highly unlikely, and after giving the situation some thought, I put in a call to the BUT office in Hull to suggest finishing the trip at Iceland. I was told to wait for a reply later in the day, and when this came through it confirmed that we could proceed to Iceland, along with a warning that we could be vulnerable to having our warps chopped, a practice that the Icelandic gunboats had used repeatedly against side trawlers.

Paying little regard to these matters, we promptly hauled and the following morning arrived in St. John's to take on fuel, stores and water before leaving that night for Iceland. Following twelve hours astern of us was another of the C class trawlers, Ranger

(Above) The Kurd, originally the Ranger Calisto, alongside at Milford Haven during her brief career fishing for mackerel.

(Left) The first of the four trawlers built at Brooke Marine was the Ranger Cadmus, delivered in 1971. She became the Arab under British United Trawlers and is seen here in Iceland in the mid-1980s under the Norwegian flag as the Pero.

Caliope, who could see no point in staying on the grounds at Newfoundland and decided to take his chance at Iceland to finish his trip.

On the whole it had been a bad period of fishing for everyone, and especially difficult for the filleter trawlers. Ships equipped to block freeze their fish were able to fill up with redfish caught in the deep water, but these wholefrozen blocks would not bring in much in the way of money, although they would help to get the trip finished and show a reasonable tonnage.

The run across to Iceland was in good weather, and when we arrived, we resumed fishing with a group of ships in a designated area under the watchful eye of a British frigate. Although this was not an ideal sort of trip, it gave us an idea of what to expect in the coming months.

Fishing at the time was spasmodic, but improved as the trip went on, and with the help of thirty tonnes of coley caught in the last sixty hours and reports of good fishing in the area around Foula, we headed for our new home port of Hull.

Initially there were few changes to the fleet after the takeover by British United Trawlers. The ships retained their original colours and names for one more trip, and as they year drew to a close it was announced that the eight Ranger freezers would take the names of Hellyer's old tribal class trawlers.

Ranger Apollo became Turcoman, Ranger Aurora became Esquimaux, Ranger Boreas became Afghan and Ranger Briseis became Hausa. Of the 'C' class trawlers, Ranger Caliope became Kelt, Ranger Cadmus became Arab, Ranger Calisto became Kurd, and Ranger Castor became Gaul.

To purchase eight freezer trawlers at a time when the fishing industry was facing a very uncertain future must have been a very brave decision on the part of British United Trawlers, as time was already running out for the British deep sea trawler fleet.

Although the Ranger Fishing Company, which had been a part of P&O, had a brief fling with the fishing industry, there can be no doubt that these ships played a major role in developing the industry in a short time. Sea frozen fillets became a highly sought-after product and in the short time that the Ranger Fishing Company was in existence, during which it built six new freezers and bought two more from Germany, it certainly made a mark that others were able to follow.

Ranger Cadmus is seen here in 2001, under the Faroese flag as the Kappinn. After fishing successfully for more than 30 years, she has recently been laid up following the crisis in the deep-sea shrimp fishery as fuel prices have risen and shrimp prices have continued to fall.

Looking Back – Faraway Places

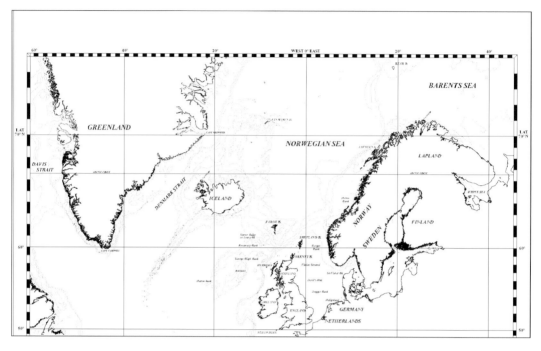

With a long steam ahead of us to the South Atlantic, there was plenty of time to reflect and look back over the years to exactly what went wrong with our own deep sea fishing industry.

Many of the older oil burning ships had given marvellous service and had paid for themselves over and over again. By the 1970s, many of those ships that had been built just after the Second World War were ready for scrapping, but a number of the diesel trawlers

British fishermen found fishing grounds all across the North Atlantic, from Newfoundland to the White Sea.

could have targeted the fishing grounds to the west of the British Isles that had over the years been fished by the Spanish fleet, and a move like this could have saved thousands of jobs. Yet our government had seemed determined on a complete destruction of an industry that over the years had served the nation well.

Britain's entry into the EEC and Iceland's decision to impose a 200 mile limit certainly did nothing to help the industry and did more to bring about the downfall of the deep sea fleet than any other factor. It is still hard to understand why the government was prepared to pay out millions of pounds in compensation to owners to decimate their industry, yet were not prepared to pay one pound to save the fishing industry and the jobs of thousands of people that were linked to fishing? Is there

One of Kingston's trawlers alongside at a remote quayside in Iceland.

any wonder at the anger that was felt as many fine ships made their final journeys to the breakers' yards?

There were some benefits with oil and gas being found over large areas of the North Sea, and many people will argue, and possibly quite rightly, that the rise of the offshore industry coincided with the fall of the fishing industry. Yet it remains a fact that nothing was done to save our industry in any way at all.

It is difficult to explain or describe the devastation that befell the two Humber ports of Hull and Grimsby, along with Fleetwood and Aberdeen to a lesser extent, where docks that had once been a hive of activity became

A winter scene as the Hull trawler Ross Trafalgar enters the Faroe Islands port of Klaksvik.

(Above)Hull trawler Ross Orion takes on pilots for the journey through the Norwegian fjords.

After a winter trip on northern fishing grounds, the journey through the usually sheltered waters of the fjords (below) provided everyone on board with a very welcome break.

graveyards full of ships with nowhere to go.

I think it is safe to say that most of the places the British trawler fleet visited during their various fishing trips would be hard to find in many holiday brochures. Yet the bleak winters in many of these high northern latitudes would change dramatically as the days lengthened, revealing some of the most beautiful scenery imaginable during the short summers.

To those who were fortunate enough to witness these changes, it all came free and was taken for granted as part and parcel of the job, or to some of us, one of the perks of the job.

The journey through the Norwegian fjords in wintertime offered shelter from the weather and a chance to prepare for a spell of fishing ahead, while the same journey on the way home offered everyone a chance to rest and unwind, sometimes before facing a very uncomfortable crossing of the North Sea.

The most popular places visited by the British fleet were Lodingen, Harstad and Tromsø, while further to the north Honningsvåg, Hammerfest and Vardø were also popular ports to call at once on the fishing grounds, either to take fuel or stores. With summer cruises to these remote and sometimes desolate places now available, I believe that few people taking a cruise like this would be able to imagine the changes that can take place from summer to winter, or even imagine the conditions that fishermen worked under around Bear Island or further north at Spitzbergen.

Long before our fishing industry went into

Boyd Line's trawler Arctic Raider alongside at Tromsø in Norway. Tromsø was a regular port of call for many British trawlers as they made their way to and from Arctic fishing grounds. In the days of coal-burning trawlers, many of these ships called at Tromsø to take bunkers for the steam home to Hull or Grimsby.

were closer to fishing grounds.

My view was that the best port to call at in Iceland was Akureyri, and I called there a number of times in different ships. The port has easy access and was convenient for trawlers fishing the north side of Iceland. I found it to be the most welcoming of all the places I visited in Iceland in the many times that I called at Icelandic ports over the years.

On the east coast ports such as Seydisfjördur and Nordfjördur were often visited by vessels seeking repairs or medical services, and although these places offered some shelter from the severe winters, I would not have recommended them as any kind of place for a long stay.

Closer to home the Faroese capital of Tórshavn was a regular port of call for many ships on their way to Iceland and was a popular place for trawlers working around the Faroe Islands, such as the many Scottish trawlers that fished those waters.

Across at Newfoundland, St John's had all that there was to offer, with good facilities and a perfect harbour that provided shelter from even the severest weather. Of all the places I visited while fishing, this was the port that was able to offer the best in facilities and provisions. St John's also provided a welcome break for freezer trawler crews on the long trips they spent fishing on and around the Grand Banks.

All of these places visited by British fishermen have seen changes take place as they are now more accessible to fleets of cruise ships manned by tourists armed to the teeth with video cameras, able to capture the beauty of the sea ice. In their everyday lives ashore, could they imagine some of these places in the depths of winter, and turn their minds to the thankless and dangerous work that trawler crews did in these high latitudes?

decline, as ships were built bigger and therefore were assumed to be safer, trawler owners did not take kindly to skippers using the comfortable passage through the Norwegian fjords to reach trawling grounds in the Barents Sea. The high cost of having to carry two pilots did nothing to help and what had once been taken for granted became a pleasant memory for most of us.

There is a little more on offer for tourists in Iceland, but most British fishermen will remember the place with very mixed feelings. The capital, Reykjavik, offered more in the way of facilities, but the two more northerly ports of Isafjördur and Dyrafjördur were the main ports of call for British trawlers as they

Harstad in Norway was another regular port of call for British trawlers that were fishing along the Norwegian coast in the spring. The trawler seen here at the quayside in Harstad is the Ross Trafalgar.

Leaving Europe Behind

On what was to be our last day in La Coruña it was explained to me that we had on board a number of items for different vessels fishing in the Falklands.

After signing for these, I decided to go back to the hotel, and to return to the vessel with my gear and belongings, leaving just the bare requirements at the hotel. Some of the crew had already joined the Fishing Explorer. Those who had travelled some distance had made arrangements to spend the night in the Seamens' Mission or on board the ship.

Back at the hotel, I made a couple of telephone calls and wrote some letters before heading for the small bar close by that had become our first port of call whenever we went out for a drink. Although we later met some of the Fishing Explorer's crew who had sailed from Plymouth, it was not a nice night to venture far from the hotel, and shortly after midnight we were back in what had become our local bar for our last couple of drinks before returning to the hotel for the last time.

Meanwhile our own ship's stores and bond were arriving, along with a number of other items which were stowed away by the crew, all of who were now on board. Many of the crew's families had also made their way down to the docks to see off their loved ones.

By 16.00, most of the families and friends of the Fishing Explorer's crew began to leave the ship, and by 17.00 it was announced that we were ready to sail. Apart from the fitters who would accompany us for a couple of short trial tows, all the remaining friends and relatives left as the crew took in the gangway and mooring ropes.

At 17.30 we were on our way, and once clear of the harbour we began to feel the swell as we made our way into the open sea. The wind was still northerly, with some heavy squalls and the prospect of a very unpleasant night.

In view of the poor weather, it was decided to have just two short tows. The first haul after just 30 minutes saw us haul aboard just five boxes of poor quality fish, and the second haul for the same length of time was about ten boxes of the same. After this we proceeded back to La Coruña to drop off the fitters, who assured us before departing that everything was fine and the winch working perfectly.

When we had dropped off the shore personnel, we once again left the shelter of the harbour and with the wind abeam at force seven to eight, we proceeded towards Cape Finisterre on what promised to be a very wet and windy night.

Once round Cape Finisterre and on a southerly course with the wind astern it was a different story. By breakfast time the weather had moderated to a force six, and by noon it was no more than a light breeze. With all the comings and goings of the previous day, it was a pleasure to be back at sea and getting used to the routine way of life aboard ship.

The fine weather during the afternoon gave me the chance to sign on the crew and complete a number of other formalities. All of those who had worked on the ship in Plymouth were still with us, while those who had joined the Fishing Explorer during our stay in La Coruña appeared to include a number of very experienced fishermen.

Our first day at sea went extremely well. The weather was fine and when I left the bridge at midnight, there were almost perfect weather conditions. It was already starting to get warmer as we left the harsh winter that was being experienced in parts of northern Europe well astern of us as we made our way towards the Canary Islands.

The following morning things got even better. The sun appeared and what little work had to be done on deck was done with the crew clad in shorts and tee shirts. This was something of a difference to the times I had made my way across the North Sea and along the Norwegian coast, at times in cold and atrocious weather conditions. Countless times we had left the Humber straight into the teeth of a full north east gale, a nightmare compared to what we were experiencing steaming south.

The third day passed just like the previous two, and by now I had got to know almost everyone on board by their first names, which in itself was quite an achievement. It seemed that my attempts to speak Spanish with a Yorkshire accent went down well with the crew.

In late evening sunshine, three days and eighteen hours after leaving La Coruña, our pilot dropped us alongside in Las Palmas, ready to take on bunkers the following morning.

Once the formalities of clearing the ship with the customs were finished, we had the opportunity to spend a few hours ashore. This was my first visit to the Canary Islands, and during the evening we had the chance to mingle with some of the holidaymakers who were escaping from the cold weather in Britain and seeking the warmth of the islands.

It was a pleasant night ashore and was made all the more pleasant for me when in one bar I met a group of people form Yorkshire, which made it a fitting way to enjoy what would be our last night in such good company.

Bunkering started the following morning and we were expected to sail at 18.00 hours. In the meantime, most of the crew were ashore having a drink and doing some last minute shopping before we were due to sail.

Everyone at some time or other had a chance to spend some time ashore during our stay in Las Palmas, and everyone had taken the opportunity of buying some of the duty free goods that were widely available. Most had purchased watches or radios. Perfumes and a wide range of other goods were all on display, and the crew began to return to the ship, each convinced that they had obtained the bargain of the century.

During the afternoon I was approached on the bridge and asked if we were proceeding to fish in the Falklands. I confirmed this, and was asked if we could take some bottles of gas to a ship already fishing there. The ship in question was the former Hull freezer trawler Pict, which had been sold to Spanish interests and now fished from Las Palmas. Much to the amazement of the owner, I told him that I was very familiar with the Pict, and went on to tell him where and in what year she had been built, and that I had been skipper of her sister ship the Dane, after the tragic loss of the Gaul.

A short time later the gas was being lowered onto the deck of the Fishing Explorer, and after the evening meal at 17.00, with all the crew on board along with the pilot, we once again prepared to sail.

By 18.45 we had dropped our pilot, slowly built up speed, and once again we were on our way. There would be no more stops now until we reached Port Stanley in the Falkland Islands.

Meanwhile on the bridge, I made myself a promise to return to the Canary Islands for a holiday, possibly when the trip was over - something I have done on numerous occasions since.

It had been a pleasant 24 hours that we had spent in Las Palmas. One member of the crew had taken care of the large amount of mail that had left the ship, and I managed to buy some English papers during my visit ashore. On being relieved on the bridge at midnight, I settled down to have a read and a few hours sleep.

Running Off

Meanwhile on the Fishing Explorer work had started in earnest, and there was a lot to be done. First of all the steel warps had to be pulled off the winch, measured and remarked. This was the first job to be undertaken by the deck crew, while the men who worked in the factory were busy marking and moving thousands of cartons in readiness for the start of fishing.

Once the work on the warps was complete, we prepared three trawls ready for fishing, and in between all this going on, there were many other jobs being done all over the ship.

Cables had to be spliced and paid to the trawl doors and chains were being cut to different lengths. It was a very busy period, but we were enjoying some glorious weather conditions, and at midday on the 20th of March 1985 our position was Lat 20°05' N, Long 19°20' W.

As we made our way down towards the equator, and the weather became warmer, most of the work on the deck was done immediately after breakfast, with the crew taking an afternoon break before commencing work again at 1500.

As for myself, with not a lot to do to occupy myself during the day, I inevitably ended up spending part of the day on the deck, assisting the crew fixing the trawls. This certainly helped pass the time away, and helped me to learn a bit more Spanish every day.

I had never experienced this type of weather, and I admit that sometimes I wished it was a bit cooler. During the night even with the portholes open it was difficult to sleep, and several of the crew chose to sleep on the deck.

On the 25th of March our position at noon was Lat 01°59' N, Long 28°08' W, and the following morning at 0335 we crossed the equator, myself for the first time after over forty years at sea.

Since leaving Las Palmas we had stopped twice, but only for minor problems caused by overheating in the engine room, and within half an hour on each occasion these were rectified and we were on our way.

Other than the two short stoppages, everything was going very well, and most days went by without any incident at all. In fact we passed no more than three ships on our run down to the Falklands.

Most of the work on deck was nearing completion, and most of this had been organised by the bosun - who organised everything on the deck with a minimum of fuss.

A tall, rawboned man, Oscar the bosun had been brought up the hard way and had hands like leather. He had been at sea since he was a boy, had served at Newfoundland in his youth. He told me he would be retiring after two more trips.

A great friendship developed between Oscar and myself, especially after I had picked up a spike and spliced a pair of cables, and helped fix one of the trawls that we would be using. This mutual respect for each other was born out of the many years we had both spent at sea fishing. Oscar never had to take a steaming watch, but his many years of experience at sea stood out as he organised the running of all the work that was carried out on deck.

Most of the crew were young men from all parts of Spain and Oscar chased them to work

Open all hours... Somewhere near the equator, the author receives a haircut free of charge from one of the crew.

every day. The younger members of the crew looked up to him and showed him a great deal of respect as he went about his job encouraging the younger deckhands. Although he was a man of few words, one got the impression he was the sort of person you would rather have on your side no matter what if the going got tough.

As my Spanish got better, Oscar took it on himself to come on the bridge with two pots of coffee heavily laced with brandy almost every night when I was on watch after the late evening meal. While most of the younger members of the crew were either playing cards or dominoes, I would listen intently as he described some of the countless trips he had experienced in the old Spanish trawlers fishing across on the Grand Banks at Newfoundland.

Knowing that I had fished these grounds myself, and being the two oldest men on the Fishing Explorer, we developed a strong respect for each other, and I looked forward to Oscar's nightly visit to the bridge to have a yarn to help pass the watch away, and it became quite obvious to me that he would play a key role in the trip.

While I was intent on improving my Spanish, some members of the crew were keen to improve their English. A number of the younger crew members had learned English at school, and never lost an opportunity to speak to me in English whenever the occasion presented itself.

Amongst the rest of the crew the first mate, who had spent most of his career in merchant ships spoke English very well, along with the chief engineer, so conversation between us was never a problem.

As ever on board a ship, football was one of the main topics of conversation, and with neither of the teams from La Coruña and Vigo doing very well, it was inevitable that when the day's work was completed most of the younger crew members would then reappear wearing the track suits of the two giants of Spanish football, Real Madrid or Barcelona. As everyone gathered on the trawl deck as the day cooled off after the late evening meal and the arguments went on, I am sure that more

goals were scored there every night than in the whole of the Spanish football season.

The two cooks and their assistant had their own rota of working hours, and one of them would always turn out at four in the morning to do the baking, ensuring that there was always fresh baked bread and rolls every morning. By and large, everything on board the Fishing Explorer was going very well indeed. I had no regrets whatever about joining the Fishing Explorer, although I was still surprised to find myself back in deep sea fishing.

Taking a bridge watch from 2000 to midnight was the ideal time to reflect on what had happened, as I had left a comparatively easy job in delivering trawlers mostly to Spain from England, Scotland and Ireland. The pay had been good, and the work both interesting and enjoyable, yet despite this I had left it behind me to return to deep sea fishing.

On reflection, it was difficult to find a reason for going back to deep sea fishing, with its long hours on deck and in the bridge, not to mention the harsh weather conditions that fishermen have to endure in the relentless search for fish.

What it is about fishing that draws men back to such a hard way of life working in places like the North Cape of Iceland with gales that make even the most experienced skipper breathe a sigh of relief when they reach shelter?

Why would anyone want to return to places like Bear Island or even further to the north to Spitzbergen, where fishermen had to endure days of gutting the mostly small fish that were often left unsold at the end of a long and tiring trip?

There is little to wonder at that fishermen preferred the relatively ice free grounds of the Barents Sea, often referred to as the White Sea. Fishing grounds further west off Greenland or Newfoundland offered little in the way of comfort. The fog shrouded banks and large areas of ice can turn the job into an endless nightmare, and the stretches of pack and field ice on Greenland's fishing grounds and the icebergs that sweep round Cape Farewell ensure that there is no room for complacency.

The summer months present a complete contrast, when the scenery can sometimes be quite breathtaking during the long hours of daylight at these high northern latitudes.

Over the years I have spoken to many old fishermen who have left the industry, frequently not for reasons of their own choice, and asked their reasons for leaving. After years spent in old ships, many with poor food and substandard living and safety conditions, most have told me that despite everything, they would turn the clock back and do it all again if given the chance.

The special bond that exists between seamen could be the main reason for fishermen being drawn back to this way of life, as the main ingredients for a happy and successful ship are the friendship and teamwork found in a good crew.

I will always remember sailing as a young deckhand in the Hull trawler Caesar, leaving for the fishing grounds only four days before Christmas. As the Caesar made her way along the Norwegian coast on Christmas Eve in cold but clear weather, the lights of Andenes and other points along the coast could be seen flashing clearly on our starboard side. In the warmth of the Caesar's bridge, it seemed to me that we were the only ship at sea that night.

I was on watch with the Caesar's bosun. Although we were close friends and had been on the same watch together for almost a year and normally had plenty to talk about, that night we all remained silent. The whole watch passed in almost total silence, each of us wrapped up in our own thoughts as Christmas morning drew closer.

The silence was broken only by the arrival of the next watch at 2300, and I feel sure that the three men who took over from us spent the watch exactly as we had.

This was a part of a fisherman's life that other people never saw or imagined. We were always glad to see a trip come to an end and the ship heading for home, yet never wanting to remain too long on shore before once again returning to the routine of life at sea.

I had been twenty-six years of age that night in the Caesar. Thirty years on, little had changed, and I had chosen to go back to fishing under no pressure from anyone, only this time heading in a completely different direction and enjoying every minute of it.

The Gaul's Last Trips

I have lost count of the number of times people have asked me the question 'what do you think happened to the Gaul?'

The first trips in the Ranger Castor, which became the Gaul when the Ranger Fishing Company became part of British United Trawlers, had seen us in the White Sea and across at Newfoundland, as well as up to Labrador and Iceland. Problems and little faults that come with every new ship were quickly rectified and the ship had fished reasonably well on these early voyages. No wonder then that when we sailed on what was to be her last complete trip, leaving Hull on the 1st of October 1973, the question everyone was asking was would we be back in time for Christmas?

Our run across the North Sea and along the Norwegian coast was a good one with a following south-westerly wind. Although we had reports from ships fishing over a wide area in the White Sea, I had already decided that we would shoot and have our first haul on Cape Bank, and tow easterly to where I thought we would possibly have our best fishing in late October and into November in the areas around Tiddly Bank, Skolpen Bank and the North Deeps.

However, some ships had already tried these grounds and reported only moderate hauls of fish, and in my own opinion this was a bit too early for these areas.

Our first few days of fishing on Cape Bank produced nothing out of the ordinary, but by keeping the trawl on the bottom and avoiding steaming or changing grounds, we finished each day with a reasonable tonnage of fillets and were still in the area of Cape Bank when we made our first significant move after two weeks of fishing. This came about because of a change in the direction of the wind and a reasonable weather forecast for the next 48 hours. Instead of steaming off to the main group of ships, I decided to steam inside just east of Vardo, and towed easterly along East Bank just off the coast of Murmansk.

The light south-easterly winds soon brought about a big improvement in the fishing, and we also had our first sighting of Russian naval craft when three ships that could have been destroyers passed us quite closely heading easterly, possibly bound for the Soviet naval base at Kildin, just a few miles further to the east along the Murmansk coast.

It was not until the third night that we had our only sightings of any submarines, when three of them steaming on the surface passed us heading to the north-west. As far as we knew, none of them paid us the least bit of attention as we went about our business and carried on fishing in the area.

By that time another BUT trawler, which had been Hellyer Brothers' Orsino, had joined us on East Bank, and the two of us enjoyed some four days of good fishing before the wind swung round to the north. We were already planning what our next move would be as soon as the fishing started to slack off.

Our move inside had been a good one, giving us some good fishing in good weather, which was just what we needed at this early stage of the trip. So far we had not had any problems, or any reason to stop fishing due to weather. As we completed our third week's fishing, Christmas at home once again looked a distinct possibility for everyone on board.

Meanwhile, ships fishing to the north between Tiddly Bank and Skolpen Bank had reported better fishing, and after steaming through the night, we towed our way towards the group of ships on the north west corner of Skolpen Bank.

There was a bit of fish in this area, and most of the ships were towing for four hours and more. While the fishing remained steady, the weather now posed the biggest threat. A north-west gale the following day brought all fishing to a halt, and rather than dodge head to wind, I decided that we would save time by steaming to Honningsvåg and refuelling while the weather remained poor.

Following a highly uncomfortable night

steaming, we entered the sheltered waters of Porsanger Fjord, and after taking on our harbour pilot, we berthed at the oil quay. We were moored alongside by 1400, where we took on bunkers and a small amount of provisions and fresh water. We then vacated the bunkering berth, as I had been informed that there would be three more freezer trawlers coming in to refuel while the weather showed no sign of improvement.

But the next Norwegian forecast offered some comfort, with the weather expected to moderate and the wind forecast to shift to the south-west. But with the heavy snow falling I was in no hurry to leave, and we remained alongside in Honningsvåg. Reports from ships still fishing indicated that none of the trawlers at sea had resumed fishing, but although the weather was due to moderate, it was the change in its direction that interested me.

It took me only a short time to make my mind up. In view of the weather forecast, the shorter trip to the East Bank would be worth another try. Our best fishing of the trip so far had been in this area, and although the weather had eased slightly, I decided that we would not sail until 2100 that night, on what would hopefully be the last leg of our voyage.

There had been some heavy falls of snow in Honningsvåg during our stay, but as we moved out into Porsanger fjord, the night was fine and clear as we made our way close in along the snow covered land eastwards towards Vardo. The East Bank was a blessing for us, as it turned out. Once again with the wind from the south-west, we once again had some very good fishing and our first encounter with some black frost during the trip.

It was in this area that we boosted our tonnage over the 200 tonne mark, which was something of a relief. But after 60 hours in the area, the wind shifted to a more northerly direction and it was not long before we were towing across Skolpen Bank to join up with four or five ships fishing in the area known as the North Deeps. The weather was now running the show, and fishing through continuous snow squalls for as little as forty or fifty baskets of fish in poor weather conditions hardly seemed worth it, yet once more the weather

forecast showed something of an improvement for the following day. With this in mind, I decided to make one more overnight steam in towards the Russian coast and shoot away off Sveti Nos in the hope that there would be some reasonable hauls of plaice there, as was usually the case at the time of year.

Our first haul was quite encouraging, as we hove on board six tonnes of good quality plaice. We were now fishing on our own, and our only sighting was in mid-morning in what little patch of daylight there was, as a plane flew low over us, turned and took another look, before turning in towards the land and did not bother us again.

What did bother us was the ever increasing amount of black frost that we were now towing through. The wind was once more from a southerly direction, blowing straight off the low lying, snow covered land. It was bitterly cold as conditions worsened throughout the day until it was impossible to see the ramp and trawl deck from the bridge. Although our last haul had been eight tonnes of plaice, we decided to leave the area. Conditions were so bad that hauling was dangerous. As the banks of black frost whirled around, it was impossible to see if the trawl was clear, and impossible to see the men at the ramp from the winch, so with these conditions, I decided to steam west.

Nevertheless, it had been a worthwhile move. Our 36 hours in the area had brought us 35 tonnes of good sized, good quality plaice. We had one more haul off Kildin for a mere thirty baskets of fish, and this was our last haul in the White Sea. The weather was still poor as we set off towards Vardo, and was forecast to deteriorate even further.

There was to be no stopping until we arrived at Malangen Bank, but resuming fishing depended entirely on the weather. Vardo Radio was asking ships to keep a lookout for a Norwegian fishing boat that was overdue, but most ships had by this time left the area on account of the weather and the slack fishing. It was not until we reached Sletnes and Nord Kyn that we came across a small group of ships, not one of which was fishing.

My intention was to keep steaming, and if

the weather permitted, shoot away again on the west edge of Malangen Bank and dock in Hull three days before Christmas. This was also the intention of the skipper of the Hull freezer Princess Anne, who was also steaming to Malangen Bank just a few miles ahead of us. At least our long steam to the south-west had given everyone a chance to catch up on some sleep. The weather over the past three weeks had been poor, making the job all the more demanding as the trip wore on, and everyone now looked forward to getting home and spending Christmas with their families.

It was during our steam down towards Malangen Bank that we received a telegram from the office informing me that they required the ship to dock on the morning of Christmas Day. I must admit that I thought this was a bit harsh, as it would mean a number of the crew having to spend part of Christmas Day travelling home to North Shields, on a day when taxis and public transport would be practically non-existent.

I had already chosen to ignore the telegram completely, and was finding it difficult to whip up any enthusiasm to start fishing once again at this late stage in the trip. Very reluctantly, the trawl went down the ramp, and we shot away on the west edge of Malangen Bank.

Fishing in this area is usually at its best in February, so we did not anticipate any large hauls of fish, and this was borne out when after a two and a half hour tow we hauled on board about 60 baskets of coley. With the next two hauls we fared no better, and with the weather still very unsettled, to everyone's delight, I decided to call a halt to fishing and we brought the trawl aboard for the last time.

The following day we had the luxury of a few hours of daylight as we passed Skomva and cleared the Arctic Circle. With our companion the Princess Anne close by, we headed to our home port of Hull.

All the talk on board was of being home for Christmas. In the end, we finished with a nice trip of fish, and there would be something in it for everyone on board. Despite the instructions from the office to dock in Hull on Christmas Day 1973, something that I found inconsiderate for the crew, we docked at 0600,

four days before Christmas with 210 tonnes of fillets and 50 tonnes of plaice on board.

Looking back, it had been a quite normal trip for that time of year for a freezer trawler fishing well within the Arctic Circle on a typical winter voyage, during which we had endured numerous gales and harsh freezing conditions in the latter stages of the trip. Throughout this, as in previous trips at Newfoundland, Labrador, Iceland and the White Sea, the Gaul had acquitted herself remarkably well, and despite all this, she failed to return to her home port on her final fateful voyage.

During the summer of 1973 the Gaul had fished across at Newfoundland and Labrador before moving across to Iceland, returning late in the year to fish well inside the Arctic Circle, where she spent the winter months at Bear Island, the Barents Sea, and would have been expected to spend some time on the Norwegian coast for the spring fishing.

What little we know about the movements of the Gaul on that last fateful voyage comes from the freezer schedule. The freezer sched, as it was known, was operated by the skippers of the freezer trawlers, and had nothing to do with the owners. It was given out in a code once the ships had commenced fishing and worked reasonably well, with reports coming in three times a day at 1030, 1630 and again at 2330 hours.

As well as giving fishing reports in either the amount of frozen blocks, or in the case of ships that filleted on board, in tonnes, each skipper would sometimes report his daily total with the number of baskets of fish for each haul during the day's fishing.

The schedule had a number of other uses, in that ships leaving their home port could make contact if they had mail or spare parts for any of the ships fishing in that area.

When fishing at places as far away as Newfoundland, it could be important to know where there was no fish, as this could save skippers a lot of time if their intentions were to go to an area that had already been tried and found to have very little fish.

It is from the freezer schedule that we know something of the last few days of the Gaul, and her movements up to that last day. Although nobody knows exactly how she met her end, we can narrow things down to the time she was lost, and we can discount the suggestions that she was engaged in spying, which is a theory that has been brought out repeatedly over the years.

Most freezer trawlers on leaving the Humber would report in briefly on the 2330 sched, stating that they had sailed and give a position, and to which fishing grounds they intended going. This was the case with the Gaul.

While at sea in 1973 the Ranger Castor became the Gaul, sailing as part of the Ranger Fishing Company and returning as a BUT ship. Although I had been due for a trip ashore, due to the change of ownership, I was asked to complete an additional trip in the Gaul, still in her Ranger colours. So by the end of 1973 I had been more than ten months on board without a proper break and arranged to be ashore for the ship's first trip of 1974, with Peter Nellist taking my place.

The Gaul sailed for the Norwegian coast at the end of January, before which I had shown Peter Nellist around the ship. Although he had not been in a filleter before, he was a man with lengthy experience in stern trawlers and had been in the Cassio for a long time.

The Gaul first appeared on the freezer schedule with a brief report that she had sailed and was bound to the NNE fishing grounds, and that her new skipper was Peter Nellist. This was brief and to the point, meaning that she was heading to the Norwegian coast, Bear Island or the Barents Sea, referred to more often as the White Sea.

This was a simple report made in plain language, but after starting fishing all reports would be sent in code. After sailing and appearing on the sched for the first time on 24th of January, the Gaul did not appear on the freezer schedule again until 28th of January, with an even shorter message of SS, meaning that she was still steaming.

Between the 24th and 28th, she would have sent her position directly to the office as she steamed to fishing grounds. It would appear that some time on the 29th of January the

Gaul started fishing, and although she did not come up on the morning schedule, she did come up at 1630 hours, and reported two hauls of very little.

On the 2330 schedule she reported very little fish, and it is possible she steamed overnight, because the following morning she came up on the 1030 sched of the 30th of January, reported a haul of 30 baskets of fish, and gave a position that was Lat 71°30' North, Long 34°30' East. On the 2330 schedule she came on again to report two hauls of 60 and another haul of just 30 baskets of fish, and once again gave a position, this time Lat 71°25' North, Long 34°50' East.

As there was not a lot of fish being reported, it would seem that the Gaul was doing some searching, and there was nothing unusual in this in the early stages of a trip.

The following day, she reported just two hauls of 50 baskets, and then one more haul of 70 baskets of fish, and on the morning of the 1st of February, the Gaul reported 80 baskets of fish on the morning schedule, and another report of 80 baskets at 1630. The day finished with a report of 70 baskets, and it would seem by the number of hauls that they were towing for a long time for just four hauls a day. Tows of around four hours would have been normal on these grounds at that time of the year.

On the 2nd of February the Gaul reported three hauls, the first of 80 baskets, followed by a haul of 60 baskets and a smaller haul of just 40 baskets, and from here it appears that the Gaul had moved to the south, because on the 3rd of February, the Gaul had changed grounds to a position off Vardo, with a report of just 40 baskets, with another 40 basket haul that afternoon. Later on the 2330 schedule, another haul of 80 baskets was reported, and a position given as Harbakken, indicating that the Gaul was moving further to the westward.

On the 4th of February, the Gaul reported five hauls for a day's fishing, two hauls of 60 baskets and another of 80 baskets in the morning, and later reported two more hauls of 50 and 70 baskets to finish the day.

The following morning the Gaul reported just one slack haul of 40 baskets, and also reported that he was steaming to the westward, which would take her to the group of ships that was fishing in the area around Cape Bank.

A number of trawlers were already fishing to the south-west, and in view of the bad weather reports, some of the side trawler skippers among the group on Cape Bank decided to leave the area and steam to the grounds around Malangen and Nordvest Bank. In February this would have been an obvious move to make, to where one would expect the fishing to improve as the month went on.

On the 1630 schedule on the 5th of February, the Gaul gave her position on Cape Bank, and later in the day on the 2330 schedule reported one haul of 100 baskets, again reporting a position on Cape Bank.

On the morning of the 6th of February the Gaul reported two hauls overnight of 90 and 100 baskets, and reported a haul of 40 baskets that afternoon, but did not report on the late evening schedule.

The position of Lat 72° 15' North, Long 24° 50' East was passed by the Gaul on the following morning's schedule, but only reported one haul of 60 baskets of fish, and on the same day reported that he had just hauled and was laid to repairing a damaged trawl.

The weather got steadily worse during that night, and the next few hours were crucial in what happened to the Gaul. There had been no reports from her that anything was wrong with the ship, or that she was making her way in to port for any reason, and indeed on Friday the 8th of February, she came up on the morning schedule, reporting like every other ship that she had stopped fishing and was laid to and dodging bad weather. This was the last time that the Gaul was heard.

The weather was atrocious during the day, and at 1630 there was no report from the Gaul, nor was there a report at 2330.

After that day's 1030 schedule, when the Gaul reported herself as not fishing and dodging in bad weather, as were all the ships in the Cape Bank area, it is quite possible that in view of the worsening weather the Gaul had not resumed fishing, since she had reported a damaged trawl and was laid to mending.

As the Gaul was not seen or heard again after reporting on the 1030 sched on the 8th of February, it is possible to assume that she was lost between the hours of 1030 and 2330, and it is equally possible that she could have been lost by the time of the afternoon schedule, on which the Gaul failed to report.

No one can be sure of when the Gaul disappeared, but there appears to be no particular reason for not reporting on the 1630 schedule. Everyone would have been rested, as it seems possible that the Gaul had done no fishing since the previous evening's report when they were laid to mending a damaged trawl.

With no obvious reason for not coming on to the schedule with a report that would have read simply laid to and dodging, as other ships had reported, my belief is that the Gaul was lost between 1030 and 1630 on the 8th of February 1974.

The Ships' Husbands

It would be a grave injustice to write about the deep sea fishing industry of Hull and Grimsby without a special mention of the ships' husbands and the part they played in signing on crews and getting the ships to sea.

Each company had its own runners, as they were best known, and there were some great characters among them. Some of these men would spend more time on the dock than in their own homes, meeting arriving trawlers arriving from fishing and being there to see ships depart for various fishing grounds at all times of the day or night.

These men had no such thing as normal working hours, as the runners and their assistants worked all hours and in all kinds of weather. At times they must have breathed a few huge sighs of relief to see the last ships disappear from the dock on their way to sea.

For forty-nine weeks of the year, the ships' husbands could look out from their offices and take their pick of men seeking employment. Until two weeks before Christmas, the runners held the whip hand, when men who realised they would miss both Christmas and new Year stayed away from the docks.

There are so many stories of men being offered bribes to entice them away to sea over Christmas that I have no doubt at least some of them must be true. As Christmas approached, the runners ventured into pubs and clubs looking for crews, while the men also remained even more determined to spend the festive season with their families and friends.

However, once the New Year had been seen in, everything changed once again and the runner could look down from his lofty perch like a Roman emperor looking down on his subjects, once again letting everyone know that he was fully in charge of the situation.

Despite everything, there were some great characters among them and I for one feel that they have been sold short, not having been given the recognition they deserved for the difficult part they played or for what was at times a thankless task in getting the many trawlers to sea at all times of the day and night. In today's modern world, when we hear so much about unsociable hours, it is hard to imagine that the ships' runners had any social life at all, as most of them would have had to consult a tide book before accepting any invitation to a sporting or social event.

During my early years as a deckhand, George Watkinson and his assistant Ernie Smailes had the task of taking care of Kingston's ever expanding fleet of trawlers. Over at Hellyer's, as many ships returned to fishing after the war, Jim Lowther and Stan Houghton looked after the ships.

After many years at sea himself, both in war and peace, Rennie Cawkwell did the job of crewing the ships for Hamlings, another company that had invested heavily in a fine fleet of trawlers. Ted Rylatt held the same position at Charleson and Smith's, and George Richardson's name is inextricably linked to Hudson Brothers, whose trawlers were always among the smartest to leave the dock past the famous swing bridge.

J Marr's impressive fleet were signed on and off by Ted Robins and Jack Waller ensured that Lord Line's ships were always the first to leave the fish dock. When the mergers came and the fleets of Hellyers, Ross Group, Kingstons and Lord Line were merged to form British United Trawlers, a good friend and neighbour of mine, Bob Northard, took on the mammoth task as others departed the scene.

I was familiar with all of them, great characters and major players in a cast of thousands, who played a great part in a big industry, but never received the recognition they so much deserved.

Looking Back – Fleetwood

None of the British deep sea ports survived for long once Iceland enforced its 200 mile fishing limits. Fleetwood, the small Lancashire port that I had visited many times over the years, had relied heavily on Iceland for its supply of fish. If Hull and Grimsby supplied the bulk of Britain's fish, I am sure that nobody could deny that Fleetwood landed the quality catches.

The notorious weather conditions that can be experienced off Iceland's North Cape and west coast during the winter months can turn some trips into a nightmare. The severe icing conditions in these areas has seen even the most experienced skippers looking over their shoulders as they have headed their vessels in towards the shelter of the land.

But to ensure the quality landings of fish into Fleetwood, these smaller types of trawlers fished these hostile waters throughout the year. I do not think that the merchants in Fleetwood, by paying poor prices for top quality fish, ever really appreciated what the men went through.

Having fished these areas myself in my early years as skipper, I made quite a number of friends of some of these Fleetwood skippers. Inevitably, when the conversation turned towards fishing, most of them were dismayed at the prices they received for their fish, compared to the prices paid in the Humber ports for some very ordinary fish.

I well remember being in Fleetwood when the first Icelandic trawler to land in the port after the dispute discharged her catch. A lot of the fish was condemned as unfit for human consumption, when my friend, a well known top skipper at the time, turned to me in disbelief and said that if we had landed trips like that, we would have been run out of town, and that the people who brought this ship here had got exactly what they deserved.

There was little wonder that feelings began

J Marr's stern trawler Jacinta FD-159 has now returned to her home port of Fleetwood as a floating museum.
Photo: Peter Horsley

to run high as Icelandic fish was once again began to arrive in British ports, only this time from Icelandic fishing vessels. British crews had only a year earlier risked their lives as Icelandic gunboats put their lives at risk while they went about the dangerous task of cutting the warps of British trawlers.

Is it then any wonder that the British fishermen felt let down by trawler owners and government alike? Despite the dispute, it is my honest opinion that Fleetwood could have survived and gone on to be the major fishing port in Britain.

The only grounds then open to British trawlers at the time lay to the west of Ireland and the south west approaches. Fleetwood had a number of ships that could have fished in these areas, Grimsby had possibly more, and owners in Hull could have switched a number of their ships to the Lancashire port.

We heard all kinds of excuses as to why the ships had to be scrapped, such as the rising price of fuel, but what about the rising price of fish?

We still had the men and we still had the ships, and we certainly still had the expertise. During this difficult period, some British freezer stern trawlers had switched to pelagic fishing for mackerel with great success, but the one thing we did not have was trawler owners prepared to back the men who had served them so well through some difficult times.

With Fleetwood's best ships boosted by more from the Humber ports, and with Flectwood practically linked to Hull and Grimsby by the M62 motorway, Fleetwood could have become Britain's premier fishing port, yet it was to go the same way as the two Humber ports.

By the time when the curtain finally came down for Fleetwood in the years leading up to Iceland extending its fishing limits to 200 miles, I can certainly say that Fleetwood had the best fleet of trawlers that had ever sailed from the port.

For many years, trawlers from Hull and Grimsby had been switched to finish their days fishing from Fleetwood and most of these could be found fishing grounds around Iceland. But by the final years came around, great strides had been made and a number of modern diesel-engined trawlers had given Fleetwood a tremendous lift. These included the factory stern trawler Criscilla, which was normally to be found fishing with the group of Hull and Grimsby freezers on north-eastern grounds.

It was a time for cool heads and some serious thinking about the future of the British fishing industry. Yet within a short time, Icelandic trawlers were back landing their catches in Britain while many British trawlers were being sold off - often only to return within a short time to fish where they should have been fishing for British owners around our own shores.

Sadly, the chance was missed and we are only left to reflect on what could have been as Fleetwood, like Hull and Grimsby, is left with only a lot of memories and a wonderful history of the men who sailed from the port.

Facilities, or the lack of them

Put on the spot to say which was the best trawler I ever sailed in out of Hull, I would have no hesitation in saying that this was the Lorenzo. I had spent a number of years in the Benvolio and her sister ship the Brutus and of the two, I had always preferred the Brutus. I later spent some time in the Lorenzo and her sister ship the Caesar, and eventually sailed as skipper of the Caesar, although I always had a soft spot for the Lorenzo.

Although I had also sailed for a number of years as mate of the Portia and the Falstaff, I can look back with all honesty on my time in the Lorenzo as some of the happiest days of my time at sea. I would not hesitate to say that this was down to the fine crew that sailed in this ship during the two years I spent on board as a deckhand.

But it had not always been like that. In my teens I had spent considerable time as deck hand in several of the old coal burners, including the Kelt and the Loch Torridon. I mention these two simply because the only thing that the Kelt will ever be remembered for is that she must have been the worst sea ship ever to sail out of Hull and it was my misfortune to sign on her on two separate occasions, and to spend more than a year at sea in her. Most of this was under water, because I simply did not know any better.

I can not find it within me to say a kind word about the Kelt. She had nothing in the way of washing facilities and a visit to the outside toilets situated right at the stern could be an ordeal in reasonable weather and in poor weather not much short of a nightmare.

A visit to the Kelt's toilet never took long. At times nerves of steel were needed. On gaining entry to the toilet, usually after having waited for the water to clear the aft part of the deck, the first thing to do was to locate the seat, which could usually be found floating in six or seven inches of water. A visit to the toilet without taking a sheet of dry newspaper could be fatal because the toilet roll suspend-

ed on a length of twine was always wet within seconds of being replaced. With some experience, you could usually judge as the trip progressed if the next sea to come over the rail would come over the top of the half door that was supposedly there to stop water getting into the toilet. There was no warning or any guarantee that the water would not sweep in over the top of the door that was about level with your chin, when in the sitting position. On a brighter note, it has to be said that if you were ever taken short or had to use the Kelt's outside toilet in a hurry, you were certain never to have to wait long.

These trawlers were usually crewed by people like myself who were in their late teens and by older deckhands who were coming to the end of their years at sea. I could hardly believe my luck when on landing what turned out to be my last trip in the Kelt, the ship's husband called me into his office and told me to sign off, as she had been sold to another company. I was hardly able to contain my joy as I walked off the dock and my only thought were: who the hell would want to buy the Kelt?

But sold she was and a few days later I walked on the dock to see the Kelt in her new company colours sailing through the lock gates out of St. Andrew's Dock. With her new crew lining the rails, I could not help thinking: 'if only you knew what you have let yourselves in for, you poor sods.'

However, the Loch Torridon was not much different to the Kelt, with the same high standard of washing facilities, which was usually a bucket heated on the galley stove or by dropping a red hot shackle into it. You could be spoilt for choice.

The Loch Torridon was painted black almost everywhere, except for a small white star on her otherwise all black funnel. Black was the most appropriate colour for the Loch Torridon, simply because everything you touched was black and my everlasting memory of the Loch Torridon is of a dirty old trawler with black smoke forever belching from her funnel and with the port side of the deck covered with old damaged nets and wires. Getting forward from aft or vice versa was like negotiating no man's land on a battle-field.

In all, I suppose I must have sailed in six different coal burning ships. I suppose this was a good apprenticeship that did no harm at all. But shortly after this I went on to the dizzy heights of sailing in the Brutus, a very fine and successful Hull trawler, before moving on to the Lorenzo with the rest of the deck crew when the skipper was promoted. I was still single at the time and being part of a success-ful ship like the Lorenzo provided me with some of the best years I spent at sea. During the short time in between trips, my only com-plaint was that while I was doing the same work and more than most, I was also paying far more income tax than the rest of the deck crew. But they were good years and I have always looked back fondly on the time that I spent as a deckhand in the Lorenzo, where I also thought about furthering my career if I intended to continue as a fisherman.

Like her sister ship the Caesar, Lorenzo was built, like most of Hellyers' ships, at Smith's Dock in Middlesbrough and in my opinion these two ships were the best of the Hellyers' fleet, the only ones built with a drying room around the funnel. These two trawlers proved to be top earning ships, and although not blessed with a fantastic turn of speed, they were both fine sea ships. This is something that was echoed by everyone who sailed in them and through the hard work there were also plenty of laughs, but on one occasion it was the skipper who was on the receiving end.

The drying room around the funnel of the Lorenzo was the perfect place to pass away the hours if you were watching the warps in case they pulled out while towing. The drying room was also well stocked with newspapers and books, and a few girlie magazines could always be found there. During my last six months in her, there were also many items to be found in the drying room that you would be likely to be asked about when going for a

mate's certificate, such as morse code, inter-national flags and the rule of the road.

All of these things could be found in there, yet on this particular trip, apart from going in there for a dry frock or oilskin, nobody had spent much time in there.

A large group of ships, mainly from Hull and Grimsby, had been experiencing some very heavy fishing on the west side of Bear Island for several days and our trip was draw-ing to a close. It was obvious that we would be on deck for a considerable time after we had taken the last large haul of fish on board and were on our way home with a fair breeze astern of us. Returning to the deck after the midday meal, it was decided that each man on deck would take a turn at the wheel for an hour and a half, giving everyone a break and the time for a pot of tea and a smoke while steering the ship along. Everything was going along fine as we set about the task on deck of clearing the fish.

Our third hand on Lorenzo was a well-known character in Hull, although he came from Fleetwood. He was a great shipmate and well thought of by everyone, but his one weakness was gambling and horse racing, and of course dominoes. Whether or not he had a good time at home between trips usually depended very much on the result of the first race, with the favourite usually carrying his entire settling on its back. If it won, things would be fine, but most times it just never happened for him. But with a smile, he never let it get him down, whatever the result, and the only one to suffer was himself as he cut back on the essential things like oilskins and the more popular rubber frocks that were worn at the time by those on deck.

Needless to say, his rubber frock that had been handed down by the mate always had prime position over the top of the engine room fidley with all the heat came through from the engine room to the drying room.

Finding your way past his two old rubber frocks that had seen better days was an expe-rience, as they hung there in the drying room with the rubber melting from the heat like the old fashioned flycatchers that hung in many people's homes at the time. Most of us were aware of the third hand's deadly form of black death in the drying room and gave them a wide berth, but the one man who never knew what fate awaited him as he ventured unsuspectingly into the drying room was the skipper.

It was close to six in the evening and my spell at the wheel was coming to an end. From the aroma that was coming from his berth, it was obvious that the skipper had been taking a bath. I shouted down and told him the time, and he appeared on the bridge and surveyed the scene on the deck, where all of the fish had been gutted and put below. He looked pleased with himself, and why not? The skipper was bathed and shaved and had put on a clean shirt and sweater and light grey slacks, so his appearance was quite different to myself and the friend of mine who relieved me at the wheel to go down for the teatime meal. Passing the mate going up to the bridge, everything seemed fine, as we were on our way home with a lot of fish on board, but in a second all the laughing and joking stopped abruptly as the skipper appeared at the mess deck door holding one of the third hand's frocks. He resembled a black and white minstrel, demanded to know who this fly catcher belonged to, before throwing it over the side some 120 miles south of Bear Island before returning to the bridge to clean himself up again. This was going to be no easy task as the black death had claimed another victim. The following day the other rubber frock got the same treatment and the curse of the black death was gone forever from the Lorenzo.

Eventually, when everyone was bathed and shaved and on our steaming watches, even the skipper was able to see the funny side of it and laugh it off. But for our third hand, it meant having to replace two rubber frocks, much to everyone's relief.

They were indeed great times. The work was not easy by any standards but it was made all the easier by the standard of the men you worked alongside. I would just like to say thanks for the memories to the men who made up the crews of these three fine ships, Portia, Lorenzo and Falstaff. These memories are something special indeed, something that will stay with me for the rest of my life.

On leaving the Lorenzo, I took an eyesight test, then sat my mate's certificate, emerging after two months at nautical college in Hull. Passing on the very same day was my older brother. It had been a very successful class, and just like at sea it had been very much down to teamwork and the willingness to help each other out.

Then it was back to sea, this time as bosun of one of the ships I had sailed in previously, the Benvolio.

After four trips, I decided to sign off and spend Christmas at home. This was something that I soon found had not been a very good idea, as with four trips still to complete before I could sail as mate, I was told that as I had signed off to spend Christmas at home, there would be no shortcut back to sea now that the Christmas and New Year festivities were over.

By this time I was married with a wife and child to support and it was well into February before the skipper of the Loch Moidart put my name forward as for the job as bosun with him. Somewhat reluctantly, the ship's husband signed me onto the Loch Moidart, but only after a stern lecture and a reminder that now I had a mate's certificate, I should think about mending my ways to some extent. He was right, and by now the party was well and truly over.

After completing my four remaining trips as bosun of the Loch Moidart, I was told within a week or so of arriving home that I would be doing my first trip as mate of another of my favourite ships, the Brutus.

Looking Back – Bear Island

It is extremely unlikely that Bear Island will ever feature in any of the glossy holiday brochures that advertise the ideal place to spend a summer vacation.

But for many years this tiny remote island miles north of the Arctic Circle between Spitzbergen and the North Cape of Norway featured prominently in the fortunes of the deep sea fishing fleets of Hull and Grimsby.

The waters in these high northern latitudes were fished with a great deal of success for many years by the Hull and Grimsby trawlers, as well as the fishing fleets of Norway and the old Soviet Union. The years after the Second World War were possibly the best, and the 1950s and 1960s also saw some remarkable catches landed from the remote waters around Bear Island.

Although fishing at Bear Island reached its peak in these years, trawlers from Hull and Grimsby had already fished these waters before the outbreak of World War 2 during the 1930s. A number of trawler owners built larger vessels that brought these grounds within range of these more modern trawlers.

Shrouded in mist for much of the time, it is possible to fish trip after trip there without catching a glimpse of the bleak island itself.

If Bear Island was a place of success for the skippers and crews who landed catches from these grounds, the island itself was the scene of some of the most dramatic sea rescues and acts of bravery told, speaking volumes about the courage and sheer determination of the rescue parties and the bond between seamen.

In Grimsby people will never forget the rescue of the crew of the trawler Earl Howe which had grounded on Bear Island in poor weather. The weather conditions ensured that there was no possibility of rescue from the seaward side by any of the ships that came to her assistance, and the first attempts at rescue were carried out by officers from the Norwegian radio station on the island.

Although a number of men managed to get ashore on the leeward side of the island, all attempts at rescue failed until a party led by Skipper Drinkall from Grimsby reached the cliff tops above the Earl Howe. These trawlermen had made the journey in pitch darkness and appalling weather across the island, a feat that had been thought impossible owing to the rough nature of the terrain and the difficult conditions that they encountered in crossing the island.

After many hours trapped in the Earl Howe's wheelhouse, every member of the crew was rescued by breeches buoy, a fitting ending for an episode which demonstrated the courage and determination of everyone concerned.

Some years later, the crew of the Hull trawler St Sebastian were not so fortunate when their ship was lost with all hands on the night of 29th September 1938 after running aground on Bear Island. They had sailed from Hull on 15th September with a crew of sixteen, bound for the Bear Island grounds.

On the 28th, the St Sebastian's position had been given to another of the company's trawlers, acting as report ship, as 20 miles north of Cape Duner. In the same message the St Sebastian reported that she would be leaving for home the following day at 1800 GMT.

From then on, the trawler's movements are not clear, but at 2015, Le Tiger and the Kingston Cairngorm picked up her radio signal to all ships requiring immediate assistance as she was aground at Cape Duner. It would appear that St Sebastian had been much further to the east than had been believed, and the skipper must have expected that his course of SW by S half S would take the trawler west of Cape Duner on her voyage home. In fact St Sebastian grounded on Bear Island's north coast in the area of Cape Kjellstrom.

The trawlers Davy, Kingston Cairngorm, Le Tiger, Loch Oskaig, Cape Duner and Mildenhall all proceeded from their positions to the assistance of the St Sebastian. The trawler's plight became clear when she was able to inform other ships by radio of the situation. The weather at the time of the grounding had been WSW, but had increased and shifted to a westerly gale, veering later to the NW and NNW, the worst possible direction for a vessel aground on the north coast of the island.

Despite the number of trawlers in the area and the presence of the Norwegian salvage vessel Jason, it was soon decided that owing to the conditions it was impossible to attempt any kind of a rescue from the seaward side. This prompted several of the ships, including Davy, Cape Duner and Jason to steam round to the east coast of the island, where a party from Davy and Cape Duner managed to get ashore in the area around Cape Levin at 1100.

The island's rough terrain made it extremely difficult for the men dressed in sea clothes and heavy thigh boots, yet by 1700 and guided by rockets fired by the ships close to the stricken trawler, these men arrived in a position on the cliffs directly above the St Sebastian.

The rescue team later told how when they arrived on the scene, the St Sebastian was intact, but was shortly after seen to break in two after being continually swept by heavy seas, and it became evident that nobody could survive in such harsh conditions.

As the rescuers reached the beach, there were hatches and wreckage to be seen, but no sign of any survivors on the beach. The rescuers eventually returned to the island's radio station at 6 AM the following morning, hungry and completely exhausted.

Skipper Wilson of the Davy, along with the skipper of the Jason and the mate of the Cape Duner, eventually returned to the St Sebastian, but found no signs of any survivors. The trawler's log was still streamed, and showed that she had steamed just twelve miles after being set.

Two bodies were found in the ship's bridge, and although one of the trawlers close to the wreck had reported sighting a man crawling over the rocks, nobody was found in the intensive search that followed.

When the Earl Howe had gone aground in 1931, everyone had been rescued, but seven years later there was no such happy ending for the crew of the St Sebastian. One can only marvel at the sheer courage and determination of the men who risked their own lives to assist fellow fishermen in distress.

Those early years around Bear Island must have been a nightmare for the men who pioneered fishing in those hostile northern waters. The intense cold and the continual darkness throughout the long winter must have stretched many mens' nerves to breaking point. With no lights on the island and only irregular radio signals, plus the areas of local magnetic anomaly, it makes one wonder what we owe to the men who fished those bleak waters around Bear Island.

Some of today's young fishermen find it hard to believe sort of conditions that their fathers sailed under, with long hours spent gutting on open decked trawlers and hauls of mainly small codling found in the waters around the island.

From personal experience, I would say that the British skippers preferred the grounds to the west of the island, as those waters have been responsible for both Hull and Grimsby markets being full from end to end.

In the years when fishing at Bear Island was at its peak, nobody mentioned the word conservation. The waters around Bear Island and further north to Spitzbergen were fished relentlessly by ships of all nations, trawlers that had to spend months on end on the fishing grounds. Inevitably, something had to give, and it did. In the late 1960s and early 1970s, there was a dramatic fall in fish catches landed from Bear Island, and at this time most of Britain's side trawlers were concentrating on the grounds at Iceland.

The few trawlers that ventured to Bear Island on occasions never enjoyed the type of fishing that was associated with fishing there in previous years. 1968 was possibly the last of the boom years at Bear Island, yet one can only be amazed at how these waters stood up to continual fishing for so many years.

The few remaining British trawlers still fish these waters, and long may they continue to do so. But the sacrifice that British fishermen made to open up these grounds for others to benefit from should not be forgotten.

The Spyship Theories

The Gaul was linked to acts of spying almost immediately after she was reported lost. Both individuals and a number of newspapers and television programmes were quick to brand the Gaul as some sort of spyship. It is my honest opinion that all the rumours linking the Gaul to acts of spying, espionage or information gathering are entirely unfounded, and have only benefited people connected to newspapers and television companies who had an interest in cynically keeping the story in the news.

From the day that I joined the Gaul, she was crewed by some very experienced fishermen, and during the period that I was skipper, nobody connected to the Secret Services, the Royal Navy, or any of the armed services sailed in the ship. She was manned solely by a crew of dedicated fishermen right up to the time of her loss.

Over the years I have spoken to a number of people from the press or television media, and it never takes me long to guess where the questions are heading. Interviews inevitably get round to the subject of spying and the part that the Gaul may have played in information gathering. My replies to the effect that the Gaul never took part in any such activities have never failed to bring about looks of amazement and disbelief, and this has normally brought interviews to a quick and timely conclusion.

After her loss, the Gaul was described by the papers and television as something of a supertrawler, and as being in a class apart from the rest of the British trawler fleet. The four ships of her class were well-built, and well thought out vessels with modern accommodation and facilities, but it must be said that at the time there were a number of British freezers built around the same time and in the same class as the Gaul. Before her loss, the four sister ships had none of this 'super-trawler' status. All this came after she was lost.

Once she had been reported missing, all kinds of rumours linked the Gaul's disappearance to Soviet activity. There have been suggestions of a Soviet submarine surfacing beneath the Gaul, but this is highly unlikely, as a collision of this type would have resulted in an obvious oil leakage and the possibility of more wreckage over a large area, but there was no sign of either of these.

Rumours that the Gaul had been arrested are even more far fetched, as nobody could ever explain how to go about the arrest of a ship in gale force winds when everyone all around is dodging head to wind in exceptionally severe weather conditions.

Practically all contact when a group of ships is fishing is by VHF, and no conversation of any kind was reported by the many ships that were fishing in the area. The suggestion that the Gaul could have been arrested in such weather conditions as there were at the time, in my opinion and in the opinion of many other experienced fishermen, is not even a remote possibility.

A retired Soviet officer went on television to speak of the Gaul as a spyship, and stated that they knew all about the movements of the Gaul and had it listed as a spyship, yet the Gaul did not sail under that name until that final voyage and had still been the Ranger Castor until only a few weeks previously.

It has also been mentioned that the Gaul had been buzzed by a Soviet aircraft during the latter stages of the previous trip, yet nobody mentioned that I had stated this at the enquiry into the Gaul's loss. This was hardly an unusual occurrence, yet the rumours and speculation have continued over the years.

For many years ships fishing in the Barents Sea in areas such as the East Bank had been requested to monitor the movements of the Soviet warships that were based at Kildin. Some skippers used cameras and took photographs, while others chose to identify what they had seen against silhouettes when they arrived home. One Hull stern trawler spent part of her trip searching for an important piece of equipment that had been lost from one of our naval ships.

These were the years of the Cold War and from this the term spyships began to be heard, frequently used by both press and television to dramatise their stories.

What was done in fact required no training, and the reporting of Soviet warships was more or less voluntary. By and large, skippers were simply observing what went on around them, as they would have done under any circumstances, rather than being involved in anything that could be described as full time spying.

On one occasion, long before the Ranger Castor had been built, I visited an office in Hull where a naval officer met a group of us and asked us to pick out of a book a number of Soviet warships and submarines. But ships that had arrived at home some days before us had also reported these same ships and I never visited the office again, and we were under no obligation to do so.

The media has continued to make a meal of the ship's disappearance, and the newspapers have never been shy of using the ship's loss when it suited them to stir up public interest, and in some cases showing no regard whatever for the dependants of the men who lost their lives with the Gaul.

After the Gaul's loss I returned to sea in one of the same type of ships, the Dane, a different build of ship, but like the Gaul, built to fillet her catch at sea. The trip in the Dane took us back to the Barents Sea, and with very good fishing we were able to return home with a full ship in quick time for the inquiry into the loss of the Gaul, which I attended and gave evidence at.

Prior to the Gaul sailing on that final voyage, I had visited the ship just once during her time in dock, and that was with Peter Nellist, who relieved me for the trip.

I had known Peter Nellist for some years, and he had spent a lot of time in stern trawlers, both as mate and as skipper. But to the best of my knowledge, this would have been his first trip in this type of filleting stern trawler.

Our visit to the Gaul lasted some two hours, with most of the time being spent in the factory deck and on the ship's bridge. I later testified on oath that after leaving the Gaul on that occasion, I never saw Peter Nellist or the Gaul again.

At the end of the inquiry that lasted a month in Hull's City Hall, the conclusion was that the Gaul had been lost in exceptionally poor weather conditions. This is a verdict that I would certainly agree with, but for years since her disappearance many people have refused to accept this as the reason for her loss.

Right: The Gaul, originally the Ranger Castor and the last of the four C class trawlers built at Brooke Marine for the Ranger Fishing Company. This is the ship as I last saw her in her newly-painted British United Trawlers colours, before sailing under Peter Nellist for that last voyage to the Barents Sea in 1974.
Photo: Malcolm Fussey.

Wild Weather
– and Some Wild Theories

Since the loss of the Gaul, British fishing activities in the area where the Gaul was lost have been greatly restricted. Politics, and the depletion of our own deep sea fleet has meant that we have only a small amount of fish to catch in these northern latitudes. Now that we only have a small deep sea fleet of trawlers operating mainly from Hull, the small quota of fish that Britain is allowed to catch is usually taken early in the year.

It was in the area of Cape Bank, a prolific fishing ground for British and Norwegian trawlers, as well as others such as the Russians, that a lifebuoy was recovered some time after the loss of the Gaul.

On its return to Hull, the lifebuoy was positively identified as belonging to the Gaul, and was easily identified by staff who had been given the task of repainting the lifebuoys.

However, forensic evidence indicated that the lack of salt water plankton on the lifebuoy meant that it had not been in the water for any length of time, and a certain television programme suggested that the lifebuoy had in all possibility been planted in a position where it would be spotted and picked up by any trawler fishing there.

With this type of scientific evidence, I would normally accept that the lack of salt water plankton on the lifebuoy is certainly a point that nobody could give a satisfactory answer to, until I had a casual conversation with a fellow skipper on the VHF when I returned to sea following the inquiry into the loss of the Gaul.

The conversation got round to the type of books we preferred to read, and it was due to this conversation that I found myself in the library, inquiring about a certain book that had been written by the great Norwegian explorer

Nansen. The book was an account of the sheer determination of these great explorers to reach the North Pole, and the hardships they endured in order to succeed. Nansen explained in the book that when his party was short of water, owing to the heavy snowfalls and the fresh water coming out of the fjords, they had been able to drink the surface water from the sea.

While not implying that one could throw a bucket over the side and drink the entire contents, but having spent many years in these areas and seen first hand some of the heavy falls of snow during the long winter months, this information could hold up a possibility of why no salt water organisms were found on the Gaul's lifebuoy.

Planting a lifebuoy in a position well inside the Arctic Circle, hoping that it would be picked up, at that time of the year when there is very little daylight, is something of a long shot. This was the suggestion at the time by the makers of the television programme, and although a long shot can sometimes come up, the fresh surface water could provide the answer to the question of the lifebuoy's condition.

Over the years I have listened to all kinds of theories as to how the Gaul was lost, at times I have been amazed at the number of people who have never taken into account the one factor that I feel sure contributed most to the loss of the ship, namely the weather that fishermen experienced during those long winter months.

The weather at that time of year can make a trip in a freezer seem endless. Stoppages for weather just prolong the trip, and the constant rolling of the ship during long periods of bad weather with no daylight simply saps the strength of everyone on board the ship.

The Gaul, however, was in the early stages of her trip, and this was the first time that the vessel had stopped fishing owing to the poor weather conditions that had worsened overnight.

At the time of the Gaul's loss, it has been estimated that she had on board no more than twenty tonnes of fish fillets, with possibly seven tonnes of meal. This combined weight would account for only half of the expended fuel and water on board after leaving Hull and steaming to fishing grounds off the Norwegian coast, but this would not have been a factor that could have seriously affected the Gaul's stability.

Unlike some of the old side trawlers that could lay between the troughs almost broadside on to the wind and sea, this would not have been the case with the Gaul, or any of the large freezer trawlers that were in the same area around Cape Bank at the time.

With very little freeboard, and the bridge slightly aft of midships, the side trawlers were the ideal design to ride and dodge out a gale of wind, while the freezers had only one option once the decision to dodge had been made. With so much freeboard and a high bridge exposed to the wind and sea, laying was out of the question. The freezer trawler would in most cases finish up with her stern ramp facing the wind and sea. This was not the ideal position to be in, and this could often result in some sort of damage.

With engines running continually, the Gaul and the other freezer trawlers would have dodged, steaming slowly head to wind with sufficient engine revolutions to keep steerage way on the ship.

As the weather had deteriorated, I feel sure that the Gaul's crew would have taken all necessary precautions once it was known that fishing operations had ceased until the weather improved.

Normal procedure would have been for the hydraulic doors at the top of the ramp leading to the factory deck to have been closed and clamped from the inside. This was all part of the normal routine for the men on the factory deck, although the survey of the wreck later showed that not all of the normal procedures had been followed.

With everything battened down, and once heading into the wind, the freezer trawlers were fine ships. This method had been used time and again, heading into the wind for three hours or more, before turning around and heading back before the wind, arriving back at the original position and turning once more. This process was repeated over and over again, usually until there was some improvement in the weather.

Using this method, ships could remain reasonably close to the area where they were fishing, and as soon as the weather improved, they would be able to resume fishing in a short time.

There were of course other methods used when dodging out a gale of wind, and this depended mainly on how bad the weather was at the time. Some skippers would cross a number of Decca lanes, while others would keep the ship head to wind for longer periods of time to avoid turning round and presenting the ship broadside to the wind and sea. Much depended on the state of the weather, and on the 8th of February 1974 the weather was very bad indeed.

My own personal view regarding dodging in severe weather is that it is best to keep the ship head to wind for as long as possible, as once the weather moderated, it generally only took a short time to run back afore wind and sea to the original position.

Normal practice when these types of ships were dodging was for one of the crewmen on watch to visit the factory deck at hourly intervals, and report to the bridge if anything was amiss. This was the routine in the time I spent in the ship, either fishing or steaming, and I feel certain that this practice would certainly have been carried on and the same routine maintained.

A year previously, while on our way to the fishing grounds, we had encountered a severe gale shortly after passing Svino on the Norwegian coast. With the wind and sea from the south west, it was not a very pleasant afternoon, and with the forecast threatening to get worse before it was to get better, I decided to bring the ship around before it got completely dark and spend the night dodging head to wind.

As forecast, the weather deteriorated even further during the period between 1800 and 2300, before we saw a very slight improvement. An hour later we were able to turn round once again and continue on our way before a big sea but with the wind strength decreasing rapidly.

There had of course been other occasions when we had been forced to stop fishing when weather was bad, and on none of these occasions had the ship ever given me any cause for alarm.

Everyone has a right to have an opinion as to what exactly did happen to the Gaul, and I have listened intently to any number of suggestions over the years as to how the Gaul may have been lost during a gale of wind that should not have presented her with any problems at all. A number of smaller ships in the area dodged the gale out as they had done many times before, while it should also be remembered that several other ships also suffered structural damage during the storm in which the Gaul disappeared.

Being familiar with the ship, I have an advantage, and I find it very difficult to imagine that whatever happened to the Gaul occurred while she was in the process of dodging head to wind with enough engine power to maintain steerage way. This had been a common enough procedure that had been used for years in bad weather.

Was the Gaul caught broadside to the wind and sea while turning around to run back? This was again a common enough manoeuvre, used by most skippers to keep close to the position where they had been forced to stop fishing in worsening weather.

During the 1974 inquiry into the loss of the Gaul, Ronnie Boughen, the highly experienced skipper of the Southella, one of the freezer trawlers on Cape Bank at the same time, mentioned that he had passed the Gaul, and shortly after he had turned around to run back before the wind and sea, his vessel had been struck by three enormous seas in succession. It is possible that whoever had been on the bridge, seeing the distance between the two ships increasing, had decided to bring the Gaul around as well to run before the weather, and while bringing the ship about, had been caught broadside to the full impact of these same three very large seas.

If this was the case, it would start to explain why a mayday had not been sent using the VHF that was located just inches away from the skipper's seat. With plenty of ships in the area within short range, this would have been the obvious way to transmit a mayday message. Whatever happened to the Gaul, one thing is certain - that it happened very quickly, as there was no distress call and both her radio and VHF sets were known to have been in order and in use earlier during the day when we assume she was lost.

During my time as skipper of the Gaul we routinely encountered the sort of weather that you can expect to encounter well inside the Arctic Ocean in the middle of winter, yet during the periods that it had been impossible to fish, I felt that we had done nothing different to what any other ship fishing same waters had done.

It was standard practice to come around quickly at full speed after a long period head to wind, before reducing speed again with the ship running before the wind and sea. Picking the right moment to come about depended very much on the weather at the time, and most skippers would wait until something of a lull in the weather presented a chance to bring the ship about. The Gaul had never given me any cause for alarm in completing manoeuvres such as to bring her before the wind.

Seldom are two trips alike. The movements of shoals of fish in the autumn and through the winter ensure that the trawlers follow the fish in their movement south-west along the steep edges of the Norwegian coast. This had been the case on the Gaul's previous trip, when steady fishing, along with a five day spell of very good fishing in good weather ensured that the Gaul was in good trim to meet the first of the gales of winter with our first hundred tonnes of fish caught in a reasonably short time.

Call it luck, or call it what you will, but this is fishing as most fishermen know it to be.

Yet with all this in mind, there were many other freezers in the early stages of their trips and in a similar condition. Apart from the normal discomfort that comes with a gale of wind, these managed to ride out the storm that claimed the Gaul, although some did suffer damage.

The tragedy of the Gaul has never been out of the news. Every year the crew have been remembered by family and friends alike, especially on the eighth of February, the day she is presumed to have been lost.

On the 20th anniversary of the Gaul's loss, I was invited to be a guest on a Radio Humberside programme to remember the sad loss of the Gaul and her crew. Towards the end of the programme I commented that advances had been made in locating the wrecks of the Titanic, the Derbyshire, the German battleship Bismarck and also HMS Edinburgh, lost in a position well known to British fishermen. I made it plain that if the money were made available, it would be a simple task to locate the wreck of the Gaul, and that this could possibly be done by a television company. My final comment was that she would probably be found on Cape Bank.

For a number of years I have had in my possession a position that I feel sure is familiar to many Hull and Grimsby skippers, Lat 72°03'5 North, Long 25°05'0 East.

On what had been good trawling ground, ships had begun reporting damaging trawls and losing full sets of gear in this region, to the extent that the position was marked on Norwegian charts and was widely thought to be the position of the wreck of the Gaul.

However, with British fishing interests in the area greatly reduced, the Gaul drifted in and out of the news until it was announced in the autumn of 1997 that the Gaul had been located and positively identified on North Cape Bank off the north cape of Norway.

The wreck was easily found by the Risøy, a survey vessel chartered for the purpose by a British television company. The ship was positively identified as the Gaul, also showing both her previous name of Ranger Castor, along with the nameplate of builders Brooke Marine, that had remained on the front of the bridge in exceptionally good condition.

The Gaul was back in the news, but for me she was back in the news for all the wrong reasons. Once again the Gaul was being linked with stories of spying and espionage by the press, radio and television, who never missed a chance to highlight anything that could link the ship to a spy story, as long as it made more headlines.

Apart from identifying the wreck of the Gaul, the Channel 4 programme in which the wreck was first shown included virtually nothing that could link the Gaul to any spying activities, but went to extreme lengths to include information about Soviet nuclear submarine activity in the 1970s.

The Soviet naval base at Kildin was seen as the likely target for British trawlers watching manoeuvres in the area, but as I have stated on many occasions, the Gaul was not involved in any work of this kind at any time.

So little did this particular television documentary reveal, that another bid to visit the wreck of the Gaul was announced, but with winter approaching, this was scheduled for the summer of 1998.

The Marine Accident Investigation Branch (MAIB) chartered the undersea support vessel Mansal 18 to carry out the survey of the Gaul. Bigger and better equipped than the Risøy, the Mansal 18 seemed to me to be the ideal vessel for this role. Among the crew of the Mansal 18 were a number of ex-fishermen, along with the MAIB team and the two men who would be going to represent the families of the crew of the Gaul.

Considering the length of time that I had been associated with the Gaul and one of her sister ships that I had skippered after the Gaul's loss, I had hopes of being invited to join the Mansal 18 in some sort of advisory capacity. I felt very strongly that I had much to offer, yet no invitation was arrived and I must admit to some annoyance at this decision.

Because this survey of the Gaul had been ordered by the Department of Transport, a number of changes had been brought about regarding filming on board, and this was now in the hands of a BBC camera crew. Once the survey was finished, the BBC wasted no time in broadcasting a programme that included a limited amount of the actual underwater footage from the Gaul.

The Mansal 18 had spent several days over the wreck, and taking into account the large amount of net strewn around the trawler, had made a good all-round series of pictures of the Gaul and the sea bed where she had been lying for twenty-four years.

Perhaps the most significant point was that the hydraulic doors leading from the trawl deck to the factory were both seen to be open, one slightly more than the other.

Another door leading into the factory deck on the starboard side of the deck was also fully open, with a large amount of net across its entrance. The programme showed little else, apart from a small amount of damage to the hull below the anchors, possibly brought about when empty tanks forward crumpled under the water pressure as the Gaul settled in her final resting place on the sea bed.

As usual when the Gaul was in the headlines, a variety of people wanted to air their views, and this time it was exactly the same following this latest television programme and the opinions flew thick and fast.

Arriving in the Falklands

With most of the work on the fishing gear now completed and the chief engineer now bringing the temperature in the hold down to below freezing, there was already a buzz of excitement on board as the Fishing Explorer made steady progress towards the Falklands. It was more than a week since we had crossed the equator, and at last things started to cool off a little.

The first indications of this were when the crew working on deck started to appear in trousers and shirts, even the occasional sweater. Gone were the shorts and flip-flops that had been the rig of the day after leaving the Canary Islands.

We had already been in radio contact with the Spanish factory trawler Arosso Octavo, where our arrival was eagerly awaited as we had on board food and stores and a large amount of mail to transfer across as they were nearing the end of their trip.

Some of our crew had friends and relations on board the Arosso Octavo. One of our younger crew members told me that his father was on the other vessel and asked if he could go across in one of the boats when we did the transfer, as he had not seen his father for some time.

We were now just three days from entering the Falkland Islands Exclusive Fishing Zone, and kept in daily contact with the fishery patrol vessel and the Arosso Octavo. Our first priority would be to hand over the large amount of stores we had on board for the Arosso Octavo, and once this was done he would then be free to do as he pleased. At that moment he was fishing in the area to the south of Beauchene Island, although the situation could change easily, depending on the weather and the fishing.

The extended trips made by these factory trawlers were very long for everyone on board once fishing had begun and the long hours worked by the crew were very demanding. Catching the large amount of fish needed to enable the ship to show a profit after coming all this way was no easy task. The first thousand tonnes would be transhipped and freighted home by a merchant ship. Then we would start all over again catching as much fish as

The Spanish trawler Arosso Octavo nearing the end of its trip and the crew were eagerly awaiting our arrival in the Falklands so that we could transfer across enough food and stores to see them home to Spain.

possible before setting off home. The first thousand tonnes would go towards the expenses of the voyage and the cost of the licence to fish in these waters.

All the fish had to be processed on board. The squid were packed and frozen, and fish such as hake were machine filleted and packed in different sized cartons. In some of the conditions that we were sure to encounter during the trip, this would be very demanding for everyone on board, physically and mentally.

By the time we were 48 hours from the Falkland Islands we had been in radio contact with both the Falkland Right and the Falkland Desire, the two fishery patrol vessels. These two former Hull stern trawlers had been taken on for the task of policing the fishing zone around the Falklands, and they were able to give us something of a briefing on what to expect when we arrived in Port Stanley.

During the day the weather gradually freshened, and it was now quite cold, not that anyone had any reason to venture on deck as all the work was finished and the Fishing Explorer was ready to commence fishing.

By midday the wind was a force six from the south west, and the occasional spray that came aboard was something we had not seen since leaving La Coruña. We had been very lucky, and the fishery patrol vessels informed us that the weather was not expected to get any worse, apart from the occasional snow shower, until we were due to arrive in Port Stanley.

During the day we had passed four trawlers, all more or less on the opposite course to ours, and probably with the worst of the weather behind them. They were all making their way home, and taking a break from the fishing grounds, but for us it was just the beginning.

The following day we entered the 150 mile fishing zone, and contacted the fishery patrol vessel to pass on our ETA, which would be passed on to the authorities in Port Stanley.

Once inside the fishing zone, we passed a number of ships, most of which appeared to be fishing and very well lit up, most likely Korean ships jigging for squid. The night passed without incident, the weather was fine, and at 04.30 we finally picked up land on the radar.

As daylight broke, after a light snow shower, we could see the land. Shortly afterwards, we had our first glimpse of the extent of the fishery in the Falklands, as we passed about twenty ships engaged in either discharging their fish to large reefer ships, or lying at anchor awaiting their turn, while a number of others were refuelling at a small tanker a little further inside the sound. It looked a busy scene, but was quickly lost to view as we continued, and shortly after we rounded Cape Pembroke. At 09.30 anchored in calm waters just outside Port Stanley, eighteen days after leaving Las Palmas.

Our first sight of Port Stanley under a leaden sky.

An hour or so later, while having coffee and a sandwich in the saloon, I was told there was a call for me on the VHF. I made my way back to the bridge, and was informed that within the hour the harbour launch would pick me up and take me ashore to pay a visit to the fisheries office.

After I had made myself somewhat presentable, the launch duly arrived and a few minutes later I was ashore in the Falklands for the very first time in the offices of the Falkland Islands Trading Company. I made the acquaintance of the agent, a fellow Yorkshireman, and we drove the short distance to the fisheries office, where we were made welcome before the debriefing began.

I have always had a deep distrust of people connected with any kind of office work, and that day confirmed my opinions. On board a ship a mistake is a mistake, but in an office a mistake is an error, and I have never quite been able to define the difference between the two.

The punchline came after the debriefing had gone rather well. I was preparing to leave with papers and charts of every description under each arm, when the bombshell was dropped. Owing to an error somewhere along the line, our fishing licence was not available, but would in all probability be ready the following day.

'What a cock-up' was my immediate reaction. We had been at sea a month, and to arrive and be told that our licence was not available left me speechless. How could these people in their nine to five jobs - who in my opinion use three sheets of paper when one would do and pass most of their work over to the ship's master, this red tape brigade who are the biggest reason for the ever deteriorating size of the rain forests - have let us down so badly?

Returning to the Fishing Explorer and being helped on board with my arms full of papers, the crew gathered on deck must have thought that I was speaking some sort of alien language as I vented my wrath on everybody who worked in government offices, local councils and shipping offices. This was the crew's first lesson in the Hessle Road English that cannot be found in any English dictionary.

We were to remain at anchor until the following day, and the first job was to send a telex asking the reason for the delay after a month at sea getting to the Falklands.

The weather was cold but fine, and the crew busied themselves by painting the ship's call sign that had to be displayed on the bridge top and other vantage points. This also gave me a chance to go through the paperwork and all the rules, regulations and schedule times when we would report the amount of fish caught each day. With something to do, it helped pass the day away and part of the night before turning in for a few hours sleep.

The telex we had sent must have woken a few people up, as while I was on the bridge after breakfast the following morning, there was a call on the VHF informing us that the error had been rectified, and that the harbour launch would pick me up later in the morning to return to the fisheries office.

The launch duly arrived, and a short time later I was back in the fisheries office, emerging shortly after with our all-important fishing licence.

We had been joined at anchor during the night by a Spanish freezer trawler, the Monte Faro, whose skipper accompanied me ashore to pick up his fishing licence. We were to see a lot of the Monte Faro in the months to come. Within half an hour of returning, both ships had hove up their anchors, and were heading out to the open sea to commence fishing.

There were still a few hours of daylight remaining, so we decided to try one tow in this area, and then possibly steam towards Beauchene Island overnight, where the bulk of the fleet appeared to be fishing at the time.

We had already informed the Arosso Octavo of our arrival in the Falklands, and expected to transfer his stores across the following night, if the weather was fine enough.

Everything was ready as we neared the area where we were to commence fishing, and within in hour of leaving Port Stanley we were shooting away the gear, as far as we knew in an area where no other trawlers were fishing.

Down Trawl

In near perfect weather, just to the east of Port Stanley, we shot away the trawl for the first time in 70 fathoms of water. Everything went smoothly, which was one of the advantages of having the first haul during the hours of daylight.

Recent reports indicated that there had been a reasonable day's fishing to be had in this area, and the other ships that had been there had left after hearing better reports from around Beauchene Island.

The trawl had been shot at 15.30, and there were some reasonable indications of fish on the sounder during the first hour of the tow, but as darkness fell there was not a lot to be seen. Nevertheless, we decided to haul after the late evening meal.

Just ahead of us the Monte Faro had decid-

ed to fish through the last hours of daylight before making his way overnight to resume fishing at Beauchene Island in the morning. Like us, he had seen some signs of fish marks on his sounder during the first hour of the tow, but these had petered out until nothing more was to be seen.

Fishing in this area did have its advantages, in that since our arrival we had been able to tune into the Falkland Island Radio to pick up the latest news from home, and also what was happening in the Falklands.

So poor was the fishing during the hours of darkness that all the ships would stop fishing

The Falklands Islands lie in the south Atlantic, as far to the south of the globe as Britain is to the north.

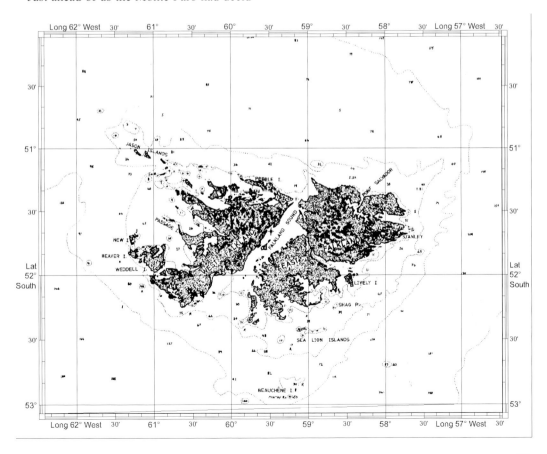

A weak and watery sun sets behind Beauchene Island, with another long night to look forward to. Just to the south of the Falkland Islands, the grounds around the tiny Beauchene Island are some of the most prolific in the world for calamari and attract fishing vessels from all over the world.

after 20.00, and wait for the daylight to resume fishing. This in itself was acceptable as long as the fishing remained reasonably good during the daylight hours.

We had plenty of time to arrive at Beauchene Island before daylight, and for this reason we decided to extend our first tow to four hours. When we eventually decided to haul, everyone expected a reasonable haul, and nobody could have been disappointed when we hauled up the ramp something in the region of seven tonnes of good quality loligo.

We had obviously caught the majority of our fish in the first two hours of the tow, and

Our first haul at Beauchene Island was a welcome sight of around ten tonnes for a tow of three hours.

it would be worth bearing in mind that we could always return here if things did not work out at Beauchene Island.

Once again we contacted the Arosso Octavo again to confirm that we would be in his area the following morning, and would make arrangements to transfer his stores across once we had finished fishing for the day.

Later on that watch as we carried on with the Monte Faro a mile ahead of us towards Beauchene Island, it was confirmed that the first haul had amounted to seven tonnes of loligo and half a tonne of hake fillets.

We arrived at Beauchene Island at 05.15, with the weather better than when we had shot away east of Port Stanley. Now there was nothing more than a light breeze as after breakfast the trawl went down the ramp in 90 fathoms of water.

As daylight broke, it emerged that most of the ships fishing in the area appeared to be Spanish, with a number of Polish and Russian freezer trawlers making up quite an impressive fleet of ships that spread as far to the west as the eye could see.

We had arrived in the Falklands some two months after the start of the new season that allowed squid to be caught in Falkland 150 mile fishing zone, and had clearly missed the best of the fishing. With the winter months approaching, we were under no illusions as to what lay ahead of throughout the remainder of our time there.

Our first haul after a three hour tow seemed to compare favourably with reports from other ships in the area, and reports from the factory deck confirmed that we had hauled about ten tonnes of squid. The next tow during the hours of daylight was even better as we hauled about thirteen tonnes of squid, but by 17.30 it was almost dark. Even though we extended the length of the tow by an hour and hauled in complete darkness, we only hauled about seven tonnes, and like the rest of the ships in the area, decided against shooting away again and lay until the following morning.

Reports from the factory suggested that the loligo we were catching were of good size and quality, and this was reflected in the evening meal when everyone sat down to an excellent meal of loligo and fish, making a most welcome change to the meat and salads that had been on the table almost every day since leaving Spain.

We had completed our first day's fishing with 30 tonnes of loligo and a small amount of hake which was filleted. Hake helped to swell the tonnage as the trip progressed, and would be our prime target if the catches of loligo became so small that it could be no longer viable to search for them.

The evening weather forecast remained quite encouraging, and the following morning we shot the trawl away near enough in the same position as on the previous day. After three hauls mainly in depths between 90 and 100 fathoms we finished the day with 27 tonnes of loligo and then proceeded to our rendezvous with the Arosso Octavo and passed across the stores that would see him through his fishing time and his long journey back to Europe.

Towards the end of our first week fishing in this area we got our first taste of weather and a reminder of what lay ahead of us. A poor weather forecast after we had completed our seventh day's fishing proved to be absolutely correct, and although we had shot away the trawl in reasonable weather conditions, by the time we hauled after a three hour tow, the wind had steadily increased to a force seven. After a reasonable second haul in the region of ten tonnes, we shot away again, even though the weather had deteriorated even further.

By mid-afternoon most of the ships had stopped fishing, as we now had a south westerly force nine gale to contend with. Although the weather had deteriorated, the fishing had improved slightly compared to the two previous days. Even though we hauled our last haul of the day in very poor weather conditions, the six tonnes gave us a total of 25 tonnes for the day. We then proceeded to dodge head to wind, as did all of the ships remaining in the area.

The Arosso Octavo coming alongside the Fishing Explorer to carry out the handover of food and stores to see them home to Spain.

Although the weather was forecast to moderate slightly to a force seven the following morning, it was still poor when we and a number of the larger ships shot away, while some of the smaller ships chose to wait for the

Our second haul was even more encouraging: with thirteen tonnes being dropped down to the factory deck. However, there was very little fishing during darkness and most ships laid to through the night.

Our constant companion during our time in the Falklands was the Spanish trawler Monte Faro. Because of her unusual markings, she was nicknamed 'the pretty ship' by the other ships in the area.

A reasonable haul of loligo is tipped down into the factory during our first few days fishing near Beauchene Island.

weather to improve. But the weather showed no signs of moderating until late in the afternoon, while our three hauls brought one of the best day's fishing, with 30 tonnes.

Overnight the weather did moderate as forecast to a stiff breeze, and as it improved, so did the fishing with ships spread over a wide area, yet we remained in the vicinity of Beauchene Island as we completed our second week's fishing with a total of 250 tonnes.

Of around sixty ships that were in the area around Beauchene Island when we arrived in the Falklands, only about fifteen remained, spread over a twenty mile area. Reports from these ships were generally poor, so the time had come to start thinking of moving on. Our

last two days had been as low as ten and twelve tonnes, including one haul in complete darkness brought only two tonnes on board for a three hour tow before we laid to for the night.

Shooting away the following morning some fourteen miles south of Cape Meredith, our long time colleague the Spanish trawler Monte Faro was now our sole companion. We towed together north west with the sounder full of good indications of fish. The Monte Faro had been a constant companion since we had left Port Stanley, and not a day had passed that we had not had a sighting of this colourful painted ship, which everyone on board named the pretty ship.

We were towing on good grounds, with a typical Spanish-style trawl made in nylon with small mesh in the codend for squid. The ground was good enough that we did not need any bobbins and the trawl was mounted on a footrope made of combination wire and bound with rope.

After a tow of three hours it came as no surprise when the codend floated well astern. Fish meshed in the wings and the square of the trawl as we brought it aboard indicated a reasonable haul of hake, and this was confirmed a few moments later as the codend came up the ramp to show a nice haul of 300 baskets - a good seven tonnes of fish.

This was the single biggest haul of hake that I had ever seen, and prior to this the largest amount that I had seen was a haul of 15 kit caught on the Rising Ground. This was an area between Scotland and the Faroe Islands where it was often possible to finish a trip if we had been forced to leave Icelandic waters due to poor weather or poor fishing.

In fact hauls like this and larger were quite common in the waters around the Falklands. After a second three hour tow through marks even closer to the bottom and showing up clearly on the bottom lock of the sounder, we brought up a haul of ten tonnes, shooting away immediately before the fish left the bottom as darkness approached.

Reports from the Monte Faro suggested that he was quite satisfied with his first two hauls, and pointed out that the fish marks were already beginning to leave the bottom, and did not hold out much hope for another good haul to give him an even better end to a reasonable day's fishing.

After an extended tow of five hours, our final haul was in the region of seven tonnes of hake. With a lot of fish remaining in the factory, we decided to clear the factory deck before tipping the last haul below and laying to for the night.

Although bitterly cold, the weather remained fine as we continued to fish in the area off Cape Meredith. Apart from a couple of gale warnings that never fully materialised, we finished most days with a reasonable tonnage of hake fillets and four or five tonnes of loligo. At the end of our fourth week's fishing we had 450 tonnes on board when we suffered our first major setback. One of the filleting machines started to give trouble, and despite continuous attempts to repair it, we eventually had to close it down until we could either get spare parts from a ship coming to the end of her fishing time, or flown out from Europe.

We had now been joined in this area by another four ships, which indicated that there was not a lot of fish in other areas, as they all seemed content to remain around Cape Meredith.

Despite numerous offers from a number of other ships to let us have spare parts we required, none of these were in our area, and the extra workload meant that the one remaining filleting machine was working practically non-stop throughout the day.

Our first daylight haul had once again been quite a good one in the region of seven tonnes, when for no other reason than that we still had fish left in the factory, we decided to shoot back to the east towards Beauchene Island. Within an hour of shooting we had practically run out of any indications on the sounder, and it came as a surprise when we hauled five tonnes of hake and five tonnes of loligo.

With one filleting machine out of commission this was the ideal type of haul, and shooting away immediately, the day finished with another five tonnes, half of which was loligo.

The following day we spent towing back easterly towards Beauchene Island, and had

The Portuguese trawler VilleDeConte had the misfortune to lose a man overboard. The man was never found, in spite of an extensive search carried out throughout that day by more than twenty trawlers of many different nationalities.

our best day's fishing to date with three hauls of seven tonnes, an afternoon haul of twelve tonnes, followed with a haul of six tonnes. A final long tow of five hours resulted in a welcome four tonnes to give us a day's total of 29 tonnes of loligo and three tonnes of hake fillets.

After shooting the following morning, we received a call from Port Stanley to confirm that we would be expected to arrive in Berkeley Sound on the 25th of May to transfer what fish we had on board to one of the reefer ships. The reefer would then travel back to Spain with the fish from a number of ships, and it would all be sold long before we arrived home.

We also received confirmation of a southwesterly severe gale, and there was to be no escape this time. Although we managed to

The sheltered waters of Berkeley Sound are an ideal place for ships seeking shelter, and to carry out repairs and any other jobs that needed to be done. Here a Spanish freezer trawler steams into Berkeley Sound.

complete our day's fishing with a total of 22 tonnes, the weather deteriorated overnight, and as daylight broke we had a full gale of wind on our hands. There was no question of shooting in the storm force winds that continued throughout the day.

Our run of good weather and good fishing had to come to an end some time. After just one haul in the morning for a small amount of hake, instead of dodging head to wind, I decided to steam before the wind and seek the shelter of Berkeley Sound. Our intention was to try the waters just east of Port Stanley where we had our first haul of the trip.

The seas built up considerably during the afternoon, and it was a welcome relief when we rounded the entrance and arrived in the sheltered water of Berkeley Sound.

Within the hour we were joined there by

Fishing Explorer's crew overhauling the trawls during a spell of poor weather, which we rode out in the shelter of Berkeley Sound.

two other ships, one our constant companion the Monte Faro and the other a Portuguese trawler, the Nauticus. With the wind gusting to force nine and ten, the evening meal was taken in relative comfort as the three ships lay under the shelter of the land, and we wondered what lay in store on the next weather forecast.

The late forecast offered little cheer, as it would be late the following day before we could expect any sign of the weather improving, and during the night we were joined by another ship which had come in to seek shelter.

Staying under the shelter of the land did give us the chance to overhaul the trawl and carry out a few minor repairs and adjustments. It was not until late in the afternoon that the wind showed any sign of moderating, and we could expect a heavy swell to be running outside. It was already dark, and I decided that we would remain in Berkeley Sound until the morning before resuming fishing.

There had been little doubt that things had

gone reasonably well during our first spell of fishing, yet one morning while fishing among a large group of trawlers, a call was heard over the VHF from the Portuguese trawler Ville de Conte, which was fishing close by.

In shooting away his trawl, one of his deck crew had the misfortune to be lost down the ramp. The skipper reported that he had a man overboard and requested immediate assistance in locating him.

Having just hauled and with our trawl on the deck when we received the call, we were soon steaming towards the Ville de Conte's position about four miles away. By the time we had covered that distance, we were joined by around twenty trawlers, most of which were Polish, and there had been no sighting of the man in the water. It has to be said that in the intense cold, things did not look good for him, even though more ships and a Naval helicopter continued to arrive on the scene to take part in the search.

With men posted as lookouts on all parts of the Fishing Explorer, and the imagination playing all sorts of tricks in the poor visibility that was not helped by the occasional light snow showers, the search went on, and with a large number of ships searching in a small area, it was getting a little crowded. Yet nobody was willing to give up the search.

The incident had occurred at around 10.30 and some three hours later, with the light getting no better and still bitterly cold, everyone realised that there was very little chance of the man surviving for so long in the water. The Ville de Conte's skipper put out a call to everyone to offer his thanks to all who had assisted in the search, saying that although he intended to continue searching, he fully understood anyone who wanted to leave to resume fishing. But there was a unanimous response that the search would continue until it became fully dark.

The response from such an international group of trawlers had been marvellous. Nobody had wasted a minute in hauling their trawls and racing to the area to join the search. Yet despite everything that had been done to assist, it was in vain and this remained a talking point on board the Fishing Explorer for days to come.

We saw little of the Ville de Conte after the tragedy. Being well into his trip, it is more than likely that they departed the scene and returned to Portugal.

It had been a stark reminder of the dangers of the job and what dangers deep sea fishermen face even in the everyday ritual of hauling and shooting the trawl. For a change, the weather had been fine, although intensely cold. The lost man had probably not been able to survive the cold for long and throughout the search there were no definite sightings of him at all.

It had been a blank day for the fleet, as almost everyone had been on the first haul of the day. But this was a small price to pay and in this instance fishing had been put into second place.

Portia's Mine

Fishing has often been described as the most dangerous job of all and of this there can be little doubt at all. But if this is the case, then I can also say honestly that there can hardly be another job anywhere that produces so much humour and so many laughs, despite the hardships and the conditions that the crew have to endure.

Now the industry as we knew it in the years after the Second World War no longer exists, and many of the characters are sadly no longer with us. The industry abounded with characters from both the shore side and the catching side and even though many of the jokes were at somebody's expense, and without mentioning any names, some of these stories are worth recalling.

I was a deckhand on the Hull side trawler Portia, fishing off Fruholmen on the Norwegian coast. During one haul it was obvious as the gear appeared that we had picked up something heavy in the trawl, which we assumed to be a large stone. After much difficulty a becket was put around the codend and the bag of fish was hove forward and over the rail, when someone shouted that the heavy object protruding through a hole in the net wasn't a stone but was quite a large Second World War mine that we had managed to pick up.

What we were not prepared for was that our very reliable fishroom hand, who was on the port side working the wires, had chosen this moment to get a riding turn on the winch drum. The ever decreasing amount of fish was being hauled over the rail and also over the bag ropes, and with everyone running about the deck like scalded cats, the codends with the mine showing clearly through a hole in the netting swung across the deck and hit the port side leg of the Portia's steel tripod mast with a resounding clang that could be heard all over the ship. It then swung back and hit the starboard leg with another shuddering bang before somebody ran to the winch to put it into reverse, but not until it had hit the port leg a second time before dropping out onto the wooden deck with a dull thud.

"It's OK, skipper," some wag called out from the deck. "I think it's a dud!"

Once normal order was restored and everyone was scrutinising our World War Two mine, someone else came out with the thought that it was just our bloody luck for it to fall out port side, as the Portia was rigged only for starboard side fishing and had no derrick to lift the mine over the port rail. This was black humour indeed.

It was another legacy from the war that gave us all a laugh when I was a deckhand on the old coal burner Davy, fishing off the west side of Iceland and not catching a great deal of fish. We hauled in the middle of the afternoon one day and as the codend was released, there were just a few baskets of fish and what looked like a World War 2 bomb that dropped onto the deck. It lay there among the few baskets of plaice, with its fins bent and damaged, and of course everyone was wary of approaching too close to it.

As the mate backed away, from what we assumed he thought was a safe distance he remarked: "Don't just stand there looking at the bloody thing, pick it up and throw it over the side."

Nobody was too keen to take the mate upon this offer, but one of the deckhands answered back: "Why don't you pick it up and throw it over the side? If the bloody thing goes off we'll tell everyone at home how brave you was."

Fatigue was the cause of a lot of accidents at sea, but also brought us many laughs. Trudging aft on the Brutus one day, after having spent many days and nights shooting, hauling and gutting, never getting off the deck, one day our deckie learner was having difficulty keeping his eyes open in the warmth of the mess deck - a feeling well known to most of us in those days of fishing around Bear Island.

His head dropped forward, and his face landing in his porridge brought him back to the land of the living with a shock.

"Why don't you use a spoon like the rest of us, son?" Somebody said as quick as a flash. "Look at the bloody mess you've made."

The unfortunate youngster spent the rest of the meal time trying to convince us that he had not fallen asleep, and of course we believed him.

Again in the Brutus and again at Bear Island, catching a lot of small fish, in one haul it was obvious that a lot of fish were escaping through a hole at the top of the codends. As we went astern to take out the first bag of fish, the skipper was screaming at the top of his voice from the bridge, suggesting that we were all blind and could not see the steady stream of codlings getting out through the hole in the net.

"Sorry skipper, from here we thought they were trying to get in," the third hand replied.

Not all the fun and humour took place at sea, as the mate of one Hull trawler found out early one morning on the fish market when showing the owner around the results of their trip.

Obviously not pleased with the catch and the quality, the owner kicked over a ten stone kit of fish, sending the fish sliding along the wet fish market.

The mate, a well known character, promptly kicked over another kit of fish, with the same results.

"Well, sir, what are we going to do now? Count the bastards?" He enquired of the owner. Needless to say, he did not sail with the ship again. But after the owner had finally seen the funny side of it, the mate was called to the office and duly signed on his next ship as skipper, very much to his surprise.

Looking Back – Grimsby

The port of Grimsby on the south bank of the Humber has over the years shared a friendly rivalry with Hull. Like Hull, Grimsby has had to pay a heavy price in both men and ships through two wars that took a toll of both North Sea and distant water trawlers.

A staggering number of trawlers from Grimsby were sunk by enemy aircraft, U-boats and mines, but this was not all one way-traffic, as numerous trawlers taken over by the Navy during the war were able to cover themselves with glory. Many more were singled out for special mention for heroics performed

These German-built trawlers are closely associated with Grimsby. The Northern Sky and the Northern Duke were among the largest and most modern vessels fishing from the Humber after the war.

under the harshest conditions it is possible to encounter.

The Grimsby trawlers that come to mind are the old Northern type that were at one time the largest fishing from the Humber after the war. These were fine, German-built vessels, and will be long remembered for the parts they played.

As things gradually began to return to normal after the war, a large number of newly-built ships began to arrive to replace older vessels. Northern built up a very impressive fleet, all bearing names that are linked inextricably with Grimsby, Northern Isles, Northern Chief, Northern Sceptre and Northern Jewel, to name a few of those that paved the way for Black Watch, Royal Lincs and others built in Germany.

With its fine fleet of distant and middle water trawlers, Grimsby was also well supplied with quality fish by the large number of Danish style snibbies working from the port. Using the seine net style of fishing, these mostly Danish-owned vessels were regular visitors to Grimsby as the war ended and the North Sea was again opened up to fishing.

As the number of seine netters has declined over the years, many boats have switched to netting or pair trawling with mixed success. It could well be that with so many seine netters

With their smart lines, the Arsenal GY-48 and her sister ships seemed to me to be in a different class to anything else sailing from the Humber at the time that they joined the Grimsby fleet.

working out of Grimsby since the end of the war, we now release the importance of their role in supplying the Grimsby market with its top quality fish.

Despite the setbacks facing the industry with Iceland and other nations imposing their 200 mile limits, Grimsby was better set to survive as a port than many. A sensible building programme meant that Grimsby had more middle water trawlers than other British ports and I am convinced that these could have saved and maintained much of the fishing industry in Grimsby and many of the jobs associated with it.

Almost all of these trawlers had years of working life ahead of them and could well have switched to fishing waters off the west of the British Isles, but instead they went on to provide the backbone of the offshore oil industry in its early years.

There is so much that comes to mind in remembering Grimsby as it was in its heyday, the many trawlers and the famous North Wall, as well as Riby Square and the pubs in the Freeman Street area that were such a part of the history of the port

For myself as a deckie learner, the trawlers from Grimsby were always the ones that caught the eye. Consolidated Fisheries' trawlers Arsenal, Grimsby Town, Hull City and Everton always looked the part, while Crampin's fleet were named after some of the most famous cricketers and always looked very fine ships, none more so than Statham and Trueman.

But the older type of Northern trawlers will always be associated in my mind with Grimsby. I have heard many stories of how these fine German-built trawlers came to this country and as a young man I once had the good fortune to look over one of these ships while we were tied up alongside at Lodingen in Norway while waiting for a pilot to take us through the fjords. At the time, I stood amazed at the size of these fine Northern ships, which had their crews' accommodation situated aft and amidships.

As I returned to my own ship, the pre-war built Davy, with accommodation three bunks high in the forecastle, I had been amazed at what I had seen on the Northern trawler that was simply years ahead of anything else in the British fleet. This has stayed with me ever since and I will always regard these trawlers as being among the best that ever sailed from the Humber.

Crampins Statham always looked the part, fine sturdy trawlers that made a big impact when they joined the Grimsby fleet.

A Flutter

Sport played a big part in breaking the monotony during a trip at sea and it was the custom in most ships to run a football sweep that gave everyone a little bit of interest as the results came down from the bridge at Saturday teatime.

However, as an addition to this, in the Brutus, there were many of the crew who liked a bet on the horses and the skipper ran a book, with the radio operator acting as the bookies' clerk. He gave us a list of the horses that was sent out each night by a radio station. The rules were very simple and the maximum bet was ten shillings. Nobody could lose more than five pounds and if you lost that, you were granted a free ten shilling bet. If that one lost, it was considered enough and you could have no more bets that trip, unless the skipper could be convinced that you could afford it. However, this never, ever seemed to be the case.

On being relieved to go for our watch below one dinnertime, my mate and I were informed by the radio operator that we had reached the crucial stage in our betting, and that the skipper, out of the goodness of his heart, had granted us both a free ten shilling bet.

With the runners written on the full side of a length of sounder paper, we both decided to go for an outside in what was the 2000 Guineas. We both wrote our bets on the blank side of the paper - ten shillings to win, Pall Mall - and duly turned in for our watch below.

On turning out at teatime, nobody knew the results of the race. With the next haul of fish cleared off the deck and now being on watch, my mate and I were told to chop up a pair of old codends that had been condemned as being no more use and were supposed to be dumped when we were finished fishing and on the way home.

After the next haul it was the same and once the fish was cleared away, some more work was found for us that would take us up to hauling time without having time for a smoke.

As midnight approached, the chief engineer suggested that we might be getting punished for backing a winner, as he had heard on his own radio that Pall Mall had won the race at 20:1.

Unknown to us, the skipper had decided that we were spending too much time studying the form book and the handicap book, so he had told the mate to keep us busy while we were on watch. This is exactly what he did right up to the time that we set off for home, so maybe it was as well that we had backed our winner so late in the trip. But we set a trend for the next trip, in which all free ten shilling bets were cancelled. That's a man you could call a good loser.

Another incident that took place on board Brutus was when we were in what we thought would be the last few days of a trip off the north cape of Iceland, along with a small group of ships that included four or five from Grimsby and the same number from Hull.

With time running out after what had been an average sort of trip, this small group had dropped down on very good fishing about forty miles north of the North Cape. But with winter getting nearer and nearer in these parts, the early November weather was threatening to spoil what would otherwise be a grandstand finish to the trip.

With tows lasting two and a half hours, the deck crew were able to keep the decks clear, but when the towing time was reduced to two hours, this became impossible and there was a bit of fish left when hauling time came around.

After hauling again before midnight and adding two good bags of fish to what was already on the deck, three of us went below for what we expected to be the last watch below of the trip. We sat in our underwear in the warmth of the Brutus' bottom forecastle, enjoying a smoke before turning in for a few hours and discussing how many more hauls we were likely to have before setting off home. Soon we were joined by the skipper, who set about explaining how beneficial it would be for everyone if we were to give up our watch below to return to the deck to finish the fish before hauling time. If we did, he promised that he would take the ship home at teatime. However, the skipper's request fell on deaf ears as we politely turned it down, explaining that we had not had so much as a break during two eighteen hour spells on deck, and how we had managed to keep the deck clear while we were towing for two and a half hours, until the tows had been shortened by half an hour.

This did not please the skipper one bit and as the argument wore on, he became more heated, with neither one side nor the other prepared to give an inch. After reminding him that we had already wasted an hour of our watch below in arguing with him, he finally left us to return to the bridge, purposely leaving the door at the top of the forecastle ladder open so that it would bang with the roll of the ship.

On climbing the ladder to close the door, I was just in time to see the skipper drenched as a huge spray swept the deck, leaving him trying to retrieve one of his slippers that he had lost as a large amount of water came through the scuppers amidships. It was all very funny at the time, but for some reason after that a large portion of the work that needed doing on the way home always seemed to get done when we came on watch, hardly surprisingly.

One of my favourite ships, the Brutus, in which I did my first trip as mate.

The Boom Years

Large deckloads of fish were a familiar sight before the introduction of the washing machine to Hull and Grimsby trawlers. Trawler crews would gut the fish for hours on end until the port side and middle section of the deck around the hatches was full, before washing the fish by hand. The fish were then stowed below in the fishroom, a backbreaking task for crew who hardly got any rest when fishing was heavy.

This series of previously unseen pictures was taken by an unknown photographer who sailed with the Hull trawler Ross Orion on a trip to Greenland in the late 1960s. These fine photographs give a very good idea of what the working conditions were like for British fishermen on the open decks on the last generation of side trawlers.

In some cases the fish was left on deck for far too long, resulting in poor quality fish landed onto the market, and this in turn resulted in poor prices paid for this low quality fish. This occurred mainly in the summer months, when there were frequently substantial amounts of unsold fish on the market.

In the years just after the war, with plenty of fish on Arctic fishing grounds, almost all the fish landed were headless. This practice was stopped eventually, and the large catches of cod and codling landed from Bear Island in the 1950s were landed with their heads on.

During this period some spectacular catches were landed by trawlers whose names became household words in Grimsby, Hull and Fleetwood. Some of the newly built side trawlers at the time really had a bonanza and this period was a boom time for the Humber ports.

With heavy landings continually arriving at the Humber markets, and much of the fish

Steaming off to the fishing grounds. During the days it sometimes took to reach distant water fishing grounds, the crew would be busy preparing the fishing gear for the days of hard work ahead. Here the crew are fixing cow hides to the codends to protect them from chafing.

Fishing in distant waters sometimes offered some breathtaking sights, such as this iceberg off Greenland.

unsold, some of the trawler owners looked for new outlets to boost the earnings of their ships, and for a time salting at sea was an attractive approach with the hope that salted fish could be sold to overseas markets.

This method of fishing meant that the crew who were there to handle the fish were recruited from the Faroe Islands. The fish were split and salted away in the fishroom.

But we still had it good compared to some people. Even in the 1960s, Portuguese cod fishermen fished with hooks and lines from open boats in Arctic waters to supply their mother ships with the cod that was salted on board.
These Portuguese dorymen spent many months on the fog-shrouded Grand Banks and other grounds and one can only admire their courage and seamanship in the difficult conditions they worked under on these long voyages.

The mostly small fish found on grounds at Bear Island were too small for salting, so the trawlers had to search around for larger and better quality fish, such as were to be found at Greenland. These grounds had normally been fished more by German trawlers, who worked all year round with a support ship in attendance, a luxury that was not available to British fishermen until three Hull trawlers were tragically lost in Iceland in appalling weather.

Several trawler owners tried salting catches at sea, but this never took off in a big way and after a few trips most soon reverted to their usual method of fishing and selling catches fresh onto the markets. Eventually it was to ensure that better quality fish was landed onto the markets that all of the new built trawlers were fitted with refrigeration plants to keep

Shooting away the trawl from the Ross Orion's starboard side in calm weather. There are no deckboards in place, the trawl has not yet been stretched and the codends are floating forward, indicating that this is the first haul of the trip.

Photo left
The skipper and mate watch carefully from the bridge as they negotiate their way around some ice.

Photo below left
Like every trawler at the time, the Ross Orion carried a radio officer who had the task of keeping the ship in touch with the office and other ships, and was also relied on by the crew for racing and football results. A good Sparks was worth his weight in gold as he listened for information and reports on the way to fishing grounds.

the temperature in the fishrooms down.

Getting to grips with a large catch meant that each fish was handled again and again before it eventually found its way into the fishroom.

The introduction of the washing machine took a lot of the backbreaking work out of deep water trawling. Hull skipper Walter Woods can claim the credit for the introduction of the washing machine, which meant that fish once gutted was dropped directly into a washer, where the motion of the ship and the force of the water pumped into the washing machine ensured that as the fish were washed out of the open end of the machine, they had been washed clean. From the washer, they went down a chute into the fishroom, where they were stowed away by the mate and the fishroom crew.

The reduction in labour allowed trawler crews to be reduced by as many as four men, and even with the loss of these extra hands on the deck, the washing machine enabled some trawlers with top crews to achieve some outstanding results in handling big catches before the next haul.

During heavy fishing most crews would work 18 hours on deck with a six hours watch below. This gave them little time to relax during this type of heavy fishing, and short tows meant that there was not enough time to get the fish below before decks before the next haul was ready to be hauled.

Hauls of gutted fish were piled on the port side of the deck until the deckhands had an opportunity to get the fish off the deck. While

Ross Orion's mate releases the codline to let a flood of cod into the pounds.

Above, left to right: The deck is watched carefully by Ross Orion's mate.
A pound full of cod to be gutted.
A young deckhand holds up a Greenland cod.
Gutting went on as long as there were fish on the deck. The lads on deck can afford a smile as they show off a few sprags with the trip drawing to a close.
Right: The mate at work on a busted trawl, and there could be plenty of this on the Greenland fishing grounds.

hauling, or if the ship was laid to while mending a trawl, some of the crew would take on the task of clearing the fish from the port side. This was backbreaking work for all concerned, not only for those on deck, but also for the fishroom men who had to prepare to receive large amounts of fish in a short space of time.

With most of the older trawlers at the time not equipped with any freezing equipment, the ice in some of the old coal burning trawlers often showed more of a resemblance to concrete than ice, and large amounts of ice had to be broken up ready to take these large hauls off the deck. A great deal of this hard work in the fishroom was carried out by young deckie learners, who worked the same long hours as the rest of the crew.

Large hauls of fish and heavy landings did not necessarily guarantee big grossings when the fish were landed, but on occasions these

The deck with a pound full of fish as the trawl is readied for shooting away again.

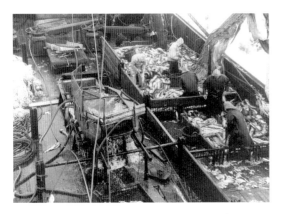

The introduction of washing machines made life easier for trawler crews. Here the Ross Orion's crew are busy gutting fish while the mate is tying the codend of the trawl ready to shoot it back for another haul. By this time the Ross Orion is clearly well into her trip, and the deck resembles a battleground with a busted trawl and some old cables on the port side.

Gutting continued day and night for as long as there was fish to be gutted.

big catches did allow some of the newer and faster side trawlers to complete some very short trips when fishing was good in places like the Barents Sea and Bear Island.

British trawlers caught large amounts of cod in these waters, and as the Russian and Norwegian fleets gradually expanded, it became clear that things could not continue for ever in the same way.

Some of the newer and more modern larger side trawlers worked further west in waters around Greenland, and although these grounds were not as prolific as those around Bear Island, Greenland provided the British fleet with some extremely good fishing that took some of the pressure off the northerly fishing grounds.

Things did not end there. The Newfoundland banks were a challenge that was soon taken up, but the long steaming time across the Atlantic limited time on the fishing grounds. A number of side trawlers made the crossing to Newfoundland, but either poor fishing or poor quality of the fish caught meant that Newfoundland was not a profitable proposition for side trawlers.

It was during these years after the war that many changes took place in the British fishing industry, and better levels of safety were introduced

The old type of towing block that was chained to the deck aft had over the years been the cause of numerous accidents when being released was eventually replaced by a more sturdy and secure type of block that reduced the accident rate when being released to haul or blocked up at the start of a tow.

Over the years there were many changes regarding the safety of the crew, but in my opinion the most important was the introduction of ships that had the whole crew's accommodation aft. Changing watches in the middle of the night in poor weather conditions could often be a nightmare, as the men had to wait for the precise moment to run aft to reach the safety of the casing ladder. This action was the cause of many fishermen being lost overboard when changing watches under poor weather conditions.

Understandably, many of the crew who had sailed in the newer type of ship with accommodation aft were reluctant to return to the older sidewinders, many of which dated back to the years before the war.

It was a hard introduction for a lot of lads, most of whom started on the deck at sixteen, working in conditions that would never have been tolerated in any other industry.

The washing machine was one of the changes that helped to make life easier, and some of the younger skippers of the time helped bring about a lot of ideas that inevitably caught on and made life easier for everyone on deck.

The old method of using quarter ropes for bringing up the trawls was eventually discarded as most trawlers changed over to the aptly named bang-bang gear that made hauling and shooting much quicker and easier.

Other methods for bringing in the trawl once the bobbins were inboard took a lot of the hard work out of the hauling procedure, and did away to an extent with the old way of pulling the trawl in by hand using nethooks.

The years between 1950 and 1960 saw a lot of changes take place which were the better for everyone concerned, such as the replacement of the old wooden fishroom boards with aluminium ones which could be picked up by the armful if necessary.

The job of deep sea fishing has always remained an extremely difficult one, but huge strides were taken during these years to make the job safer. Most of the old wooden lifeboats, which were both heavy and difficult to handle in bad weather, were replaced with inflatable liferafts. The old type of davits were also no longer needed as the old lifeboats were replaced. These old davits were highly prone to icing in severe weather, which meant that a crew had little chance of launching a boat in an emergency or in rough weather.

Most of these changes had already been long overdue by the time they came about, and many of the older trawlers had certainly seen better days by then. I don't believe that many tears were shed as many of the old pre-war trawlers made their way to the breaker's yard, even though many of them had served their owners and the nation exceptionally well.

It wasn't always calm and sunny. The view from Ross Orion's wheelhouse as a fresh breeze sweeps spray over the deck as she makes her way to Greenland.

The Islands

It was while we were laid in Berkeley Sound that I realised how little I knew about these islands, so with time to kill as we waited for the weather to improve, I took some time to read up on the history of the Falklands.

Port Stanley lies at the eastern end of East Falkand, a tiny city of immense charm and a living relic of the British Empire. Set amidst starkly beautiful and tranquil moorland, it officially became the capital of the Falklands when the seat of government was moved from Port Louis in 1845 to the area formerly known as Fort Jackson, and subsequently renamed after the secretary of state for the colonies, Lord Stanley.

The site was well chosen, with an abundant supply of fuel in the form of peat, which is still used by most households, with water, shelter and a natural harbour.

During the 1850s, as seaborne traffic around Cape Horn increased with the California Gold Rush and the Peruvian guano trade, ships began calling in for repairs and all kinds of supplies. Some of the vessels attempting to round the Horn were overloaded, some were unseaworthy and others were simply unlucky, and as a result many limped back to Stanley with the prevailing westerly winds to lick their wounds.

Not all of these ships recovered, as many had taken a severe battering. A few were deliberately wrecked and their cargoes sold, or otherwise distributed by unscrupulous operators. The port gained a notorious reputation, and many of the hulks which lie in Port Stanley harbour today date from this period.

A natural abundance of wildlife in the Falkland waters gave rise to the whaling, sealing and penguin oil industries, while on shore the sheep farming industry became established. Port Stanley became established as the centre of commerce and the only settlement of any size in the islands, and grew in

Top: Although it was only mid-afternoon, we were shooting away in the dark near Beauchene Island towards the end of our time in the Falkland Islands.

One of the Fishing Explorer's crew releases the codline, allowing loligo squid to stream down to the factory deck.

A very nice haul of loligo squid being released from the codend down into the factory deck to be processed, packed and frozen.
Middle: A good haul of hake comes up the ramp for the first haul of the day off Cape Meredith. With very little fishing during the hours of darkness, it was essential to get the fish down to the factory as quickly as possible so as to make the most of the remaining hours of daylight.

importance. Today only the sheep farming industry survives, and the wool is still exported through the capital, which remains the only port and business centre in the Islands.

In two world wars the Falklands have demonstrated their strategic value. In December 1914 at the battle of the Falkland Islands the Royal Navy Squadron at Port Stanley vanquished the German fleet under Graf Spee, and thereafter retained control of the South Atlantic.

In 1939 the battle of the River Plate was won by a Squadron that used Port Stanley for repairs after the action, and once again for the rest of the war Britain controlled the region.

On the second of April 1982 a massive invasion of the Islands by the Argentine armed forces took place, as residents of Port Stanley awoke to the sound of gunfire at dawn. Within hours the capital and with it the islands, defended by only 80 marines and a local volunteer force, were taken by several thousand enemy troops and placed under foreign rule.

By the following day a combined British task force was on its way to restore British sovereignty and within eleven weeks and with a brilliantly conducted campaign, this was achieved. 258 Britons, including three Falkland Islanders lost their lives, and 12,000 enemy troops, most in Port Stanley, surrendered.

The scars of war are still visible, but as a result of rehabilitation and development, and aid from the British government, services damaged in the conflict have been replaced and repaired.

Waiting for the weather to improve while we lay in the shelter of Berkeley Sound had given me an opportunity to glance over the history of the Falklands. The shelter also gave the crew the chance to overhaul the trawl and

In the early stages of our time in the Falklands we were fishing with an international group that includes ships from Spain, Italy, Greece, Japan, Poland, Portugal and other nations. Here the French factory trawler Commandante Rey tows alongside us.

to carry out a few minor repairs and adjustments. But as the weather only began to moderate late in the afternoon as darkness was already approaching, and with the prospect of

Italian freezer trawler Maria Michele fishing through some fine weather.

The old Portuguese side trawler Nauticas must have spent many years fishing for cod on the fog-shrouded Grand Banks at Newfoundland. Here in the Falklands she was just one of an international fleet of vessels fishing for squid a long way from home.

Spanish freezer trawler Pesca Puerta Cuarto shoots away alongside us.

a heavy swell running outside, I decided to remain in the shelter of Berkeley Sound until the morning before resuming fishing.

During the night the wind eased steadily, and at 0500 made our way out of our shelter and into open sea again. Within the hour the trawl was once more going down the ramp in 70 fathoms of water. The weather was by now quite reasonable, and moderating all the time as we shot away before the wind and towed to the north east with just enough indications on the sounder to keep one interested.

Our first haul after a three hour tow was quite a reasonable one as we hauled aboard six tonnes of good sized loligo and shot back over the same tow, hoping for a repeat of this haul at least.

Our second haul was not quite as good as the first, but was in the region of five tonnes. This was pleasing as this was the first sign of loligo that we had seen for a number of days, and a very welcome sight.

We remained in this area, between seventy and ninety fathoms, and for the first time since resuming fishing our twenty-four hours amounted to 28 tonnes of loligo with a small amount of hake.

With our rendezvous to transship our catch getting closer, we still had a number of options open to us, and if need be we could return to Cape Meredith. But for the time being we were content to spend some time in this area just a few miles to the east of Port Stanley.

Meanwhile the weather remained fine, and although we had no spectacular hauls, with six and sometimes seven tonnes, we finished most days with a reasonable amount of fish. A week before we were due to transship our fish, we had on board 900 tonnes of frozen fish.

Even though there were not a lot of squid in this area, fishing day and night meant that we were sure of around twenty tonnes a day, and with less than four days to go to transship, there now seemed little point in leaving these waters.

From reports we were getting, there seemed to be only around four fishing vessels remaining in the Falklands. Most had left the zone, and were fishing well to the north off

Argentina, and like us they had endured some very poor weather, forcing them to stop fishing at the same time as we were sheltering in Berkeley Sound.

We had now towed to a position forty miles to the north of Port Salvador, and although we still averaged three tonnes of loligo each haul, we were also picking up a tonne of hake fillets. During the hours of daylight this could be as high as two tonnes.

The main thing was that we had been able to continue fishing since leaving Berkeley Sound, and as we were only two days from transhipping, the forecast was not good. Heavy snow made the job no easier, with the snow squalls getting more frequent, and with the wind now reaching gale force, we hauled and made our way once again into Berkeley Sound, some twelve hours before we were due to refuel the following morning.

Our last haul had been about four tonnes, and as we closed the land on a bitterly cold night with some heavy falls of snow in the last few days, everything resembled a real winter scene near the snow clad land.

The following morning we contacted the small tanker anchored further inside Berkeley Sound and tied up alongside her with a real biting wind coming straight down from the snow covered mountains. Refuelling was expected to take all morning and well into the afternoon, and it was not until 14.30 that it was announced that we could disconnect the hoses. After signing the necessary papers, we slowly covered the short distance to the reefer where we would unload our fish.

A familiar sight - the former Hull freezer trawler Pict, now fishing for new Spanish owners and seen here towing alongside the Fishing Explorer in Falkland water.

This former Hull stern trawler took on the role of a fishery patrol vessel in the Falklands.

Fishery officers from the fishery patrol vessel Falkland Right pay a visit to the Fishing Explorer during a spell of fine weather while we were fishing near Beauchene Island. These visits usually resulted in some news from home and a parcel of English newspapers.

Hard Work On A Cold Day

Transferring our fish across to the reefer ship was expected to take more than four days, with most of the work done by our own crew and the crew of the reefer working their own derricks and winches.

Work started as soon as we were tied up alongside, and continued until midnight. The hatches were then put on again until 06.30 the following morning, after that we worked in watches day and night until the job was finished.

There was quite a bit of mail waiting for us, and a fair number of English newspapers, which made for a quiet evening, even though some of the papers were quite old.

The weather remained bitterly cold in Berkeley Sound, with men working constantly on deck and relieving each other for hot coffee as often as not laced with brandy. The temperature dropped well below freezing during the hours of darkness.

Under the circumstances, and despite having to stop for the occasional snow shower, things went well. We had arrived in Berkeley Sound with a total of 1040 tonnes on board, and at midnight on our second day we had transhipped 480 tonnes, almost half of our catch.

Meanwhile on the bridge I was getting reports from ships 250 miles to the north of the Falklands. Although the weather was very bad there, some ships had caught good hauls of illex squid, a different species to the loligo squid we had been catching in the Falklands.

The other reports that we would rather not have heard were of the weather. The day before we were due to finish transhipping our fish, the forecast was for severe south-westerly gales. To the best of our knowledge, there were now no ships at all fishing inside the Falklands zone. With the best reports coming from ships well to the north, I decided to move to that area once we had finished our transhipment.

It was at 20.00 the following day that the last few cartons of fish were hove across to the reefer ship, and after the final paperwork was completed and the hatches secured, the crew prepared for what looked like being a very uncomfortable night. At 21.30 we slipped our ropes and were once more passing Volunteer Point and making our way out of Berkeley Sound.

Heading north as we moved away from the land, we soon started to feel the full weight of wind and weather as the sea continued to build up. The few reports we received confirmed that few ships were fishing, and judging by the morning forecast, it was obvious that it would be while before any of them would be fishing.

Our first sightings of other ships were at mid-afternoon, when we passed a group of ten ships dodging head to wind. By that evening there were just the slightest signs of the weather moderating and at midnight,

Cartons of frozen squid and fish being swung across from Fishing Explorer to the reefer in Berkeley Sound. The job of trans-shipping our catch of over a thousand tonnes of fish was a long, tedious and cold job.

although the wind had eased, a very heavy swell was still running. At five the next morning we shot away the trawl among a group of what appeared to be mainly Polish and Spanish trawlers.

Almost six days after we had steamed into Berkeley Sound to start transshipping our catch, it was something of a pleasure to see the trawl go down the ramp again.

The wind was now no more than a force five and the swell had dropped considerably. From the conversations over the VHF, it seemed that most of the trawlers were on their first tow since hauling to dodge out the spell of bad weather.

Our first haul with this group of ships was a very good one, consisting of some twenty tonnes of illex squid, which is much larger than the loligo we had been catching further south around the Falklands. Although illex would not fetch such good prices as loligo, this was a welcome sight as we now had a large empty fish hold to start filling once more

This was the deepest water we had fished in so far, and our first haul was in 200 fathoms. As we towed along, we had ships on either side of us, indicating that some ships were deeper than us, and other working in a few fathoms shallower.

Nevertheless, it had been a reasonable first haul, and the next one in the early afternoon was even better when we hauled on board something in the region of twenty-five tonnes, which consisted entirely of illex.

It was in this position that we witnessed an amazing sight, as after dusk, as if by a prescribed signal, the entire horizon lit up as the massive fleet

of ships using the jigging method of fishing switched on their lights as they prepared to start fishing for the night.

This large fleet of ships using this highly effective method of fishing, mainly from Taiwan and Korea, illuminated the horizon as far as the eye could see.

On board the Fishing Explorer things were going very well indeed as the two further hauls that we had before midnight brought our total since 05.00 to almost a hundred tonnes. But all this came to an abrupt and sad end the following day.

There is surely no other job on earth that brings you down as suddenly as deep sea fishing can. One minute you are up in the clouds, and the next you are brought down to earth with a bang, and sometimes a big bang.

Our first day since resuming fishing had gone well, and early indications were that it would get better still. We had dodged back through the night and shot away once more in 200 fathoms. The weather was still cold, and now reasonably fine with just a moderate breeze from the south-west. When we started to haul everything seemed normal, and it was soon obvious that we had a good haul as the cod end was at the bottom of the ramp. But even with extra beckets around the trawl and extra wires to the winch drums, we were

Polish stern trawlers transshipping their catches to a reefer in the sheltered waters of Berkeley Sound. Poland had a large fleet of trawlers fishing in the Falklands at that time and had made a big contribution to the development of the fishery there.
British interests in these waters came far too late. A modern fleet of Spanish trawlers and an ageing fleet of Polish vessels had already been fishing there successfully long before British companies showed any signs of interest in South Atlantic fisheries.

clearly going to have trouble getting the codend up onto the deck. The winch stopped and then started, and agonisingly slowly the bag of fish inched its way up the ramp while part of the codend remained in the water. Only by releasing some of the squid as it came up to the top of the ramp were we able to get the bag of fish onto the trawl deck. It had taken us almost two hours to get the haul of squid up the ramp, and after almost everyone had guessed at the size of the haul, it seemed by general opinion to be in the region of sixty tonnes of squid.

Inevitably over the midday meal there were remarks to the effect that ten days of this fishing would see us on our way home, and I must admit that the thought had crossed my mind just like the rest.

But within a matter of hours we left wondering just what might have been. Hauling at 16.30, after shortening the length of the tow to just two and a half hours, it was evident that once again we had a very good haul and would have problems getting it up the ramp.

Only by repeating the process of the previous haul and releasing some of the squid were we able to get the haul some of the way up the ramp. By now there was quite a lot of smoke coming from the winch motor, yet by cutting the net and releasing even more squid onto the deck, after a long struggle we at last got the haul onto the deck. It was now time to count the cost. Little could be done until the winch motor had cooled sufficiently to allow any

sort of discussion on whether it would be possible to resume fishing, or whether we would have to seek repairs.

The situation did not look good, even though the chief and second engineers worked through the night, making a number of adjustments and small repairs. Deep down it was obvious to everyone that we had little option other than to make arrangements to have the winch motor repaired ashore. The only problem was where?

We contacted our agent in Port Stanley indicating what sort of repairs were needed, and we were informed that they had no facilities for this type of repair, and we would have to look for a port in South America.

We had already been in touch with our own offices in England and Spain, and it was not long before we were instructed to proceed to Montevideo, where repairs would be carried out on our arrival. It would take us five days to reach Montevideo.

It seemed so unreal to end a spell of good fishing, brought to an untimely end by a burnt out winch motor. So with fish still in the factory from the previous haul, and the last haul of sixty tonnes still laid out on the deck waiting to be tipped down into the factory, we made our way towards Montevideo.

The factory was not fully clear until the following day, and from our two hauls we had processed and frozen 127 tonnes of illex, leaving us to reflect on what might have been had we been able to carry on for a few days more.

The winch motor would obviously have to be taken ashore to be repaired, and although the engineers had done everything possible to have the motor ready for removal as soon as we arrived in Montevideo, there was little else to do for the remainder of the journey. It did at least get a little bit warmer each day as we progressed northwards.

This large haul of squid and a second even larger were to cost us dearly, with twenty-eight days spent in Montevideo getting our winch repaired, plus a further ten days spent steaming from the fishing grounds and back again.

The Trip with the Devil

At the time I'm referring to, it is a fact that the skipper of the Hull trawler Caesar was without doubt the most unpopular skipper that I ever had the misfortune to sail with.

After a two week spell at Chatham to do my Royal Naval Reserve training, I had been asked by the ship's husband, with something of a wry smile, if I fancied a trip in the Caesar instead of waiting for my regular ship, the Brutus, to arrive home. Along with a close friend, I decided to give it a try. As the old saying goes, you can do one trip with the Devil.

Hellyer Brothers' trawler Caesar. The author spent a difficult trip in the Caesar and some happy times in her sister ship Lorenzo as deckhand, before going on to skipper both of these fine ships.

I did my one trip and I found out in that trip that the Devil himself certainly has a rare old sense of humour. Years later I sailed again in the Caesar, as mate and also as skipper, but even with all the years in between, I could not help but think back to that one trip, and I can still recall it as if it were yesterday.

There was a short run to the south-west of Iceland, which meant that every day was spent fixing a trawl and bobbins either side. We would be working two gears in this area and all our time was spent fixing trawls or altering gear that had already been fixed.

When we started fishing, after having spent the day on deck carrying out tasks that could have been done with half the number of men, and after the second haul, the skipper - God bless him - announced that he had completely forgotten to start watch below. He went on to demand of the crew why should they always have to rely on him to think of everything? By the time that last watch below did finally go below, they had been up for almost two days.

As the trip went on, nobody got off the deck except for meal times and their watch below. Regardless of how long the trawl had been on the bottom, when the last fish was gutted, it was hauling time once again. So it went on for day after day. Standing in the pounds cold and wet, I remember thinking just who did William Wilberforce free from slavery? After all, we were from the same bloody place, so why were the poor bloody fishermen not included when slavery was abolished?

One day we were hauling when there appeared to be something very heavy in the trawl. This was not helped by being laid broadside onto a moderate swell. With about half of the trawl inboard, a rather larger than usual swell made it difficult to stop the trawl pulling out and as it did so, it took the mate out with it.

Fortunately the mate had the presence of mind to hang to the trawl, but was now a short distance from the side of the Caesar, with some of us trying to pull the trawl in, while others tried to throw a line to the man.

It was obvious that he was being affected by the cold of the water and would certainly not be able to hold on for much longer, and as the Caesar rolled to starboard, someone managed to grab him by the neck of his oilskin and held on for dear life.

It was a difficult task indeed to get him back on board, with everyone getting in each other's way on deck, but eventually he was safely up to the ship's rail and back on board. In the warmth of the galley it was some time before the mate was able to speak, due to the cold and the shock of what had been a very close call. However, when he assured everyone that he was able to go back to his normal duties, he paid a visit to the skipper in the bridge.

The skipper sat there and listened to the mate tell him how lucky he had been because he could not have lasted much longer in the water.

"Yes, very lucky," the skipper replied. "But in future, Mr. Mate, never leave the ship again without my permission."

When the torture was finally over and the Caesar was full up and on her way home, still with a lot of fish on the decks, not surprisingly there was not a bit of the usual joy or joviality when a ship leaves the fishing grounds for home. Although our beloved skipper has forgotten to start watch below at the start of the trip, he certainly never forgot to stop the watch below at the end of the trip.

With the decks clear of fish by the time of the midday meal, we then returned to the deck to prepare the bobbins and secure the trawls after they had been overhauled, and in general swill the ship down as we made our way home. All this had taken eighteen hours by the time the poor bloody deck crew trudged off deck at teatime on the stroke of 1800 hours.

But it did not all end there. From an old newspaper we learned that there was a title fight on the radio, and although the radio had not been heard during the entire trip, we wondered whether or not it would be worth asking the skipper if he could find it in himself to put the fight on in the mess deck for a few of us to listen to. As I had no intentions of doing another trip in the Caesar, I duly paid a visit to the skipper with our request, but left the bridge without knowing if the fight would be on or not, but fully aware that there was a lot of work to do tomorrow and we should get some sleep instead of sitting there listening to fights on the radio.

As the time of the fight drew closer, there were fewer and fewer of us left on the mess deck as men made their way to their bunks. The last of us departed to their bunks around the time that the fight was about to start, and slept right through until going on watch after breakfast time. Yet at breakfast time, to my surprise, the engineer told me who had won the fight. He told us that the fight had come on the radio in the mess deck at the sound of the first bell, not a minute before, and was switched off the very second that the decision was given. I could only remark that I was surprised he had kept it on long enough for the decision, after having listened to the fight.

I was making my way up to the bridge for my turn at the wheel, rolling a cigarette and surveying the damage to my hands, a feeling well known to many fishermen at the end of a trip, when I was soon confronted by our skipper, who wasted no time in telling me that it was deckhands like me who got him a bad name. Out of the goodness of his heart he had tuned into the fight, only to find that there was nobody remaining on the mess deck to listen to it. Some sense of humour our skipper had.

The Caesar was lost when she went aground near Ísafjördur in the north-west of Iceland in 1971. Although she was recovered from where she had grounded, she later sank under tow. One of the Caesar's life rings is to be seen in the museum in Ísafjördur.
Photo: The Westfjords Folk Museum.

Piecing Together The Evidence

By the time the Gaul had dropped from the headlines some weeks after she had been located and surveyed, I received a call from the MAIB that took me by surprise, to say the least. George Petty, who had been mate on the Gaul, and I were invited to travel to the MAIB headquarters in Southampton to view the entire video footage from the survey, including all the material that had not been released for public viewing.

Since the loss of the Gaul, George and I had gone our separate ways. Following the decline of the deep water trawler fleet, George had spent several years doing seismic survey work on a number of ships, while I had fished out of Spain before venturing down to the Falklands and later spending a few years with the offshore oil industry.

Now with our long sea careers well and truly behind us, we continued to meet from time to time, and quite often the conversation would turn to the Gaul.

As the MAIB's invitation to Southampton had been made at short notice, I forfeited a week's holiday in the sun, but convinced myself that I had made the right decision. George and I travelled down to Southampton in September 1998, along with the thousands of people who were visiting the Southampton Boat Show at the same time. We had little idea of what to expect, but we were both intent on keeping an open mind on anything that we were to see on the following morning.

After a night in a hotel in Portsmouth, we were collected and driven to Southampton, where we were warmly greeted and thanked for giving up our time.

After a short briefing on the equipment that was at our disposal, we were handed the tapes that would keep us glued to the screens for the following four days.

The first tape we viewed revealed very lit-

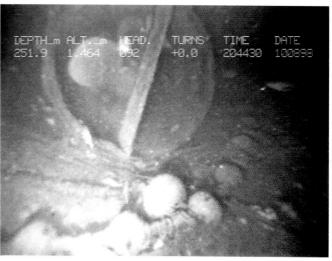

A full set of trawl gear can be seen here laid across the Gaul's stern, left there by a trawler unlucky enough to come fast on the wreck. The propeller and kort nozzle can be seen, with the rudder almost amidships. (MAIB)

tle, and started on the foredeck where we could see that hatches were secured correctly as were both of the anchors. Moving aft along the foredeck the access doors that lead through to the winch and trawl deck were both closed and clamped down, and close to these doors the spare anchor was clearly visible in its normal position. The foredeck of the Gaul showed nothing unusual in a vessel prepared to dodge out an arctic gale. The first real signs of damage were apparent as the camera centred on the bridge top. Almost all of the handrails were missing, as were the whip aerials, and there were no radar scanners to be seen. It seemed that a lot of this damage was caused by the numerous trawlers that had towed into the Gaul, leaving a considerable amount of trawl gear on and around the wreck.

The port bridge door was missing and was found on the floor, while the Gaul's lifeboat was also missing, leaving a davit with no lifeboat at the end of it.

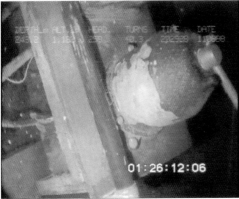

twenty years before – 72° 03'5N, 25°04'0E – as the position of the wreck of the Gaul, had turned out to be right, with the ship found on Cape Bank, as I had predicted all those years before. Judging from the sheer amount of fishing gear that had been lost over the years, including warps with twenty years of growth on them, the Gaul must have become a well-known fastener for Norwegian fishermen and I have a strong suspicion that the Risøy and the Channel 4 crew did not go to the area on spec - they had known exactly where to go.

When the hydraulic doors leading to the factory had been found to have been open, a lot of people jumped to the conclusion that the Gaul had been fishing when the tragedy occurred, yet as we came along the port side to the stern, we were able to identify the port side trawl door, indicating that she could not have been fishing at the time of her loss. Moving across the stern, we were not able to locate the starboard door, but had no difficulty in identifying a full set of bobbins left

There was nothing on the first tape we viewed that we could link directly to the loss of the Gaul, but what was becoming clear was the vast amount of net that was draped over the wreck, and the further aft along the port side that we moved, it became evident that the Gaul had claimed more nets and gear than we had imagined.

The position that had been given to me

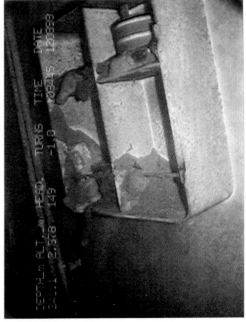

around the stern of the Gaul by another trawler that had obviously towed straight into the wreck. The same sequence also showed the kort nozzle and propeller undamaged, and the rudder to port of the midships position.

Despite a large amount of netting everywhere, access on to the trawl deck was gained close to what we called the five ton winch, used for emptying the codends, located just forward of the aft gantry.

Once again the hydraulic hatches leading to the factory were given a lot of attention, as was a lot of net leading down through the hatches into the factory deck. Like every other part of the ship, the funnels were littered with net and bobbins, and also on the trawl deck was a trawl door of the type that we had used in my time on the Gaul, and was possibly one of the spare doors carried on board.

As the camera moved slowly forward over the trawl deck, the arena around which the bobbins would normally be secured came into view, but without any bobbins to be seen. At this point it seemed that this was as far as the camera was going to get, but after a while it moved a little further forward, and then clearly showed the port side dan leno and the butterfly attached to it. Laid across the arena in front of the winch was a mass of net and bobbins that I feel was certainly the working trawl that the Gaul had been using and intended to use again when fishing resumed.

At the time the Gaul was lost, the days of the old sisal trawls had just about come to an end, and most of the trawls in use at the time were made from polyethylene. This was the case on board the Gaul, except for her codends. When the Ranger Castor arrived in Hull after the takeover with a large amount of fishing gear on board, most of the trawls were made to a standard design, with the codends made of nylon and protected by chafers made of older nylon netting.

This was what was needed to establish beyond doubt that the Gaul was not trawling at the time she was lost, as had been suggested on numerous occasions.

If there was anything to be learned from these tapes, George and I were in agreement that it would be from the trawl deck. So far we

The hand basin in one of the cabins on board, with what appears to be the door of one of the cabinets resting on it. The Gaul's fitting were showing signs of disintegrating, as can be expected after 30 years on the sea bed, but we were able to identify tables and other small items inside cabins. This task was made no more pleasant by having a set of photographs of the ship as she was when new, as she had been when George and I knew her and how we would prefer to remember her. (MAIB)

had been able to identify some nets that we felt sure belonged to the Gaul, as well as part of a pelagic trawl.

Initially George and I had been asked to spend two days looking over the tapes, but it was soon evident that this would not be enough to do full justice to the amount of video material that we had to view and comment on. After running the tapes back on numerous occasions and clarifying many points, the first tape alone had taken a full day,

On the deck, the port side dan leno bobbin can be seen, with more fishing gear laid across the arena. (MAIB)

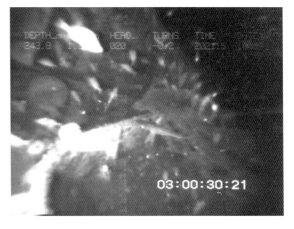

so after a discussion with Keith Dixon, the principal inspector, we both agreed without hesitation to stay on for the rest of the week.

Our short discussions at the end of each morning and at the end of each day enabled us to point out the items that had caught our eye, and also for George to have a well-earned smoke. The second tape was of the trawl deck, and we were certain that here we would find out anything that could be learned.

A cable close to the wreck of the Gaul was just what had been needed to rekindle the spying allegations, and this had featured prominently in the Channel 4 documentary the previous year. At the time the journalist involved had gone to great lengths to get one of the Risøy's crew to agree that this was a submarine cable of some kind, and this was one of the items that the Mansal 18 took a closer look at when surveying the wreck and the sur-

rounding area, showing that the mysterious cable was nothing more sinister than a discarded trawl warp.

It is hardly surprising that on a heavily fished area such as Cape Bank that a wreck should regularly claim other trawlers' fishing gear, especially in the first few years after her loss, before skippers were able properly to chart the new obstruction on the sea bed precisely. In the event, the mysterious cable was another of the spying theories that fell apart as the survey continued.

George and I felt that we had built up a good working relationship with the staff at the MAIB offices in Southampton, and with everyone working on the Gaul project. It was clear to us that no stone was being left unturned, regardless of cost, to come up with the correct reasons as to how the Gaul had been lost.

Our third day took us inside the bridge, the most familiar place on the ship to George and myself. Access to the bridge was through one of the broken windows, and we were quickly able to make out the ship's wheel. A number of the other instruments, including the spare radar, were still in place, and despite some of the deck head panels that had fallen out of place, the bridge interior was much as I remembered it all those years back.

As the day wore on, we returned to the deck of the Gaul, and the large amount of net that covered much of the ship.

The usual procedure on a freezer trawler

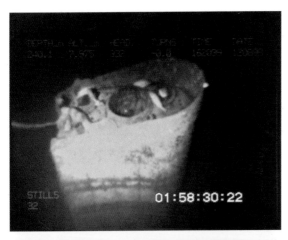

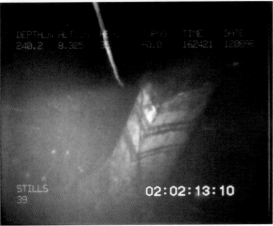

Pictures from the Mansal 18 survey show damage to the Gaul's port funnel, with damage visible on the outboard side. (MAIB)

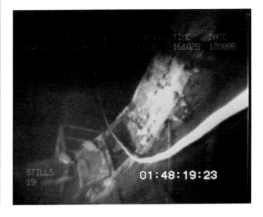

when the trawl in use had sustained some damage was to cut it away from the bobbins and heave the trawl aft. From there it was usual to open the doors to the factory deck, and lower the trawl below, leaving the deck clear for another trawl to be attached to the footrope. Once this trawl had been shot away, the damaged trawl could be retrieved from the factory deck and stretched out on the trawl deck to be repaired. This repaired trawl could then be stowed away, ready to replace the trawl in use as soon as it sustained any damage needing substantial repair.

This was the Gaul's routine and much the same procedure was used on the other Hull and Grimsby stern trawlers. The method of working was a time saver for everyone, as most vessels were not fitted with net drums at this time.

On the 7th of February 1974, the Gaul reported on the 2330 schedule that she was

The Gaul's name plate, showing the original name of Ranger Castor and the name of Brooke Marine in Lowestoft. This name plate and the ship's bell were recovered by the Mansal 18. (MAIB)

repairing her trawl, which to me seems a strange thing to be doing with the weather deteriorating. The Gaul's trawl had been reported to have been paralysed, meaning that the gear was so badly damaged that a considerable amount of time would be needed for repair to get it ready for use again.

Nobody knows for sure what the skipper's intentions were. His intention could have been to repair the trawl quickly, which could have been possible if it had been damaged but with none of the net missing, allowing it to be laced together. This would have been a practical option, allowing him to change trawls again some time later when they had hauled or when the weather had moderated enough to allow them to continue fishing.

Nobody knows for sure what happened on Cape Bank in February 1974. I have listened intently to peoples' views of what happened to

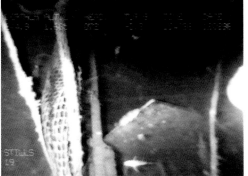

The clamps to the two hydraulic doors leading from the Gaul's deck to the factory are clearly undamaged, but it appears that these doors had not been clamped shut. I am convinced that this would have opened as the Gaul laid over on her side and that this contributed in no small way to the factory deck flooding, more than the open door on the starboard side leading to the engine room. (MAIB)

the Gaul, and since the day she disappeared I have never stopped looking for the reasons behind her loss. I have always had plenty of ideas on the subject, and one of them could be the right one, but when I returned to our hotel from Southampton after the second day of viewing tapes, I could not with my hand on my heart say for certain how the Gaul had come to be lost, and it would have taken a brave and clever man to do so.

The tape that had covered the Gaul's trawl deck had thrown up a number of interesting points that had kept George and myself glued to the video screen, but for the moment the only thing we could be sure of was that the Gaul would not give up her secrets easily. We had already made up our minds to spend our last day at Southampton viewing again the tape of the Gaul's trawl deck, as well as some of the interior of the ship.

Entry into the cabins on the port side through portholes again revealed very little. Parts of some of the cabins were understandably starting to disintegrate, but we were able to make out the small table, wash basin and cabinet in the bathroom of one of the cabins. Although the camera was able to highlight and dwell on a number of items, it would have taken a brave man to say for certain that these were human remains.

In fact it was announced ten weeks later that the forensic evidence had been research thoroughly and the survey had not returned with any human remains. If the Gaul had been lost at the time of the midday meal, as I have always thought was likely, then hardly any-body would have been in any of the cabins. The cooks would have been at work, the engineers would have been handing over watches and especially if there was work being done on a damaged trawl, the deck crew would have been at work as well.

The Gaul had given us a lot to think about, and our visit to the south coast made me think long and hard about things that I had not previously imagined could have brought about the loss of the Gaul.

From all the evidence we had seen on the screens, it seemed that the Gaul had laid over to starboard at the time she was lost. We had seen enough evidence to support this, and in my mind I came up with a number of things that may have contributed to the sinking of the Gaul.

We had seen enough evidence to say for certain that the Gaul was not fishing at the time she was lost, and had been dodging as weather brought fishing to a halt on Cape Bank. With the wind from the ESE at the time with snow showers and heavy squalls, it would seem that the Gaul was ready to dodge out a storm that presented no problems to any of the other trawlers in the area at the time. The Gaul was in regular contact with other vessels in the area using VHF, a normal procedure for several trawlers fishing together.

Taking into account the last radio contact with Wick radio at 1130 that day, it would seem that all was well with the Gaul. There were reports of the Gaul and a number of sightings, including one which put the Gaul on a course that would have taken her in towards the land. If the Gaul's skipper had intended to seek some sort of shelter, this would have been a perfectly normal course of action.

There would have been no sort of shelter in an ESE gale on Cape Bank. Once clear of Sletnes, the contour of the land runs away in a south-easterly direction across Tana Fjord, Omgang, Bass Fjord, Maakur, Baarlevag and further on to Vardo. With no chance of closing

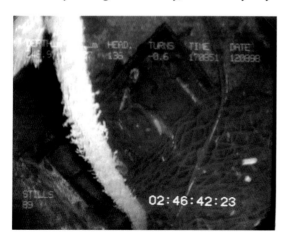

The open door on the Gaul's starboard side leading to the engine room, partly blocked with netting. (MAIB)

with the land on a course of ESE, the best chance of obtaining a lee of some sort would have been to put the wind on the port bow and make good a more southerly course, seeking some sort of shelter west of Helsnes. The North Cape, Yjelmsøy, Storr Stapen and Fruholmen would have offered a break from the weather as long as it stayed ESE, but to reach this area, the Gaul would have had to expose more of her port side to the weather.

We had seen on the first video that the Gaul had been securely battened down, and with this in mind, I feel that the Gaul would have filled up by the stern. The combined weight of the engines and the large amount of machinery on the factory deck, plus the spare trawl doors and sets of spare bobbins on the deck would have contributed a great deal to how she sank, but this still tells us nothing of how she came to lay over to starboard in the first place.

An open door leading to the engine room would possibly support the theory that the Gaul could have filled by the stern and sunk stern first, as I believe she did.

However, I cannot believe that the hydraulic doors leading to the factory deck could have been opened by air pressure. The clamps for these doors were examined closely, and there were no signs of damage to them. This supports the theory that it was not sheer force that opened these doors, assuming they had been clamped down in the first place and not opened for some specific reason.

But these doors being unclamped and able to open as the Gaul was swamped by three large seas in succession could have been the critical factor in the ship being lost so rapidly that there was no time to transmit a distress call.

It was obvious to George and myself that everyone concerned with the Gaul project had gone out of their way to assist us in any way possible, and clearly every effort was being made in the search for any piece of information that could be linked to the loss of the Gaul.

Despite the good relationship we had built up with the MAIB staff, on our final afternoon as we went through our final debriefing at the

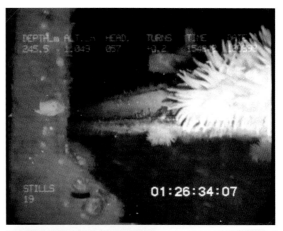

Clamps on the hatches are shown to be clearly undamaged. (MAIB)

close of the day we both felt annoyed and frustrated that we had not been able to identify what had happened to the Gaul and brought about her loss.

We both felt that there had not been enough information obtained from the survey. Although we knew we had highlighted a number of points, there were still nagging doubts about the trawl deck video, and these doubts remained with me all through the train journey back to Hull.

Heavy Weather

I will always have a soft spot for the Barnsley, a former Grimsby trawler that I skippered as a standby vessel in the northern sector of the North Sea. I had also many times fished alongside the Barnsley in Iceland. In this ship I experienced some of the worst weather I have ever encountered, including a huge sea that could easily have swamped the ship one December afternoon. This is an experience that I feel sure I shall never be able to forget.

A number of years after the loss of the Gaul, and five or six years before the wreck had been located, I had been skipper of the Barnsley, a former Grimsby trawler, on stand-by duty in the North Sea in the middle of December and looking forward to being home for Christmas. We had been given a severe weather warning for the following day, with the wind expected to reach force twelve and more.

With plenty of time to prepare, everything was secured on deck, including the hatches leading to what was now the survivors' space, which previously had been the Barnsley's fishroom for many years.

Throughout the night the weather remained reasonable, but early in the morning the wind settled and began to freshen from a northerly direction, and so began a day that I have remembered clearly ever since.

I arrived on the bridge at 0630, after we had remained to the south of the rig overnight. It was my intention to keep to the south of the rig until the weather became so dangerous that it would have been dangerous to bring the Barnsley around any more than was necessary. At 0900 and five miles south of the rig, we brought the Barnsley around and started heading back on a northerly course into what were by this time storm force winds that were forecast to get still worse during what promised to be a very uncomfortable day indeed.

Some two hours later we passed the rig at a range of about one mile and in view of the conditions, were told to look after ourselves until there was some sort of moderation in the weather.

As the weather worsened further, I decided to change from automatic steering to hand steering, and although I had a very experienced mate with me, I decided to remain in the bridge throughout his watch as well. During the afternoon we spent our time steering the Barnsley as we dodged relentlessly head to wind with the Huddersfield Town, another old Grimsby trawler, three miles abeam of us on our starboard side.

It had been one of those days with very little daylight at all, and throughout it all the Barnsley had dealt with it all remarkably well. I was sure she had seen it all time and time again. However, staring into the gathering dusk, I was finding it very hard to define what was the sea and what was the sky.

Finally, I knew that the mate was staring hard at me, and without looking across at him, I said "OK Bill, I've seen it."

Rolling towards us in what seemed like slow motion was what seemed to be one of the biggest, if not the biggest sea that I have seen in my life.

On sighting this mass of water, I took the wheel myself and had time to adjust the engine revs before the Barnsley started to climb up the monstrous sea that stretched out endlessly right across her stem. The Barnsley was still climbing and pointing towards the sky when the sea broke over her, and how high was the amount of green water that broke over her nobody will ever know. I will never understand how the bridge remained intact after it took the full impact of that mass of water.

Once the Barnsley reached the peak of this monstrous sea, we started the descent into the trough that followed behind it. Stealing a glance through a slit in one of the boarded up windows showed an awesome sight, nothing but white water lay ahead of us and an eerie noise as if we were getting some sort of shelter in the trough of the giant sea.

Once again we started to climb out of the trough to meet the next wall of water. With nothing of the foredeck of the Barnsley visible from the sheer amount of water, and shaking herself vigorously, the port and starboard rails came clear of the water as the Barnsley cleared herself and the decks came into view after what seemed a lifetime, but had in fact been a few minutes.

These were two or three minutes that I shall never forget, and neither will Bill the mate, long past retirement age and with years of experience behind him. On the way back to the rig, Bill said to me: "Skipper, I think it's time that I called it a day." To the best of my knowledge, that is exactly what he did.

When we eventually turned the Barnsley round in what was by now a mere force eight or nine and slowly moderating, we were 28 miles from the rig. When we arrived back on station we were asked jokingly if we had enjoyed our day off, to which I replied that I would not have missed it for the world.

Several ships suffered some damage that day before the weather improved, and the main talking point among the crews was the size of the sea that had broken over the Barnsley as we dodged through the storm.

Those of the crew who had been aft in the mess deck told me how they had been thrown along the seats until they had found themselves pressed against the aft end and were helpless until she slid down into the trough of the sea. The bosun, another very experienced old fisherman, arrived on the bridge fully expecting it to be extensively damaged and could hardly believe his eyes when I told him that everything was all right up there, apart from being a little shaken.

That was a day I will never forget, and I will never forget the Barnsley and the way she handled the weather. To the best of my knowledge that was the Barnsley's last trip on standby duty, as new regulations had come into force and such vessels were not thought to be up to the standards required by the offshore industry.

I had been skipper of the Barnsley for about a year before moving on to a much larger and more modern type of ship, but I will always have a soft spot for the Barnsley and her sea keeping capabilities - high praise for a Grimsby ship from a Yorkie. I have no doubt that being battened down and the buoyancy of the air space in the survivors' accommodation contributed to the Barnsley surviving that particular storm, and being able to meet that giant sea head on was also important. Had she been struck beam on by the power of that huge sea, I feel certain that she would not have survived it, and I do not believe that a larger vessel caught beam on to that sea would have survived.

The incident comes easily to mind because ever since the loss of the Gaul, some people have searched for excuses to link her to anything sinister, but the obvious thing that could have brought about her loss - the weather - has been largely ignored.

It is believed that because of the poor weather the Gaul had hauled her trawl to dodge out the imminent gale of wind that had been forecast, and there is nothing out of the ordinary about this.

From 0430 on the 8th of February 1974, when it was thought that the Gaul had hauled her trawl for the last time, nothing amiss had been reported, and there is no reason to assume that anything was wrong at that time.

There had been no reports of heavy fishing in the area at the time, so I feel it is safe to assume that the fish from that last haul was processed within an hour and a half of being tipped into the factory. In view of the schedule reports from other ships in the area, this would have been the maximum amount of time needed to clear the fish.

This would have brought the time close to breakfast time on board the Gaul, and it would have also meant that watches would have been changing, along with the cooks, who would have turned out an hour earlier. To all intents and purposes, this would have been a normal day like any other. The skipper would have taken over the watch from the mate on the bridge, and the chief would have been on watch in the engine room.

Although they may not have been required to work on the deck, the watches would have been changed for the deck and factory crews. Any fish that had to be packed and frozen I feel sure would have been dealt with by 0800 and stowed in the hold.

On the bridge the skipper under normal circumstances would have had the second mate with him, along with a deckhand who would take turns with another hand spending hourly spells on watch.

During poor weather there was not a lot to do once the ship had stopped fishing, but one thing that was required was that the factory deck should be checked every hour for fire or a build up of water. Being familiar with the ship, almost all of the crew and the everyday routine, I can see no reason why anything would have been changed, as this routine was the same on all of the freezer trawlers operating from Hull and Grimsby.

Not only would the watchmen have had reason to visit the factory, but any number of others would also have had work to do there, the men who packed the last haul of fish, the Baader mechanics, and I feel sure that the chief engineer would have had call to visit the factory at least once in his watch.

Knowing the Gaul and her crew, and the routine on board, I find it extremely difficult to imagine that a large amount of water could have entered the factory deck over a long period without it being noticed.

As hard as I have tried, I cannot convince myself that the Gaul could have been lost due to large amounts of water taken over her trawl deck. During my time on the Gaul I had seen her take water up the stern ramp on a number of occasions, and on most of these occasions, this happened while we were dodging in poor weather with fishing brought to a halt. We had experienced plenty of this in November and December immediately prior to the trip in which she was lost.

Although at first it may have seemed that the ship had taken a very heavy sea up the ramp, by the time it had run the full length of the trawl deck, the water remaining was only a few inches deep, and certainly not enough to have a serious effect on the Gaul's stability. With this in mind I feel it is highly unlikely that with the high step on the door that was found to be open on the starboard side and leading down to the engine room, that enough water could have entered the door to cause her problems when taking a sea up the stern ramp. However, I feel that the open door could have contributed in no small way to how and why she sank.

We can hardly rule out the possibility that the Gaul was steaming, as she had been reported to have been doing, and heading in towards the land to seek shelter. With the wind on her port bow, in the murk, snow and constant darkness, she could have been struck by a series of seas that laid her over on her starboard side.

If the Gaul had been steering on autopilot, and was struck heavily on the port bow, the autopilot could have been thrown out, exposing the port side of the ship fully broadside to the next heavy seas that followed. This may also explain partly why the ship's workboat was missing from the Schat davit on the port side, which would most likely have taken the full impact. I have never been able to rule out the real possibility that this was the reason why the Gaul came to be lost.

Model ships and tank tests may not support this theory, but tank tests do not throw up the heavy squalls of snow that can whip the sea to a frenzy in a few seconds. How many of us have spoken or heard the words 'where did that one come from?' when a big sea larger than all the rest rolls along to keep everyone on their toes.

Although I am sure that tank tests can provide us with a great deal of information, let us not forget that in the case of the Gaul, these were only required because she had already been lost. Contrary to what has been said in the past, I and several other people believe that the Gaul could have been lost, even without her watertight integrity being breached.

That December afternoon in the Barnsley was enough to convince me that this is a real possibility and again answers the question of why no distress signal from the Gaul was sent.

Theories are plentiful. Only a fool would dismiss the fact that the open door would contribute in no small way to her loss, but this could hardly have been the sole factor that brought about her loss.

It is believed that because of poor weather, the Gaul had hauled her trawl to dodge out an imminent gale that had been forecast, and there is nothing out of the ordinary in this. There is no reason to believe that anything was amiss on board when the Gaul hauled for the last time, at or not long after 0430.

There had been reports that the Gaul had been experiencing problems with her steering and had been hand steering for some time, but we must also remember that in many ships it was customary to switch to hand steering in poor weather.

However, I feel that the open door contributed in no small way to the Gaul's loss, in that it provided an entrance for large amounts of water when the Gaul was laid over to starboard after being struck by the three large seas that also damaged the Southella, while the failure to clamp shut the fish hatches was undoubtedly the critical factor in the Gaul being unable it right herself.

More Tests - And Some Conclusions

Late in 1998, the relatives of the men who were lost with the Gaul had a chance to see for themselves and draw their own conclusions as to what may have happened when the tapes from the Mansal 18 were brought to Hull and a private viewing was arranged for them.

Once again the Gaul was in the news, and the damage to the stem of the vessel below the anchors was singled out for attention.

As Christmas and the New Year

The author on the left, with George Petty and MAIB inspector Owen Brown on the right, taken during the session at Gosport during which the model of the Gaul was subjected to a variety of tests. (MAIB)

approached, things became quiet as people waited for a date when the findings of the latest survey would be made public. George Petty and I had seen for ourselves the amount of painstaking work that had gone into bringing all the pieces of this amazing puzzle together once and for all. Whatever the findings, I thought they would never be acceptable to everyone, whatever the outcome.

In the first few days of 1999 I received another surprise telephone call. While I had thought that all the loose ends were being tied up, George Petty and I were once again invited by MAIB to travel to Portsmouth to

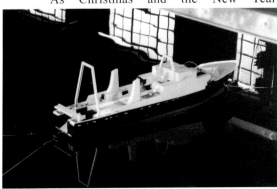

The model of the Gaul in the tank at Gosport during the MAIB tests. (MAIB)

observe tank tests that were to be carried out using a scale model of the Gaul.

In order not to miss the first day of the tests, I brought forward a planned birthday dinner, accepted the invitation, and travelled south on my birthday.

The tank where the tests were to be carried out was more than 200 metres long, and only those people directly involved with the tests were actually present throughout. On the 8th of January 1999, almost twenty-five years after the Gaul had been reported missing, the tests finally got underway while George and I looked on with great interest.

The first tests were carried out using a model of the Gaul remotely operated from the side of the tank, and the model had no difficulty in coping with everything it encountered. The model made a number of runs both running head to sea and with a following sea, programmed as far as possible to represent the same conditions as the Gaul would have experienced on that day twenty-five years before.

The first day's tests looked very realistic, and I was quick to point out that the wind factor that the tank was not equipped to provide would have made the test even more accurate. Taking into account the cost of hiring this sort of tank, it was no surprise that testing continued well into the evening. Nevertheless, by the end of the day, we were all agreed that it would have taken something out of the ordinary to put this model into any sort of danger.

The wreck of the Gaul had been found with her hydraulic doors leading to the factory open, and another door leading to the engine room also open. With these same doors left open on the model, the second day's testing began.

With these doors left open, the model inevitably started to take on water. Seven minutes later the model had only a slight list to starboard and was recovered. It was explained told that these seven minutes in the tank represented a seventh of real time, which would indicate that it would have taken the Gaul 49 minutes to reach this condition. Once again this had me wondering why no mayday had been transmitted and convinced me that the Gaul was not lost in this way.

Here the model is running before a simulation of a heavy following sea. (MAIB)

The model, still running before a following sea. (MAIB)

Here the model is running before a simulation of a heavy following sea. (MAIB)

Tethered to face the waves from a variety of different angles, the model of the Gaul proved herself to be very durable indeed. After taking on board large amounts of water time after time, the model was each time retrieved, but the time factor told the same story every time.

With wind and sea on the port bow, this could have been the direction the Gaul was heading when she could have been hit by a series of heavy seas that also damaged another trawler. (MAIB)

Pictured from above, the model of the Gaul is struck fully broadside. The model was tested in almost every position possible during the tank tests. This session was undoubtedly the most interesting part of our two stays with the MAIB in Southampton. (MAIB)

The final series of tests on the model of the Gaul were carried out with various doors and hatches left open. This picture shows the Gaul listing heavily to starboard after taking in water through the door leading to the engine room. (MAIB)

Nothing that we had witnessed so far had taken us by surprise, and we now had to wait while the model was thoroughly dried out before being tethered in the tank once again to see how it would react broadside to the waves.

During this sequence, the wave height was gradually increased, and the model was hit by a number of very heavy waves that eventually laid it over on its starboard side. Even from this angle, the model managed to right itself to an extent. This was the first time during the tests that we had seen the model in any serious difficulties, and also the first time that I did not agree with the suggestions and conclusions being drawn around the tank.

The findings of the survey of the Gaul may differ from my own conclusions, but I have had the benefit of having seen the video footage of the wreck. After what I had seen during the two days of tank testing, I could not agree with those who thought that the Gaul could recover and right herself after a full ninety degree knockdown that laid her on her starboard side.

As no wind was used or taken into consideration during these tank tests, I find it hard to believe that she could have righted herself, knowing what she would have had to come back against.

This would have been a full gale of wind and seas of the same type as had laid her over on her side to begin with. We should also not forget that the machinery in the factory deck could well have broken adrift, and we had already seen on the video tapes how all of the nets and bobbins that the Gaul had been using had rolled to the starboard side. I feel that these factors, plus the movement of anything else that may have been loose on the Gaul, would have been sufficient to ensure that she was unable to right herself from this particular situation.

On the third day of testing there was no reprieve for the model. Knocked over with the door to the engine room left open, the model quickly filled up with water by the stern before it lifted its bows and sank stern first.

For years the Humber ports have suffered some horrific losses in terms of men and ships, and most of these have occurred in the winter in appalling conditions. Ships from both ports had disappeared without trace, while others had succumbed to severe icing conditions, and others had grounded and been lost. Yet out of this long list of ships, the Gaul has remained in the public eye ever since she was first reported missing.

Over a drink at the hotel in Portsmouth, George and I had a chance to reflect on our two visits to the south coast. This also gave us a chance to look back on happier times in the Gaul and the fine bunch of men who made up her crew, rather than the groundless allegations of spying that we both knew were completely untrue.

George told me how when he was put ashore at the start of the trip, a Norwegian doctor had instructed him to fly home to seek further treatment. After helping him ashore with his bags, some of the crew had jokingly reminded him that he would be home in time to see Hull RFC play an important fixture at the Boulevard the following week.

This had left the Gaul with an experienced skipper in Peter Nellist and an experienced mate, Maurice Spurgeon, who was flown out to Norway to replace George Petty. But this also left the Gaul with her two senior deck officers, the skipper and mate, all making their first trip with the ship. Also the chief engineer was making his first trip in this capacity, although he had already sailed previously as the Gaul's second engineer.

Quite understandably, George had chosen to remain silent about the Gaul through the years, and after seeing for myself the way that the press, radio and television go out of their way to misinterpret your words, I can fully understand George's decision.

I did not have to remind George of the time we were alongside at Honningsvåg waiting for some spare parts when the chief of police complimented me for having a man at the gangplank to prevent the crew from going ashore. I replied that the crew were free to go ashore if they wanted, and the man at the gangplank was there to prevent the wrong sort of people from coming on board the ship. This is how I feel that we both wanted to remember the Gaul.

On that final day of testing, we visited the MAIB offices for a final analysis and to talk over what we had seen during our time observing the tank tests.

Despite everything that I had seen and heard during our two visits, I think that my mind was already made up as to how the Gaul was lost. What I had seen did nothing to alter my first thoughts, and confirmed in my mind much of what I had always thought had played a major role in her loss.

The publicity that the loss of the Gaul had created over so many years, especially in her home port of Hull, can only mean that some people will not accept the findings of the MAIB officers, and there will always be people who have their own ideas about what happened, and who knows? They may just be right.

My own thoughts on the Gaul's loss have changed little since she was first reported missing. However, I have had my doubts, and have been privileged to have seen the videos and tank tests, and these have gone some way to help me build up a picture in my own mind of what happened to the Gaul. I feel that my views will not be shared by everyone, and that they may also vary somewhat from the findings of the MAIB.

It is now well established that the Gaul was not fishing at the time of her loss. One trawl door and a set of bobbins were identified as belonging to the Gaul, and she had already reported herself to be laid to and dodging on the freezer schedule.

There also seems little doubt that anything could have happened to the Gaul all the time that she remained head to wind and sea. The problems that the Gaul encountered could have started in any number of ways that caused her to fall off the wind, finishing up broadside or almost broadside on to the wind and sea.

We can not underestimate the force of the weather at the time the Gaul was lost. When dodging head to wind on automatic steering, most of us have seen exactly what can happen when the wind gets on either bow, and how quickly the ship can fall off the wind. I have seen this happen on numerous occasions, and so have many others. When dodging in this situation, the ship will not respond to rudder alone to come back to her original course, and the only option is to increase the engine revolutions or the pitch of the propeller to get back to the original heading.

All this could have happened very quickly, and as we saw during the tank tests, this put the Gaul into the most vulnerable position of all those that we had seen, regardless of whether this happened if she had been knocked off her course or if she had been broadside to the weather while coming about.

With her port side exposed to the severe weather, the Gaul may well have been struck in succession by the three heavy seas that were reported by other skippers in the area. A dent in the Gaul's port side funnel suggests to me that she was struck by more than one big sea at this time, and once laid over on her starboard side, I am sure that this spelled the end for the Gaul. The large aft gantry and heavy top blocks would have gone some way to ensuring that she could not have righted herself from this position, and the movement of some of the heavy machinery on her factory deck is something that I feel would have contributed much to her loss.

With all these odds stacked against her in a gale, I feel that this was too much for the Gaul to be able to right herself. With the one door open and leading down to the engine room, she would have started to take in water, and laid to with a list of as much as 100°, the two fish hatches could have opened with nothing to prevent them from doing so.

As there is no damage to the clamps on these doors, it would not appear that they were forced open by air pressure, as has been suggested.

Nobody will ever know why the fish hatches to the factory deck had not been clamped shut. It is possible that there could have been some disruption to the usual routine, or simply that someone thought that someone else had already done this after the last haul.

With the Gaul filling up by the stern, any build up of pressure would have been in the forepart of the vessel. As more water entered the Gaul, she would have sunk stern first rather quickly, hitting the sea bed heavily. My final conclusion regarding how the Gaul sank covers the damage to the bow or forefoot. In my own opinion, this was caused by the build up of hydrostatic pressure inside the vessel as it filled with water, combined with the shock wave of the Gaul hitting the sea bed travelling through the ship, causing some of the plates to rupture.

If I needed any more convincing of how the Gaul came to be lost, it came when the model was retrieved from the tank and the weight of water inside was calculated to be equivalent to 180 tonnes. My thoughts are that the Gaul was unlucky to have been in the wrong place at the wrong time, and what happened to the Gaul could have happened to any of the ships fishing on Cape Bank at that time.

Montevideo

Our arrival in Montevideo after five days steaming was a relief in itself. At least we would be able to find out to what extent the winch motor was damaged and be given some idea of how long repairs could take.

Although I had never visited any of the South American countries, I did have some idea of what we could expect on arrival. No sooner had the pilot who brought us down the river and put us alongside disappeared with his bottle of whisky than we were boarded by representatives of the Army and the Navy. I am sure that somewhere there must have been someone from the Air Force, as well as the customs and police. Of course everyone had brought along a friend just to swell the crowd.

Fishing Explorer entering Montevideo

After shaking hands with everyone who came aboard the ship and signing an endless amount of paperwork, the only man I had not managed to meet so far was the one who would be repairing the winch motor.

He eventually arrived, and promptly told me that the next day was some sort of fiesta, and it would not be possible to start work until the following day. It was a day off for everyone, with people singing and dancing in the streets.

I had assured him that under the circumstances it would be very unlikely that I would be singing and dancing in the street, and he told me that this type of work could take up to four weeks, but I should not worry as tomorrow would be a good day for everyone.

Once the holiday was over, things did eventually start to get moving. The motor was removed from the Fishing Explorer, and later in the morning our worst fears were confirmed, when after it had been thoroughly checked over, it was confirmed that repairs would take four weeks as predicted.

At first it took a little time to sink in, as we had already lost a week, and with four weeks ahead of us in Montevideo, plus a week steaming back to the Falklands, we would lose a total of six weeks and have to start practically all over again. These were six weeks that would have seen us back in Spain with almost a full ship, and going back to the Falklands would mean arriving in the middle of winter.

Boredom played a big part in our stay in Montevideo once the initial novelty had worn off. Watches were maintained on board the ship, and to ease the workload for the cooks, fresh bread was delivered to the ship at seven every morning.

Money was available in US dollars, and I had arranged for a certain amount to be delivered to the ship every Friday. Nobody asked for more than they could afford, and by and large the morale on board remained excellent throughout the first two weeks. Most of the crew went ashore every day, if only for a walk or to do a little shopping. Some preferred to go ashore at night for a few beers, but some-

Our friends from Poland...

And friends from the east. We were berthed with a Russian trawler one side a Polish one the other. Although the crews of both of these ships went out of their way to be friendly and speak to us, it was clear that they never spoke to each other.

one always remained on board, either reading or writing a letter home, which for everyone seemed a long way off.

Most of the time the weather was fine, and we could go ashore casually dressed in shirt and slacks, giving the crew plenty of opportunity to go ashore and not keeping them confined to the ship.

As for myself, during a walk ashore with the first mate, I had come across a small newsagent not far from the docks who sold a number of English newspapers. Although my Spanish had come on in leaps and bounds over the last few months, with the help of the mate I was able to place an order for a paper for every day that we remained in Montevideo. Every day I could take a leisurely stroll to the newsagent, with a coffee or a cold beer in one of the many small cafes in the area.

Another place where I often called was the workshop of the company repairing the winch motor. They were always polite and very friendly, always greeting me with coffee and brandy, the like of which I have never been able to buy anywhere else. This has convinced me that if coffee is one of the main exports of this part of the world, then they must save the best for themselves.

Not being a cigarette smoker, in Montevideo I was able to purchase enough hand rolling tobacco and cigarette papers to see me to the end of the voyage - hopefully.

Into our third week it was obvious that more and more of the crew remained on board every

One of a number of Japanese trawlers fishing in the South Atlantic. This one had berthed in Montevideo to change crew and is seen here leaving just ahead of us to steam back to the Falklands.

A group of Taiwanese jiggers moored in the large harbour in Montevideo, waiting to change crew.

night, playing cards or passing the time reading a book, and preferring to go ashore for a night out at the weekend.

As we entered our fourth week in Montevideo, our agent let me know that repairs to the winch motor were going well, and this was confirmed the following day when I paid a visit to the workshop. Over the customary coffee and brandy, I was told that repairs would be completed on time and we would soon be back at sea.

This was good news for everyone, as this had been a long time to spend in port. This was also a late stage of the trip, when we should have been on our way home instead of facing the winter months in the Falklands to catch the remainder of our voyage.

Late on our twenty-sixth day in Montevideo, the winch motor was returned to the Fishing Explorer, ready to start work the following morning. Throughout the night blocks and chains were made ready to manoeuvre the winch motor back into position. Finally it was wired up ready to be tried out.

Not surprisingly as this was our last day, most of the crew required a few extra dollars for last minute shopping, and a final night ashore that was well deserved by everyone.

It was the mate who told me that as this was our last night, we had been invited out to a club which most of the younger crew members had frequented during our stay. Not wishing to disappoint anyone, we both duly turned up along with our chief engineer, and thoroughly enjoyed our last night in Montevideo. After stopping out a bit longer than we had expected, and also after a few more drinks than had been anticipated, it was back to business.

A few small items remained, such as water, some fresh food and the inevitable final paperwork to be completed. With the pilot on board, we headed out into the River Plate and some pleasant afternoon sunshine, and as darkness fell we were heading southwards back towards the Falkland Islands.

Montevideo harbour, with two old Spanish side trawlers moored up in the distance, waiting to be broken up for scrap.

Our time in Montevideo had gone remarkably well. Morale had remained exceptional throughout our stay and although duties on board had been light, Fishing Explorer remained spotlessly clean and must have impressed anyone who visited the ship. Although our stay had at times been enjoyable, as we made our way though weather that became gradually colder the closer we came to the Falklands, everyone on board was glad to be back at sea.

A Japanese jigging vessel steaming out of Montevideo to make her way back to fishing grounds.

Tragedy

On board the Fishing Explorer everyone must have reflected at some time on what might have been if we had not had the misfortune to lose so much time and so much good fishing that would almost certainly have seen us on our way back to Spain. Yet here we were again on our way back to the Falklands.

Two hauls in the area where just a few weeks before we had struggled to get large hauls up the ramp now proved to be a waste of time, with around two tonnes of poor quality fish in each haul.

We did see some improvement when we arrived and shot away once more just outside the Falkland Islands fishing zone. Our first haul saw us bring on board eight tonnes of good quality loligo and two tonnes of hake.

We were now fishing alone in this area, and to the best of our knowledge there were only about six ships fishing around the Falklands, and all gave their positions in the Beauchene Island area.

Since we had resumed fishing the winch was working perfectly and had given no cause for alarm. Although it must be said that we had seen nothing like the amount of fish that had been the cause of us losing so much time earlier.

Owing to the time that we had lost in Montevideo, we had been granted another

A good haul of hake to start the day.

licence for two months that would allow us to fish inside the Falklands zone, but it was decided we would not proceed to Port Stanley unless the fishing slacked off or the weather deteriorated enough for us to have to stop fishing. Although most of our hauls were in the region of five tonnes, inevitably it was the weather that made our minds up for us, and a force nine gale saw us slowly making our way once more towards Port Stanley to collect our fishing licence, and hopefully some fresh reading matter and mail from home.

At 0500 we anchored outside Port Stanley, and another stern trawler, the Beatrix Nores, anchored a short distance from us. She had called in to Port Stanley to pick up some spares, and was now waiting for the weather to ease off before resuming fishing just outside.

That morning I was summoned ashore to pick up the two-month fishing license that would come into effect at midnight and enable us to fish inside the 150 mile fishing zone. We had built up a good working relationship with the two fishery patrol vessels during our previous spell in the Falklands. A number of the patrol ships' crew were from Hull, and saved us papers and other news from home, along with any amount of books and magazines that meant so much to us during these long voyages.

After a short briefing ashore in the fisheries office, and a talk about our time in Montevideo, it was time to pick up a large amount of mail from the agent, and after more coffee and talk it was time to say our farewells once again and return to the Fishing Explorer.

There was mail for almost everyone on board, and after it had been distributed and the late evening meal was over, it was decided that we would remain at anchor. Although due to moderate, the weather was still quite fresh, and the Beatrix Nores, which had sailed a few hours before, had not shot away and was still waiting for the weather to ease off a bit more.

It was a chance for everyone to relax for a

few hours. Some tried to sleep, while others chose to answer the letters they had received a few hours before in the hope that we might be able to pass them across to the one of the fishery patrol vessels, which also acted as our postmen.

At 0300 on the 1st of August we were once more heading out from Port Stanley, in the middle of winter in these parts, and facing possibly the worst two months of the entire trip.

The wind had moderated to a force six, and the swell had dropped considerably as we shot away the trawl once more. Towing to the north with just the lights of the Beatrix Nores ahead of us, we had covered this stretch of water many times before during the trip, and although catches had varied from time to time, the quality of the loligo in the area had generally been good.

Apart from an occasional snow squall, by the time it came to haul the weather had dropped to nothing more than a force four and our first haul was a reasonable six tonnes of loligo. Shooting back to the south in the daylight, we picked up some very good indications of loligo early in the tow, but when the time came to haul we brought on board a disappointing ten tonnes.

The five ships in our small group were now spread over a twenty-five mile circle, and it was encouraging as each ship reported a reasonable haul, indicating fish spread over a wide area. With this in mind when we brought in another haul, it was no surprise when we brought aboard something in the region of twenty-five tonnes of loligo.

At the moment we were enjoying a spell of fine weather, with the wind no more than a force four from the south west, and apart from the occasional snow flurry, ideal for fishing.

According to the fishery patrol, with which we were in daily contact, we were the only ships now fishing in the Falklands. Although not in our area, the fishery patrol expected to see us the next day before making his way into Port Stanley.

We had another reasonable haul of ten tonnes for the remaining daylight, and finished the day with a smaller haul of six

A second haul of hake after a two hour tow.

tonnes. By and large, it had been a satisfactory day's fishing for all the other ships in the area.

Overnight we experienced a lot of heavy snow, and while the weather was still reasonably fine, we had towed to a position 40 miles north of Stanley. Again our first haul was in the region of six tonnes, and our second ten tonnes. An hour into the third tow, we received an urgent call from one of the ships in our group, just a few miles ahead of us.

The Beatrix Nores, towing about five miles ahead of us, had apparently come fast on some obstruction, and while trying to free his trawl, there had been an accident in the engine room. One of the engineers had suffered a serious injury. The skipper was clearly very upset, and asked us if we could arrange for a helicopter to come from shore with medical backup.

This was done immediately, and we also made contact with the fishery patrol vessel, which was now just a few miles away and preparing to take a sick man off one of the other ships in the group for medical attention in Port Stanley.

We were informed by the authorities that due to the same heavy snow that we had experienced overnight, there would be a short delay, but the chopper would be with us as soon as possible. After relaying the position of the casualty, we were now only two miles from the Beatrix Nores and towing directly towards him, and were able to inform the skipper that the helicopter would be on its way.

When we were less than a mile from the Beatrix Nores and in VHF range, the helicopter crew asked us to instruct the Beatrix Nores to lower all aerials and remove any obstructions, as he intended to lower a medic on to the ship's deck, no easy task between snow squalls and with the Beatrix Nores rolling heavily.

In the meantime we hauled, and laid to just to the port side of the Beatrix Nores, and passed on the message that the helicopter would have to jettison some fuel before lowering the man down onto the deck, and requested that they bring the casualty up to the deck. Once this was done, the helicopter made its approach, and amidst a cheer from our crew, who were all on deck despite the intense cold, the medic landed safely on the deck of the Beatrix Nores. Within minutes, and with an even greater cheer from our crew, both the medic and the casualty on a stretcher were winched up to the helicopter, which immediately turned and left the scene.

It had been an eventful afternoon. We had laid close to the Beatrix Nores during the transfer of the casualty, but with the helicopter returning with the injured man and the fishery patrol vessel heading for Port Stanley, we once again shot away the trawl and towed to the south west.

As the gear went down the ramp it was almost dark, and it had been about two hours since we hauled about ten tonnes of loligo and had been informed from shore that we would be notified as soon as there was any news of the injured man. All talk on board the Fishing Explorer was of the events of the afternoon, and although we did not know the extent of the man's injuries or the cause of the accident, it was obviously very serious. We were still in touch by VHF with the Beatrix Nores, who steamed past our stern making her way into Port Stanley shortly after we had shot away our trawl.

It was just minutes after I had gone down into the saloon for the late evening meal that I was asked to return to the bridge. In a brief message from shore, I was informed that despite everything that had been done, the injured man had died in the helicopter just before it arrived back at its base. I was asked to inform the captain of the Beatrix Nores, and

A good start to the day as this haul of hake comes up the ramp after a tow of two hours. Three or four hauls a day like this were enough to ensure finishing each day with a reasonable tonnage of fillets.

Unlike the haul of hake above, this moderate haul of five tonnes of loligo was the result of a five hour tow in the area around Beauchene Island.

to request him to continue in to Port Stanley.

The lights of the Beatrix Nores were still quite clearly visible no more than five miles away when we broke the news, expressed our regrets and after asking as briefly as possible if we could be of any further assistance, left things at that. This was the one piece of news we had not wanted to hear. Shortly afterwards I broke the news to the crew, and this was received in complete silence by everyone.

The evening meal that the cooks had prepared was left mainly untouched, such was the effect the news had on everyone.

Almost everyone had been on deck when the casualty had been lifted off the Beatrix Nores. Cooks, engineers, and even men who should have been sleeping below, all came up on deck as if to add their support. The youngest crew member had spotted the helicopter first even though it was still some distance away, and there had been cheers when the medic was lowered onto the Beatrix Nores, and there were bigger cheers when he was winched back with the casualty on a stretcher. Everyone had played a small part, and yet it had all ended so sadly.

Later, alone on the bridge with my thoughts, I remember thinking sadly of the man's family, who would as yet have no knowledge of the events of the afternoon, and the sad news that would be broken to them the following day.

This was the saddest day of the entire trip on the Fishing Explorer, as well as undoubtedly on the other three ships in our small group. Just what is it about this bloody awful job of deep sea fishing is it that was so difficult to break away from? During my time at sea I had seen more than my fair share of accidents, yet this job with the highest accident rate in the world was just like being hooked on some sort

A fatal accident on board Spanish trawler Beatrix Nores cast a shadow over everyone on the Fishing Explorer for a long time. Beatrix Nores is seen here close to the Fishing Explorer shortly after the casualty had been lifted off by helicopter.

of drug and being unable to kick the habit.

Everything was unusually quiet. There was none of the usual chatter on the VHF that usually followed the evening meal, just an eerie silence as we carried on towing to the south.

Aboard the other three ships would be just the same. This small group had been close together to offer any assistance during the afternoon, but now everyone would be collecting their thoughts, just as we were, hardly able to believe what had happened.

But what would it be like on the Beatrix Nores? Any accident at sea is bad enough, but a fatal one such as this would be absolutely devastating for the whole crew, as to lose a crew member and shipmate would affect everyone. We heard the following day that the Beatrix Nores was returning to Spain.

My Worst Day at Sea

Sometimes even working under the harshest conditions can raise a laugh. I have no hesitation in saying that the worst day I ever spent at sea while I was on deck was during the time I was mate on the Portia.

Sat in the mess having a mug of tea after coming up from the fishroom, all the talk was of what an easy trip it had been so far. One of the more experienced deckhands went so far as to say that it had been the easiest trips he could remember.

We were fishing off the Norwegian coast in February, after having steamed from the Humber to the Malangen Bank in only four days with a following wind. Luck had certainly been our side and everything had gone right from the very first haul. As fishermen will testify, these things do happen, occasionally.

A few of the crew had been asking me already: would he take her home and give us a long weekend at home? I must admit the possibility had already crossed my mind. Even if we made a little less money by landing on the Friday, the long weekend at home would be very welcome indeed. The crew appeared to share these thoughts and I had already mentioned in the mess deck that with the Portia's speed, we would have to leave the Malangen Bank by the following breakfast time to reach the Humber in time, but my own gut feeling was that we would stick it out and fish a bit longer to land on Monday.

Very much to my surprise, while I was down in the fishroom, one of the crew shouted down to say that the skipper wanted a tally of what fish we had on board. On going to the bridge, I could tell him that we had about 2400 kits, which was very good for what would be a sixteen day trip. This counted for a good trip at that time of year, or indeed at any time of the year.

I had been with the skipper for long enough to know his ways and before I turned in after teatime, the skipper told me that the forecast for the following day was 'not so good.' That I had learned meant force eight or more, while 'not so bad' meant force six or less. In his opinion that was all you needed to know, that was all you got to know.

On turning out again at midnight and going to the bridge to relieve the skipper, I was told to steam the Portia at half speed to just south of the Bight of Malangen, remain in that area and to call him at 0600. With the wind now at force four or five from the north-west, the Portia made light work of these conditions. However, there were a lot of heavy snow showers about and not a lot to do but sit in the chair and have a cigarette while the lads on deck were making inroads into what had been another good haul of fish. My only visitor on the bridge was the engineer who brought me a pot of coffee, asking - inevitably - if I knew what the skipper's intentions were, to which I could honestly reply that I did not know, although I could see that the weather had deteriorated over the last hour to what was now a force seven. This made me think that there was a distinct possibility that we would carry on home. What little conversation there was on the VHF was all about the weather and how it had freshened during the last hour or so.

I called the skipper at 0600 and informed him that the weather had freshened quite a bit during our steam back, and on arriving on the bridge he told the crew to get their breakfast while he had a look at the conditions. These were now quite bad and no other ships had yet shot their gear away. But as soon as breakfast was finished came the order through the speakers to put the trawl over the side and from that moment what had been the easiest trip many of us had spent at sea came to a very abrupt end. Any hopes of our long weekend at home vanished.

Fishing in bad weather was nothing new to any of us and within a few minutes the codends were over the side, quickly followed by the bobbins. With a little bit of daylight starting to appear, it was clear that the weather had taken a nosedive and we now had a full gale of wind to contend with, but worse was to follow. Shooting under the lee of the ship was no easy task in this sort of weather and with twenty lengths of warp out, the Portia lifted on a large sea. With a sudden bang, we had chopped the forward warp with the propeller, and with that started what I have never hesitated to recall as the worst day I have spent on the deck.

Scarcely able to believe what had happened, we started hauling the gear back on the aft warp, but with so much weight still over the side, even getting the aft door to come up at a reasonable angle to put the door chain in was almost impossible. This was eventually achieved with the help of a huge sea as the Portia lay there with the wind and sea on her starboard quarter.

I had served in the Portia for a long time as a deckhand before sailing as mate and if there was one fault I could find in this otherwise fine ship, it was that the aft derrick and the forward codend derrick were too small for a ship of her size. With so much weight over the side, the aft derrick would not have been able to withstand the strain as the Portia rolled in a full gale, seemingly anchored to the weight of gear in the water. With the gilson wire and the forward tackle wire relayed aft, we did eventually succeed in getting the bobbins hove up forward and the hove up aft in their normal position along the starboard rail. But all this had certainly taken a long time and many of the crew, myself included, had taken one or two knocks. In fact, we were lucky that nobody had sustained any serious injuries. There was no damage to the trawl and pulling in the empty trawl was the easiest part of the whole operation, but now there was the small problem of 250 fathoms of warp and 50 fathoms of cable to deal with, as well, of course, as the forward trawl door. By this time there was not a man on the deck who was not soaked to the skin, cold and totally pissed off with the proceedings so far.

With the bobbins and the trawl now inboard and chained down, the hardest was over. We eventually got to our forward cable followed by the trawl door, so that we could finally start on the 500 fathoms of trawl warp. While this was being hove onto the winch, some of the crew had a chance to get changed into dry clothing and some had the chance to take their dinnertime meal.

Measuring and splicing the Portia's warp under the whaleback did at least give everyone the chance for a cigarette and eventually, at about 1400, I was able to go to the bridge and report to the skipper that everything was ready to shoot the gear away if this was what he wished to do.

Very much to my surprise, this was exactly what he chose to do, going on to explain that we had missed the best part of a day's fishing, so we had better try to salvage what was left of the day. With the weather no better than when we had shot away that morning, we stopped and put the gear over the side once again. Just as we had done seven hours earlier, the propeller once again fouled and chopped the warp, this time in the eighteenth length. I think for the first time in my life I was speechless, completely lost for words when I realised that what we had just gone through we would now have to go through again, and now in the gathering darkness it would be even more difficult. Yet we set about the task in hand and went through the same procedure all over again.

With one eye on the weather as it grew darker, working close to the ship's rail was no picnic and certainly no place for the faint-hearted. But apart from everyone on deck getting a good soaking, just as we had done previously, we managed, after a titanic struggle, to get the bobbins inboard without any serious incident. This was something of a miracle, but really was down to the brilliant bunch of deckhands who knew exactly what they were doing and what was required of them. For their work that day I can only describe them as extraordinary seamen. We had not caught anything or put a fish below for eighteen hours, yet this had turned out to be the hardest day of the trip so far. It was 2100 when I was finally able to make my way to the bridge to report to the skipper that we were once again ready to shoot away.

I stood there trying to roll a cigarette, cold, hungry, pissing wet through and absolutely pissed off with the day's proceedings, and I think that the skipper finally got the message about how everyone felt.

Without another word, he produced a full bottle of rum.

"I don't suppose you'd say no to a little dram, would you?" He asked.

Looking at the full bottle of rum in his hand I replied that I wouldn't say no to a f***ing big dram, never mind a little one. This must have done the trick, because the skipper changed the small glass in his hand and produced a big one, handing me the hardest dram of rum that I have ever earned in my life.

The evening meal, normally taken at 1800, was a little later than usual and was at 2200. It had been one of those days that were so familiar at sea, but once again within a few minutes the crew who had performed miracles on deck were joking about it.

After the day we had spent on deck, our skipper found it in himself to hand me the bottle of rum so that I could give the lads on deck a well-earned dram as well, but not before replacing the large glass once again with the small one to dish out the drams, remarking that we wouldn't want anyone falling about the deck drunk in that sort of weather, something that would have been a near impossibility with a dram glass of that particular size.

Hellyer Brother's trawler Portia, seen here making her way through the lock gates. The author is one of the group on the bow.

Looking Back – Kingston upon Hull

I was born in the City of Hull, just a stone's throw from Saint Andrew's Dock, referred to by everyone in Hull as the Fish Dock. I was born in Eton Street on Hull's famous Hessle Road, and after an education interrupted by World War Two, like many others on leaving school at fourteen years of age, I found work on the Fish Docks. As the trawlers that had fought with such courage and distinction throughout the war returned to their home ports, work on the Fish Dock was plentiful.

Distant fishing grounds, virtually untouched during the war, were reopened, and as the size of the fishing fleet grew and as fish was plentiful, the Fish Docks became a hive of activity. In those days Hull was a city that never slept.

As the trawlers returned with some spectacular catches, work on the Fish Docks went on continuously, day after day, week after week. Trawlers landed their catches from Monday through to Saturday, yet people could still be found at work on Sunday as they prepared for landings on Monday morning. To add to this,

Above: St Andrew's Dock in Hull in the 1970s, crowded with ships, including the Kingston Pearl, the Cordella, a small foreign trawler and a seine netter. This is a typical scene of how many people will remember the docks to have been.

Below: In contrast, a solitary figure watches as J Marr's Swanella leaves Albert Dock for the fishing grounds in 1996.

Plenty of work for everyone, with fish as far as the eye can see. On a day of heavy landings the kits of fish would stretch from one end of the fish market to the other.

This barrow lad delivers fish to his place of work. Young lads of fourteen, straight from school, did this kind of work and many moved on to go fishing.

A busy scene on St Andrew's Dock, with a kit scrubber washing the kits in readiness for the next day's fish. The kits of coley in the foreground show the tallies of one of Cawoods, one of the well-known names on Hull's fish docks. Each company on the fish market had its own colourful tally that could be placed on the kits of fish as they were sold during the auction as it progressed from one ship's catch to the next. On a busy landing day with a full market, it was an advantage to be among the first few ships landing, as a better price could often be aid to get fish early.

work spilled over into numerous fish houses that could be found in the streets along Hessle Road.

Trains were leaving Hull's Fish Docks morning, afternoon and night, loaded to capacity with fish of all varieties to supply all of the major cities in Britain as the nation started to come to terms with life after the war.

The bobbers who landed the trawlers from Hull began work shortly after midnight. The streets along Hessle Road would come alive to the sound of clogs as the bobbers made their way to the Fish Docks to begin landing the catches at 2 AM, to ensure that fish was on the market in time for the first sale.

According to the amount of fish she was expected to land, a trawler would be allocated a number of gangs, with each gang made up of eight bobbers. Often when landings were heavy, casual labour would be used to ensure that the fish was on the market as early for the all-important first sale of fish.

During wintertime discharging fish would continue in some very unpleasant weather, and when most people were thinking of getting up to go to work, the bobbers would be making their way home with a hard day's work already behind them.

Not only trawlers from Hull landed their catches on the Fish Dock. As the minefields of the North Sea were cleared away, a number of Danish vessels, better known as snibbies, began to land their catches to the Humber ports of Hull and Grimsby. As most of these catches were good quality plaice, it ensured a better variety of fish on the market. Add to this an Icelandic trawler and the occasional Norwegian vessel landing boxes of herrings, and it was a familiar sight to see the fish market full from end to end.

This unique workforce, often at work until late in the evening, would see the market cleared in readiness for the next day's landings, and so it went on day after day and week after week.

The other side of St. Andrew's Dock was known to most people as the dry side of the dock. Here the trawling companies had their offices situated so the front overlooked the dock and the rear overlooked the Humber.

On the dry side, the ships were turned around and once again made ready for sea. Once a trawler had discharged her catch onto the fish market, she would be towed across to the dry side for bunkering with coal or oil. Then ice would be taken on in readiness for the next trip. Any repairs needed would be carried out while the ship was laid on the dry side. No time was lost, and water was taken on while a ship's catch was being discharged onto the market.

New trawls, bobbins, wires, ropes, and anything the trawler required, would be put on board while lying at the dry side. Most of the trawling companies had their own rigging and blacksmith's shops adjoining or below their offices, and here a large amount of gear would be kept ready for the trawlers to have their complement of trawls ready for when they sailed once again.

On the old St Andrew's Dock there was no protection from the weather for the men who stood there filleting fish for hours on end with only a few short breaks during the day. This was skilful work, but tiring. The steel for sharpening the filleting knives can be seen stuck in the end of the filleting tray and the transport of the day, a bicycle, can be seen hung up in the background.

Not all of the nets were made or fixed on the dock. Some of the net making companies had premises just off the dock, and a large proportion of the nets were made up in people's homes. Companies delivered the twine that was used to make the trawls, and the women would braid the different parts of the trawls that were required. Nets were often braided in people's back yards, or hung over the front door if the weather was fine. There were hundreds of children at the time who could fill a braiding needle before they could write their names, and I could never recall a fisherman who could match one of these women for speed of braiding these nets that were so important to the ever increasing number of trawlers that were joining the Hull fleet.

There was so much more that went on around the dry side of the dock. Men sought work on the trawlers that were once again preparing to sail, while others would be arriving at their offices to settle and pick up the money that was due to them from the proceeds of the catch after spending three weeks at sea.

Further along the dock the fish meal company was busy handling any poor quality or unsold fish remaining on the market, and the heads and fish bones that remained when the filleters had finished after a long day's work.

Once all the trawlers had returned after the war, it was not long before the owners set about rebuilding the fleet, keeping the shipyards of Cook, Welton and Gemmell at Beverley and Cochrane's at Selby busy with a constant series of orders.

J Marr were ahead of many with their build-

Above: A sad sight - St Andrew's Dock as it is today, with the practically empty Lord Line building, still carrying its British United Trawlers Limited nameplate.
Below: It is hard to take in the scene as it is today, with the sorry state of the entrance to St Andrew's Dock. This area was once a hive of activity, providing work for thousands of people in dozens of different trades.

ing programme and the Southella, Lorella and Borella were the first new trawlers to arrive, as were Kingston's Kingston Peridot and Kingston Sardius, followed by the Kingston Garnet and the Kingston Zircon.

Along the dock at Hamling's, their new trawlers were the Saint Apollo and Saint Leander, followed by the Saint Britwin and the Saint Alquin. Hellyers went to the Smith Dockyard at Middlesbrough for the Benvolio, Brutus, Lorenzo and Caesar, while Lord Line added the Lord Ancaster, Lord Wavell, Lord Willoughby and Lord Rowallen to swell the fleet that docked in front of the newly-built Lord Line offices dominating St. Andrew's Dock.

Such was the speed of development that some owners went to Scottish or even German yards with their orders for new trawlers, while older trawlers disappeared gradually, either to other ports or to breaker's yards.

The fishing industry was a huge employer, supporting jobs and businesses both on and off the dock. The estimate was that for every fishermen, there were eight jobs ashore, but I have always believed that this was a very conservative estimate. In the years after the war, work was plentiful and business was good for everyone,but there remained a heavy price to be paid for all this success in men and ships.

Albert Draper's scrapyard in Hull's old Victoria Dock was the graveyard and last resting place for a large number of fine trawlers from both Hull and Grimsby. Not only did a number of top earning side trawlers end their days here, but Hull's first factory trawler, the Lord Nelson, made the short journey and was scrapped here in 1981. As far back as 1972 some of the older oil burning side trawlers that had served the industry so well had ended their days being scrapped in Hull.

Household names in Hull such as the Benvolio, Loch Inver, St. Apollo, St. Alquin, Newby Wyke, Kingston Jade and the Kingston Amandine all ended their days being broken up in their home port of Hull.

Equally famous names from across the river, such as the Vanessa, Northern Sky, Northern Eagle, William Wilberforce, and the twice Silver Cod winner Lord Beatty returned from Grimsby to be broken up at Albert Draper's scrapyard in Hull.

Every year people from far and wide gather on the Lock Head at the entrance to the old St. Andrew's Dock in Hull, where in a moving ceremony the lost trawlermen are remembered.

Old and young alike gather around the plaque to remember and pay their respects to the many brave men who sailed from the City of Hull and never returned.

There are the elderly with their memories, men and women who have over the years witnessed and experienced so much grief and tragedy. Those of us who were at sea recall their feelings when news filtered through that a trawler had been lost or a member of the crew was missing.

And the children, too young to remember, will hopefully grow up and look back with pride when they read about the price that was paid by the lost trawlermen of Hull.

It is also a day when whole families gather, and old friends and shipmates arrive every year to pay their respects, have a yarn, gaze around at the old derelict buildings on the St. Andrew's Dock, and reflect on how it all used to be in its heyday.

But it is not all tears and sadness. Like the men they come to remember, they are a tough breed of people who have had to face up to so many tragedies, yet they can still put on a smile when they greet an old face from the past, or someone who has come back to Hull for this special day, to this very special city.

Although Hull's fishing fleet brought a lot of success to the city, it did not come easily or cheaply. The cost over the years in human life was staggering, as fine men and ships sailed and never returned to St. Andrew's Dock.

Even when the two World Wars were over, it was left to the fishermen to do the clearing up as mines, torpedoes and other weapons of destruction that had been left on the sea bed proved to be as big a danger as the weather itself.

The North Sea trawler Rochester never returned from a trip after picking up a mine, and these deadly leftovers of the war were to be found all over the north Atlantic as the

Another trawler with the same name, Spaniard H-366. This ship was lost off Sletnes in Finnmark in the north of Norway in 1949. All of the crew were taken off and survived.

trawlers began to fish on grounds that had been closed during the war years.

In the distant northern latitudes where Arctic convoys had suffered from bombing and U-boat attacks, these grim reminders of the war were still being presented to fishermen long after the end of the war itself. Most fishermen admitted to being more than a little concerned whenever a heavy object or something unknown appeared in the trawl.

These fishing grounds inside the Arctic Circle were a constant and sinister reminder of what had happened in these bleak northern latitudes only a few years before.

Few will forget the shock waves that swept through the city when the St. Hubert trawled up an object that later exploded, killing the skipper and three of the crew while fishing off Norway in 1960. Years after the war ended, the cost was still being counted.

If the years of war took their toll of both men and ships, so did the weather that fishermen experienced and worked under. One of my earliest recollections of when I was a young lad working on the fish docks is of the trawler Sargon being lost at Iceland, and later when I was fishing myself, the loss of the Norman on rocks at Greenland.

These too were constant reminders of the dangers that went hand in hand with the catching side of the fishing industry, and yet worse was to follow.

The loss of the two Hull trawlers Lorella and Roderigo in some of the worst weather conditions ever experienced off Iceland's North Cape in 1955 stunned the entire fishing community along Hessle Road and the entire city of Hull.

The story unfolded of how the two trawlers had battered their way through hurricane force winds that showed no signs of easing off, and with both vessels now top heavy with ice. After continually dodging head to wind. Both ships capsized within a short time of each other and forty men lost their lives in the worst conditions experienced for many years.

Yet Iceland was like a magnet to Hull ships. Over the years they and the ships from Grimsby began to fish further off the land as Iceland extended her fishing limits to twelve miles and later to fifty miles. Not deterred by this, the trawlers moved out and enjoyed some successful years fishing on these grounds.

Although Iceland took a heavy toll of men and ships from Hull, the Hull trawler Arctic Viking was just a few hours from her home port, sixteen miles from Flamborough Head, when she capsized in a gale. Other ships were lost in individual groundings and collisions, and men were lost off ships not only during fishing, but as the trawlers made their way to and from the distant fishing grounds.

Yet Iceland was to feature very much once again in the next triple tragedy that once more shook the old city of Hull.

Along with the stunned and shocked women, hardened old seamen wept openly as news began to come through of the loss of three ships within a few days of each other.

The winter of 1968 brought about the loss of three Hull trawlers, St. Romanus, Kingston Peridot and Ross Cleveland. At the same time, it seemed that everyone you spoke to either had a relative or a friend in one of the three ships.

St. Romanus was probably lost as she made her way to the Norwegian coast or White Sea fishing grounds. Once again, the notorious weather of Iceland's North Cape claimed the Kingston Peridot and the Ross Cleveland. It is thought that the Kingston Peridot was lost as she tried to clear the area where they had experienced so much bad weather by steaming easterly along the north coast of Iceland. When her sister ship Kingston Sardius called her on the radio the following day there was no reply, and later some small fragments of wreckage washed up on the north coast of Iceland were identified as belonging to the Kingston Peridot.

Meanwhile the ships still off North Cape were still having to endure weather that showed no sign of easing. Although some ships managed to steam into Isafjördur, the direction of the wind gave the ships nothing in the way of a lee, and here the Ross Cleveland capsized, and just one man, Harry Eddom the mate, survived...

Ships fishing in other areas were aware of the tragedy that had occurred as news came through mainly from ships heading for the grounds along the Norwegian coast after being told prior to leaving to avoid Iceland. The full story started to unfold.

Men who had friends or relatives in any of the three ill fated ships sat around in deep thought wondering if a certain friend or relative had sailed on those last fateful voyages.

Ships fishing along the Norwegian coast had worked in reasonable weather conditions, and on the Kingston Pearl, the ship I was skipper of at the time, we had experienced nothing out of the ordinary for fishing off Norway's North Cape at that time of year. Here the fishing and the weather presented no problems until a poor weather forecast forced us reluctantly to leave the area and join the ships fishing to the south west in the area of Malangen and Nord West Bank for the final two days of our trip.

Right: Hellyer's Silver Cod winner Falstaff won the trophy in 1959, seen here badly in need of a paint-up.
The regular crews of these top-earning ships spent as much as 330 days each year at sea.
Falstaff and her sister ship Portia were the last side trawlers that were built for Hellyer Brothers and were built at Middlesborough. Noted as fine sea ships capable of a good turn of speed, both remained in Hull until there were no more grounds for them to fish.
photo: Hull Daily Mail

It was not until we had shot away amongst this group of ships that the full extent of the triple tragedy at Iceland was made known to us.

Raymond Wilson, the skipper of the Kingston Peridot, was my cousin, and had spent the previous year with me as mate in the Kingston Zircon. We had spent every trip at Iceland.

Phil Gay, the skipper of the Ross Cleveland, had a lot of experience and like myself, rarely fished anywhere but Iceland. Both men came from Hessle Road, and had attended famous old school of West Dock Avenue. Both had been extremely popular in Hull's fishing community.

On returning to Hull, the quayside was full of people waiting with news of the men who would not be returning. Ashore in the pubs and clubs that surrounded the fish dock area people could speak of nothing else, and sat in a daze, dumbfounded as ships that had been in the area returned. They had maybe not fished very well, but were just glad to be home from a trip to Iceland that had turned into a nightmare.

So bad had the weather been that it affected men in different ways. Some took time off before returning, while others never went to sea again and sought other ways of earning a living ashore. But most of the men knew nothing other than fishing, and as it was their life or a family tradition, in most cases just a few days passed before they were heading back once more to those distant water fishing grounds with memories of that last trip that would stay with them for years to come, if not for ever.

Not surprisingly, the mood ashore turned to anger as people confronted the trawler owners, and demanded to have Iceland, and in particular the area around North Cape, banned during the winter months. Women confronted members of Parliament, demanding assurances that standards of safety would be vastly improved. There was a lot of anger in the city. It had been a harsh winter, and a very costly one.

For many years the fleets of Hull and Grimsby had fished in some of the remotest and harshest areas that can be imagined, with no back-up or support ship when medical assistance was needed. All this changed when the Miranda joined the distant water fleet as a support ship. Although it had been a long time coming, there is no doubt that Miranda was a welcome sight as she did some sterling work assisting the fleet. This was sometimes in appalling weather conditions and the Miranda was very much appreciated by the many trawlermen who came to her for assistance.

Looking Back – the Crews

With Britain's deep water fleet laid up with nowhere to fish, nobody suffered more than the crews.

The men who had sailed in these deep water trawlers received the worst possible treatment from both the government and the trawler owners. The men who had over the years given everything that it was possible to give to an industry had been left to fend for themselves after the industry collapsed.

In an industry that had seen so many tragedies, it is difficult to imagine why this treatment was handed out to fishermen who had served the trawler owners and the national interest for so long and with such loyalty. Yet the biggest insult of all was to come when the trawler owners and the government classed fishermen as casual labourers.

Being classed as a casual labourer was the biggest insult and was something I have personally always resented deeply and still do to this day. I have always seen this as a method that was used by many people to deprive fishermen of any redundancy payments that they were certainly entitled to. Many of these men spent well over three hundred days at sea each year, under some of the harshest conditions that would never have been tolerated in any workplace ashore. Yet we still heard news of factories where the entire workforce walked out when the central heating failed and the temperature dropped by a couple of degrees.

Although the trawler owners had been well treated in terms of compensation for having to lay up their ships, not a penny of this money found its way to the crews as compensation for the loss of employment after the years and decades of loyal service they had given to the fishing industry.

Some of these men had served in trawlers in wartime as well as in peace, often spending years in one ship, and in many cases their entire working lives with a single trawler company, yet all received the same harsh treatment.

There is little wonder at the resentment felt by the crews, most of whom had known little other than fishing for their entire working lives. Many of these men were in the prime of their lives, yet were never able to return to sea. The general feeling was that we had been betrayed, stabbed in the back, as many preferred to put it.

I spoke to one young British fisherman in Spain before we sailed to the Falklands, and found that I had sailed with his father, and known him as a good deckhand and an excellent seaman. This man had given up all hope of going back to sea. After seeing the treatment that his father had received, the son was now earning a living for himself and supporting his young family by fishing from Spain, only managing to get home every six months.

'Hardly the type of people you would want to have watching your back when the going gets tough,' was how another young man chose to remember the trawler owners. 'They took the money and ran for it.'

These are just the thoughts of two young men, both of whom had started fishing shortly before it all started to come apart at the seams.

Evidence produced over the years has shown that the fishermen were entitled to redundancy payments, yet over the years the trawler owners have fought the men in the courts, and various government have chosen consistently to ignore the men whose livelihoods they chose to sign away and throw on the scrapheap.

Some chose to go ashore to find work, while some managed to find employment fishing from Spain's two main fishing ports of Vigo and La Coruña. Others drifted into the offshore oil industry, often serving again in the ships that they had known in waters off Bear Island, Iceland and the Barents Sea. Yet most of the men would freely admit that these less demanding jobs were a poor substitute for the work that they had become used to and that had provided both for them and for many thousands of others in related industries.

The author at the memorial that overlooks the Humber from St Andrew's Dock. A service for lost fishermen is held here every year.

Being classed as casual labour was something that many men and women refused to stand for without a fight and a very long fight it turned out to be as evidence was produced form both sides of the country. The wrangling has continued for many years, and despite setbacks, fishermen have doggedly refused to give up, even taking their case to Parliament. At long last a breakthrough was made and in 2000, West Hull MP Alan Johnson, who has fought the fishermens' case since his election to the area, was able to announce to a packed house in Hull that the long battle had been won and compensation would be made available. Over on the other side of the Humber at Grimsby, Austin Mitchell, who had also supported the fishermen through their long campaign, was able to make a similar announcement.

It was a great night for many on both sides of the river, yet tinged with sadness for so many friends who had passed on during the long campaign. At last the slur of being cast as casual workers had been lifted.

We have already seen the folly in the decision to sell or scrap the fleet of deep sea trawlers. The conflict over the Falklands with Argentina saw a few remaining stern trawlers quickly assembled to accompany the Royal Navy to the south Atlantic, where they played a significant role.

Perhaps most important of all, we have lost a generation of young men who would have turned to the sea like their fathers for careers in fishing. As a maritime nation and with a history such as ours, we are the poorer for this loss. The expertise that could have been handed down to these young men is rapidly being lost, and this is something that our country could yet come to regret.

As the loss of deep sea fishing has been followed by a decline in the rest of the fishing industry, it can be said that no other industry has paid such a high price as fishing has for our entry into the EU.

The Special Guest

Going down the dock to settle one day, along with two other members of the Portia's crew, we were informed that we were to go upstairs at the company's offices where a member of the office staff wanted to say a few words to the entire crew.

Once everyone was present, we were told that a close friend of the owner's woul d be on board with us. Our special guest was to be treated with the utmost respect by everyone on board and that anyone who failed to comply would be signed off when we returned home - sacked, in other words. So important was our guest that we even had an extra day in dock to give him time to arrive. Without knowing who our guest could be, we could only thank him in his absence for the very welcome extra day.

Leaving the dock on a glorious August morning, Portia was soon heading up the Humber. As was usual, once all the work was done and everything was secured on deck, the deckhands gathered aft in one of the larger cabins to have a few tins of beer and the odd dram of whisky or rum, and in general to talk over what had happened during our time in dock, and not least be thankful for our extra day at home.

With the first case of beer gone and well into the second one, much to everyone's surprise, our distinguished guest appeared in the doorway and introduced himself and was in fact a real gentleman. With most of us lost for words for the first time, it seemed the only thing that we could do was to offer our new friend a tin of beer, which to our relief, he gladly accepted and sat down with us deckies. He told us that the reason for our extra day ashore was that he had recently returned from a round the world cruise before his chauffeur had driven him to Hull to join Portia.

Soon another case of beer appeared, and then another bottle of whisky appeared, with our new friend matching us drink for drink, our afternoon session came to a late close and the crew made their way to their berths, while it was quite obvious that our guest was having quite some difficulty in climbing the stairway from the lower accommodation.

Two of the lads thought they had better give him a hand to the owner's berth, hoping that the skipper would be turned in for the afternoon. Unfortunately this was not the case, and opening the door that separated the crew's accommodation from the skipper's and owner's berths as quietly as possible, our luck ran out entirely and the skipper appeared. He realised immediately that everything was not right as we helped our guest to his berth.

"I should have known better than to send anyone aft to introduce themselves to you lot. If I'd sent Jesus Christ himself and the ten disciples to meet you lot, I'm sure you would have got them drunk as well," he told us in no uncertain terms.

The following morning all the lads were working on deck as usual and our new found friend persuaded the skipper to let him purchase two cases of beer from the bond and promptly sent them down to the deck to be shared between the men, which was much appreciated by everyone.

So impressed was our special guest with the crew on the deck and the amount of work that they put in during the days we were fishing that he continually sang our praises to the skipper, telling him how fortunate he was to have a crew like this. Yet I think the skipper knew this, although he would never have said so himself.

I feel sure that our guest enjoyed every minute of his trip, and after he had shaken hands with every one of us when we arrived back in Hull, the bosun informed us that our departing friend had left fifty pounds for a drink on our next trip. This was a great deal of money in those days and a rare gesture from a real gentleman, as without a doubt, we had made a great impression on him. One could not help the impression that he was genuinely sorry to be leaving. In that one trip he had seen plenty of fine weather, plenty of fish, and when he told us that he had enjoyed his trip with us more than his cruise around the world, I felt sure that he meant it.

Looking Back – Iceland

If any one country can be blamed for bringing about the end of Britain's deep sea fishing industry, this must rest well and truly on Iceland. True, Britain had relied heavily on Icelandic caught fish over the years, with good quality fish generally bringing top prices in the major ports.

The comparatively short journey to the Icelandic fishing grounds enabled some trawlers to make very short trips and turn in some excellent grossings from Icelandic waters.

Icelandic fishing limits had been extended over the years and British trawlers still maintained some excellent catches, despite having to fish further afield, which often during the harsh winter months gave cause for concern.

But if Iceland had been good to our deep sea fleet, it is just as true that the British markets had been just as good to the Icelandic trawlers which often landed their catches into the Humber ports of Hull and Grimsby, sometimes affecting the prices paid for fish caught to our own trawlers that were unfortunate enough to land on the same days.

With the political situation as it was in the 1970s, it was obvious that we were fighting a losing battle once the Icelandic government decided to extend the fishing limits out to 200 miles. It has been said that the United States air base at Keflavik was under threat of closure, and with the early warning system installed there, this could have been a major threat to NATO.

Keflavik was an important base, bearing in mind the situation as it was throughout the Cold War. This could have been the main reason why the British government bowed to pressure and eventually ordered all British trawlers to leave Iceland.

Towards the end the situation became farcical. Those of us who were there at the time witnessed some amazing skirmishes as the trawlers used any methods available to thwart the attempts of the Icelandic gunboats to cut their warps as they carried on fishing to the very end.

During this period tempers flared, and ably assisted by the frigates of the Royal Navy, and backed up by the tugs which did sterling work, almost every Icelandic gunboat had to return to port at some time or another to carry out repairs. The skippers of some of the trawlers showed their contempt for the gunboats and inflicted damage on them by ramming them on numerous occasions.

Our entry into the EEC had cost us dearly. Not only had we signed away our entire deep water fleet under the terms of entry, in 1972 we were also left with a situation where we also signed away the waters around the shores of Britain. The downward trend that started in 1972 has continued since, leaving us an island nation with no say in the waters around our own coast.

Within a year of Iceland extending its fishing limits to 200 miles, a further insult was heaped on the British fisherman when Icelandic ships were once again allowed to land their catches in Britain, much to the disgust of the many men who, after a lifetime in the industry either at sea or on shore, found themselves out of work and facing a future that looked very bleak indeed.

There was no welcoming committee for the first Icelandic ship to land her catch in Hull or any other of the deep sea ports after the conflict between the two countries.

Men whose lives had been put at risk by the dangerous actions of the Icelandic gunboats protested vigorously and feelings ran high. It was assumed that none of the crews of the trawlers ventured ashore to use the pubs and clubs along Hessle Road in Hull, such was the feeling in the city at the time.

It was an obvious reaction from people who had been badly let down by the series of events that had taken away not only their livelihood, but also a way of life. There are people today who can not find it within themselves to forget or forgive the actions that brought about the end of Hull as a major fishing port.

The docks at Hull, Grimsby and Fleetwood became a sorry sight within a short time. Trawlers that had sailed from these ports were now tied up. First class ships that had worked through some of the hardest weather imaginable were now laid idle. They had sailed smart and freshly painted from the Humber and Fleetwood to provide work for thousands of people throughout the country.

In terms of unemployment many people found themselves out of work for the first time in their lives, and the roll-on effects showed exactly how many people had relied on the fishing industry for a livelihood.

The engineers, riggers, netmakers, ice manufacturers, the men who worked on the fish docks, along with the bobbers who had unloaded the trawlers - British and Icelandic alike - found themselves facing a bleak and uncertain future.

This was their reward for the years of loyal service and devotion that they had given to the fishing industry. The downward trend was not long in starting away from the dock as well. Pubs and clubs that had been meeting places for fishermen began to feel the pinch, and shops that had been household names along Hessle Road went out of business. This was the most depressing time for the close-knit Hessle Road community. The picture was just the same across the Humber at Grimsby and at the other side of the country in Fleetwood.

The small number of deep sea trawlers that now operate out of Hull are very restricted in what areas they can fish in Norwegian waters, and Iceland, which has also chosen to remain outside the EU, limits foreign trawlers to a tiny amount of fish on grounds where there is little to be found. Iceland is a country that benefits very much from the high British and European market prices, with free access to the European markets that are the best customers for Icelandic-caught fish, yet the situation remains the same. This is a country that takes everything it can but gives nothing in return. Many people wonder why things have been made so easy for Iceland to benefit from the EU, while it chooses to remain outside the community.

In the 1970s Iceland had offered Britain a quota in its waters, although nothing was said about how long this would be available. The offer should have been accepted at the time, as this would at least have given the industry time to adjust. Instead of a panic situation, many of the old side trawlers could have been scrapped, leaving the more economic diesel trawlers to catch the amount of fish allowed. This would have saved many jobs ashore and at sea, but sadly the offer was not accepted by the British government and we were left to wonder why.

Winter In The Falklands

It took a few days to get back to normal. The weather remained fairly fine, and the fishing remained reasonable with most of the loligo we caught being of good quality, so there was no question of leaving the area, at least for the time being. We managed to complete a full week's fishing without any disruptions from the weather, which in itself was a bonus and very welcome one.

If anything, the last two days had seen a bit of an improvement in the fishing, and a week later, after we had completed our second transhipment, we had close to 200 tonnes of loligo on board and the weather had been kind to us.

So fine had the weather been up until this last week, that nobody had mentioned returning the Beauchene Island to see if things had improved. The little group of ships was quite content to stick it out in the same area all the time there was something to show at the end of each day's fishing.

It was not until our tenth day that the weather took a nosedive as the forecast for the following day was for the wind to increase to gale force from the south west, and we would possibly have to stop fishing once again.

We managed three more hauls, and although the weather was nothing more than a force six or seven, midway through our third haul the weather deteriorated even further. Seeing no point in increasing the distance between ourselves and the land, I decided to haul after three hours and made our way in towards Berkeley Sound.

That evening the forecast brought no joy at all, as the wind was forecast to increase to severe gale force during the night and would show no signs of decreasing for at least twenty-four hours.

Hauling just a short distance from us was our long time companion the Monte Faro. Like ourselves, he hauled and kept his trawl on board, and he soon felt the weight of the wind and sea coming round head to wind half a mile from us. The wind and sea had increased even more since we had hauled, and the two stern trawlers began to plough into the large seas and storm force winds. Glancing across to our companion, her lights cast a ghostly glare in the sky as she disappeared completely from view into the troughs before once again climbing and emerging to plough into the next gigantic wave, sending spray cascading aft the full length of the ship, illuminated by the powerful lights on the deck as both trawlers once again headed towards the land for shelter.

It was almost daylight when we were able to increase speed and make our way into Berkeley Sound once again. It had been a very uncomfortable night making our way in, only picking up a lee when we were less than ten miles from land. The Monte Faro, which had spent the night dodging with us, arrived shortly after us. The Nauticas had been sheltering since midnight, but now the three ships laid in calm waters while we wondered what the next weather forecast held in store for us and if there would be any comfort in it.

It was obvious that the weather would play a major role during what fishing time we had left in the Falklands, and stoppages like this one did nothing to help as the trip grew longer. Yet despite everything, the morale amongst the crew remained excellent.

There was some comfort in the midday shipping forecast. Winds were expected to decrease during the day, but the outlook was not too good for the next few days, with the weather forecast to stay unsettled for some days to come.

Overnight there was only a slight improvement as the wind eased a little, and even though we made our way to the entrance of Berkeley Sound, it was clear that there was still a very big sea running a few miles off the land. So we turned around and decided to wait a little longer.

The wait turned out to be longer than we had expected, as the wind increased again during the night and there was nothing to do but be patient and wait for a definite improvement.

Fishing Explorer's trawl deck with a reasonable haul of around eight tonnes coming up the ramp. These were the bread-and-butter days of fishing, with long hours spent on the bridge and sometimes not a great deal of fish to show for those long hours.

In all we lost almost three days before we were once more able to resume fishing, with a reasonable forecast for the next few days. Within an hour of leaving Berkeley Sound we were once more towing and back in business. There was still a bit of fish in the area, and our first four hour tow was in the region of eight tonnes.

This was a lot more than we had expected, even though we had seen some good indications to begin with, but not a lot towards the latter part of the tow, which made this eight tonnes a pleasant and welcome surprise. The next haul, in complete darkness, saw us haul on board only three tons of loligo for five hours, but at least we were fishing again and things did look encouraging as the daylight approached.

The Monte Faro reported a nice haul of loligo, so it was no surprise when we hauled two hours later, and brought something in the region of fifteen tonnes up the ramp, for a five hour tow in mainly seventy fathoms of water.

We were now enjoying some fine weather again and a spell of reasonable fishing, which was very welcome indeed, and as we fished out the daylight hours we were rewarded with a good haul, which when processed turned out to be seventeen tons of loligo and a tonne of hake fillets.

Apart from the daily visit from an aeroplane which usually came over to take a look at us, and a call on the radio from the fishery patrol vessel, things were very quiet. To the best of our knowledge, there were no other ships around here or down at Beauchene Island. Although we had no intention of leaving the area, if the fishing did slack off, we had no fishing reports to act on and would just have to hope that things had improved around Beauchene Island.

During the afternoon we were joined by the Monte Faro and the Nauticas. Both reported poor fishing around Beauchene Island, where their last hauls had been around two tonnes.

It seemed that we were in the best spot, even though catches were not spectacular. At the end of the day we had put below almost thirty tonnes of loligo and followed this up the next day with twenty-seven tonnes. When we had bettered this the next day with thirty tonnes,

Nothing is more tiring on these long trips than the long periods of bad weather that the crews of most ships experience at some time or other. These pictures illustrate the difficulties that the men working on the deck had to contend with during the every-day routine of hauling and shooting the trawl that goes on day and night.

we received a telex to proceed once more into Berkeley Sound for our second transhipment of what fish we had on board. This came as quite a shock to everyone and a big disappointment. The weather was fine, although bitterly cold, the forecast was reasonable, and the fishing was still steady, but nevertheless, we made our way in to Berkeley Sound to transship the 510 tonnes that we had on board.

Although we had a short licence for only two months, it was obvious that a considerable amount of time would be lost through poor weather, and we had already lost a considerable amount of fishing time during the voyage. I was disappointed and my personal feelings were that this transshipment was badly timed and not necessary.

Before commencing the transhipment, we took on enough fuel to cover the remaining fishing time and enough for our long journey back to Spain. We were well sheltered in Berkeley Sound, but it remained very cold. Apart from stopping for the occasional snow squall and a hot drink, the transshipment and refuelling in Berkeley Sound were completed in just over 60 hours. After signing numerous papers, we made our way out of Berkeley Sound to resume fishing once again, with just a little light snow falling as we headed out to the open sea. The weather was still fine, and we soon picked out the lights of four ships when the snow passed over.

Much to the delight of the crew, a small amount of mail was delivered while we transshipped, which was once again very welcome, especially for those who had received no mail a few days previously. With all our mooring ropes stowed as we left the land astern, and the lights of Port Stanley lighting up the sky, the trawl was shot away smoothly with no hitches, and we were fishing once again.

Once the trawl was shot away, it was decided that we would tow for most of the night to give everyone the chance of a few hours sleep. It had been a hard and tiring day, which had not been made any easier by the bitter cold of Berkeley Sound. In spite of everything, the crew had done extremely well to complete the transhipment in such a short time.

Fishing in this area just a few miles east of Berkeley Sound meant that in poor weather there was no need to dodge head to wind for long periods in discomfort, when for the sake of a short steam the sheltered waters of Port Stanley or Berkeley Sound could be reached in comfort.

Everything was working as near to perfection as possible on board the Fishing Explorer. The winch had given us no cause for concern at any time since we resumed fishing, and down in the factory everything was working more efficiently than at any time during the trip. This in itself was a bonus, as we needed no further stoppages at this late stage of the trip.

On deck the trawl was being hauled and shot away again in seldom more than thirty minutes, unless there were any repairs to be made. But the areas we had fished in the Falklands were mostly good trawling grounds, ensuring the trawl was only on deck for about two hours in a full day's fishing. Reports from the galley indicated that we would have enough food to see the trip almost through, except for a few small items that we could be in need of to see us through the long journey back to Spain to discharge our catch in Cadiz.

As we entered our last few weeks of fishing the morale on board remained excellent,

Our second transshipment to a reefer in Berkeley Sound was something we could have done without. In view of the time that we had already lost, transshipping while the weather was reasonable and the fishing was good probably lost us sixty hours of fishing time and maybe seventy tonnes of good quality loligo squid.
Here a small Spanish freezer can be seen waiting to begin discharging as the last few lifts of fish are swung across from Fishing Explorer.

despite the countless gales of wind and the generally poor weather conditions that we had experienced in recent weeks.

As the trip came towards a close, everyone began to show signs of weariness and some sort of fatigue. The long hours that everyone had worked throughout the trip began to show that there was not the least resemblance between us and the sun-tanned crew who had arrived in the Falklands some months before.

Men went on watch and relieved other crewmen who went below to grab a few hours sleep, and in turn they would be called out to take the places of the next watch to go below. In between, if the fishing was slack, once the fish was cleared from the factory, most of the men would take the chance to lie down for an hour or so until it was time to haul in the trawl once more. So it went on, day and night, fine weather and foul, and we certainly had more than our fair share of that.

But at the moment we were enjoying a good spell of weather, and had done so for a few days. One could not but feel that this was an uneasy truce before the next gale of wind came along and once again brought proceedings to a halt. Although the fishing was not spectacular, on most days we averaged twenty-five to thirty tonnes of good quality loligo, along with a few tones of hake fillets.

The Monte Faro was still in the area, and her skipper seemed quite content with the fishing in this area, and made it plain that they had no intentions of leaving unless there was a drastic change in the fishing.

Along with the Portuguese trawler Nauticus, which was also close by, to the best of our knowledge, there were no other trawlers fishing in Falkland waters

We entered our last weeks of fishing with about five hundred tonnes of loligo on board, and the countdown had begun as everyone looked forward to the day we would be leaving for home. No sooner did a new day break, than it was crossed off the calendar by one of the younger members of the crew, who were now eagerly looking forward to going home.

Three weeks can seem a long time as a trip comes to an end, and once again the weather did us no favours, as the forecast was for another gale.

By Thursday of that week we were towing through a force eight gale, but as we had seen before in these parts, the fishing improved slightly. The squid appeared to be more prevalent in rough weather and it had often been possible to take some very good hauls in some of the worst weather conditions. After hauling eight tonnes of loligo at midnight after a five hour tow, we chose to dodge back to the south-west through the night as the weather had deteriorated over the last two hours of the tow. The forecast was for the wind to decrease a little the following morning, and that is just what it did.

After breakfast we were once again shooting away the gear. The wind stayed from the south-west, and had eased slightly to a force seven as we faced up to another day of fishing, just like any other.

Through to the end of the week the weather remained unsettled, but never presented a problem and we were able to keep towing. Although it was a bit uncomfortable at times during the squalls, there was always something to show for our labours at the end of each day's fishing.

As the week drew to a close, there was no improvement in the gale force winds, and as the days were crossed off the calendar, we entered our last fourteen days with seven hundred tonnes of loligo and a small amount of other species, mainly hake, on board.

Our two companions still fishing in the area, like ourselves, were also coming to the end of their trips. Both the Monte Faro and the Nauticus were smaller than the Fishing Explorer, and their crews, like ourselves, must have been looking forward to an end to fishing and a rapid improvement in the weather.

Our last haul of the day, just before midnight, was in the region of seven tonnes, giving us a reasonable total for the day, and just what was needed at this stage of the trip. We expected to lose more time through weather, but the two good hauls during the daylight hours had been a real tonic for everyone.

Since resuming fishing after leaving Berkeley Sound, the wind had moderated we had enjoyed some very good weather with just the occasional light snow shower. This was the best spell of settled weather we had seen for some time, and towing along with the sea flat calm, it was difficult to imagine that just a few days before we had dodged into Berkeley Sound through the teeth of a full gale and hoping for a better forecast.

The enduring good weather was a big help, and so was the ground we were fishing on. Unlike Greenland, Newfoundland and some parts of Iceland, I cannot remember any other fishing grounds to compare with those in the Falklands. Any damage to the trawl was just down to wear and tear, with no time lost repairing nets, as this was usually done when sheltering and took no more than an hour's work to put things to rights.

The best fishing in this area to the east of Port Stanley and Berkeley Sound had all been between sixty-five and ninety-five fathoms, with non of the trawlers venturing deeper than one hundred fathoms. Our best hauls had been taken in around seventy-five fathoms of water, and during our time at Beauchene Island the best hauls of loligo were caught in water no deeper than ninety-five fathoms.

We did at least have a few options open to us if the fishing were to slacken considerably. We had been getting something of a reasonable day's fishing before the weather intervened, and just before we had called in to Port Stanley to pick up our fishing licence, so we could not rule out the possibility or returning to that position, or trying Beauchene Island once more. The waters between our position and Beauchene Island had been only lightly fished during our time in the Falklands, as there was so much scope in these waters.

But we were in no position to lose any time trying fresh grounds and experimenting, and this also seemed to be the case with our two companions, who seemed content to take the good with the bad and remain in the area as long as the fishing remained reasonable and the weather fine.

Since we had obtained our short licence to complete our trip, we had done very little steaming, only stopping fishing when the weather was too bad. With just eight days fishing to go, we passed the 1000 tonnes of fish on board, mostly loligo, making it diffi-

cult to imagine a grandstand finish to the trip.

There was one bit of excitement when after towing for only an hour, and not being too happy with the gear and the way that we were towing, we decided to haul the trawl to see if any part of it had been fouled or damaged. To everyone's surprise, we brought on board six tonnes of loligo. Yet despite staying in the area for the rest of the day, we were not able to repeat what had been our shortest and best haul for some time.

There were still a number of things to take into consideration as we neared the end of our fishing time. Orders for food to be obtained had to be arranged for us to pick up when we called into Port Stanley before setting off on the long journey back to Spain.

We had been informed that there was a large amount of mail waiting, and an even larger amount of newspapers, which would be welcomed by everyone on board.

During an extended period of fine weather, the fishing remained slack. No matter where we towed between sixty-five and ninety-five fathoms, the end result was much the same with hauls of only three or four tonnes of good loligo.

To venture deeper than ninety-five fathoms resulted in more hake and less loligo. As the loligo fetched a far greater value, it was our policy to stick to the shallower water for the rest of our time.

With only a few days fishing time left,

This haul of around five tonnes was taken just east of Port Stanley. This area not far from shelter was a blessing for us when fishing slackened off dramatically around Beauchene Island.

everything that we would require for the journey had been taken care of, as we were within VHF range of Port Stanley, with little chance of us leaving the area.

There was very little fishing activity going on in the Falklands area at the time, apart from a few jiggers going in and out of Port Stanley to discharge catches and take on stores, and everything remained very quiet.

The two last hauls of the day that took us into the final week caused no excitement, with two four tonne hauls, each after four hours towing. As we passed into the final week, for everyone on board the Fishing Explorer, myself included, those seven days could not pass quickly enough.

As we started the last week's fishing there was not much of a change in anything. Fishing remained very spasmodic, and although summer was surely just around the corner, there was as yet no sign of it.

After two very slack hauls in succession, we towed further to the south, and despite a bit of improvement, the best haul was just four tonnes, and the following day after trying four hauls between sixty and a hundred fathoms, we could only finish the day with fourteen tonnes, of which three were hake fillets. In the early hours of the morning we steamed the short distance to Beauchene Island.

We had towed most of the way and had seen little fish of any description, and there was no

reason to expect any improvement in this area, and this was the case when after a four hour tow we hauled no more than four tonnes of loligo. We carried on towing westerly, hauled only four tonnes and again towed north-westerly to Cape Meredith where we had seen some good hake fishing earlier in the trip. Sure enough, after picking up some good fish marks, we hauled in a reasonable ten tonnes, all of which was hake. The next haul was better, and from the two hauls we processed seven tonnes, of which five tonnes were hake fillets and two tonnes loligo. The following morning we were back south of Beauchene Island.

Our two companions to the north reported no improvement in their fishing, and our reports stopped them from joining us, as we told them that we intended to tow back to the north-east the following day if things did not improve.

We were now going through a very slack period, and trying tows in different waters, mainly deeper than at any time during the trip. However, it appeared that every time we went deeper than a hundred fathoms, we caught more hake but less loligo.

This slack fishing was all the more annoying as the weather was now once more good, yet no matter where we towed, the best hauls were only in the region of three to four tonnes of loligo between seventy and ninety fathoms.

As we towed back to the north-east, we saw the lights of our two companions during the night, and as daylight broke we towed past the Monte Faro, whose skipper informed us that he would be on his way back home the following day, and asked us our advice on the procedure to follow once he had finished fishing.

After a short conversation we hauled once again what was becoming the inevitable four tonnes for a tow of four hours, and with nothing more to do, shot again to the north-east, holding to seventy fathoms.

Back once again in the area of Port Stanley, we were once again able to catch upon the latest news courtesy of Port Stanley Radio which had served us well during the trip. But right now, all thoughts were on going home.

With the trip in its final stages, this was not the time to be searching around for fish. Although there was not a great deal to be had, by keeping the trawl in the water and with occasional hauls like the ten-ton bag in this picture, we were able to maintain a reasonable daily tonnage.

The Home Stretch

The morale on board the Fishing Explorer was as good as it had been throughout the trip as we entered the last seven days fishing time. The trip had gone extremely well, despite some severe weather and we had come through without any injuries except for the odd cut or bruise, and on a long fishing voyage this is a bonus.

Although maybe slightly premature as we entered the last week, the weather was forecast to remain quite reasonable until we were due to set off for home.

There was still a few days fishing to get through, but the two hauls before midday produced only eight tonnes of loligo and a tonne of hake fillets.

Things were going just as smoothly at this late stage of the trip as they had done at the beginning, and some of the young men who had started out on their first trip just a few months ago now began to take on the look of experienced deckhands who had spent years at sea.

Under the ever watchful eye of Oscar the bosun, the work on deck had gone extremely well. The younger men, some on their first trip, had been urged on by Oscar, and although at times everyone on deck had received an ear bashing from him in a language I could not understand, everyone had come through with flying colours.

Nobody on a trawler has a worse job than the cook, or in our case, the cooks. Despite some of the atrocious weather that we had fished and dodged through, and the rough conditions we had steamed through as we sought shelter in Berkeley Sound and other places, the meals had always been of good quality and served up on time by our two cooks and their assistant.

We had lost very little time through stoppages, and below in the engine room things had gone very smoothly. Although the problem of the winch motor had cost us dearly, it was nobody's fault, and simply highlighted the hazards of fishing in isolated places such as the Falklands, where at the time there were no facilities to carry out repairs of this nature.

The day's third haul was a poor effort of only three tonnes and there was little improvement in the four-tonne haul just before midnight, allowing us to finish the third day of our final week with a disappointing sixteen tonnes. Despite trying different waters the following day while staying in the same area, we fared only slightly better and finished the day with eighteen tonnes of loligo and two tonnes of hake, and the prospects for the next five days looked bleak indeed.

During this slack spell we had the opportunity to get the Fishing Explorer tidied up a bit, with some of the spare gear on deck stowed away, leaving the bare essentials for the unlikely event of us damaging the trawl.

There was no improvement in the fishing for the remainder of our time, and at the end of the sixth day we hauled on what was our last haul of the trip. This haul was just the same as many others over the last week, but was enough to send us heading the short distance in to Port Stanley, where in the morning I could go ashore and deliver our fishing log to the authorities.

In the meantime we laid to, waiting for the daylight, while the rest of the fishing gear was cleared off the deck to prepare for the long journey to Europe.

At 1030 I was on my way ashore, and after delivering the logbooks and talking things over as to how the trip had gone and making a few suggestions as to how things could be improved, it was time to say a few goodbyes before picking up the mail and a few other items and returning to the harbour launch. A short while later I was climbing back onto the Fishing Explorer, and within minutes Port Stanley was astern of us. With no more than a south-westerly force four breeze behind us, we were at last heading for home and it was a great feeling to be at last on our way.

The only thing working overtime was the showers, as everyone took the opportunity to unwind and ease their aching limbs under a hot shower, knowing that they would not be called out on to the deck to haul or shoot the trawl.

On watch after the evening meal all was quiet, as most of the crew slept. There was an eerie silence, and although we saw the lights of two ships in the distance, the watch passed without incident. We could have hardly hoped for better conditions to see us on our way since we left Port Stanley at 1500. After being relieved on the bridge at midnight, and going aft for a cup of coffee before turning in myself, I thought how different everything was to just twenty-four hours previously with so much going on. Now the ship was quiet, as everyone except the engineer on watch was either laid down reading or catching up on some well-earned sleep.

My Spanish had improved sufficiently for me to be able to hold a conversation with almost anyone, and after an hour talking to the engineer, who assured me that we would have a good time once we were tied up in Cadiz, I turned in for the night. It had been a long day, but an enjoyable one.

The next morning was fine but clear, with just a light breeze astern of us. Most of the crew appeared for breakfast bearing little resemblance to the men who had dragged themselves wearily on to the deck just a day earlier.

Gone were the beards and the drab working clothes used during fishing, and now it was back to track suits and the casual gear as everyone relaxed and licked their wounds after being given some time to themselves.

The atmosphere on board was completely relaxed as we made our way homeward on a north-easterly course in near perfect weather conditions that got better as the days passed.

The temperature gradually rose, and our main job was to get the Fishing Explorer to resemble the ship that had sailed from La Coruña eight months before.

We had spent a full winter at sea in the Falklands, and in that time we had taken quite a battering from the weather and the countless gales of wind that had certainly taken a toll on the paintwork.

As the weather got warmer, it was during a walk around the deck that I noticed the sorry state of our red ensign. Although it was made of metal and freshly painted before we had arrived in the Falklands, wind, rain, snow and even the occasional sunshine had contributed to its rusty and weather-beaten appearance. But for now it was all behind us, with plenty of time to put everything to rights during the long journey home.

The Last Visit to the Gaul

Although the Mansal 18 survey had rvealed a number of very important findings during its time spent over the wreck, I had always believed that the time spent there had simply not been long enough to answer the many remaining questions that were being asked following the location of the wreck.

Once it had been announced that another survey was to be carried out, there was much speculation as to what sort of survey the return to the wreck of the Gaul would be. Many people were of the opinion that a manned dive would be carried out, but this was considered too hazardous and it was decided that the survey would be carried out using Remotely Operated Vehicles (ROVs) and side scan sonar.

In recent years there had been vast improvements in this type of technology, resulting in the location and identification of some of the finest ships ever built that had long been thought to have been lost for ever. These include battleships and submarines from two world wars, as well as tankers and other merchant ships that had been located under difficult conditions and in some of the most desolate places in the world.

It was early in 2001 that I was first notified that another survey of the Gaul to be carried out. Many people had campaigned for this, not least the Gaul Families Association. Although the timing of the survey was not announced immediately, it was widely assumed that the summer of 2002 would be the ideal time for it, and this turned out to be the case.

Throughout 2001 I attended a number of meetings in London, Southampton and in Hull regarding this proposed return visit to the Gaul, but it was not until early 2002 that I was formally invited to join the trip, subject to a medical check-up. The same offer had also been sent to George Petty, and after discussing it between ourselves, we both agreed and accepted the invitation.

Both George Petty and I had been retired for some years, and until the wreck had been found and identified, neither of us had been asked for our opinions on the Gaul, except on the anniversary of her loss. During all those years we had never approached the MAIB or any of the solicitors representing the Gaul Families Association, and eventually it was only at the invitation of these parties that we came to be asked for our views on how the Gaul had been lost.

It therefore came as something of a surprise, when, after it had been announced by the MAIB that George Petty and I would be sailing as fishery advisers, there was quite an outcry from some of the committee members representing the Gaul Families Association.

Remarks were made that we were untrustworthy and that we were so set in our views that we would not be open to new concepts as to what had happened to the Gaul. It was also remarked that we had never attended any meetings of the Gaul Families Association, yet there was no mention of the fact that we had never been invited to attend any of these meetings. Out of respect we had never wished to do so without having been invited.

Of course, I had my own views as to what happened to the Gaul, as have many people who are quite entitled to hold views. I had also openly stated that until such a time as I saw something that would change my mind, my views would remain unchanged.

These remarks had been hurtful, untrue and totally unnecessary, and are something that I would not forget in a hurry. Yet when I was later asked if I would be prepared to meet the full committee of the Gaul Families Association, on my own and in the offices of their lawyers to answer any questions, I readily agreed. I was pleased to be able to come face to face with my accusers and left the meeting with the feeling that those who had made these accusations were in the minority of those present that afternoon.

During the time that I spent with the Gaul Families Association, I pointed out the mistakes that I felt had been had been made on the

Mansal 18 survey. One engineer and one factory hand had accompanied the team on this trip, yet it was obvious from the outset that entry would not be gained to the areas of the ship that they had been familiar with. The one place that would definitely be entered was the bridge, yet there was nobody in the team on the Mansal 18 who had any idea of the Gaul's bridge layout, including the chart room and radio room that were located inside the bridge.

I also pointed out that the engineer who sailed on the survey should never have been put in the position of having to answer questions as to whether or not the Gaul had been fishing at the time of her loss, when it was quite clear to anyone with knowledge of the deck that she was not. I was also able to point out that simply because we knew where to look and exactly what we were looking for that George Petty and I had been able to identify all of the sounders and other instruments that we had seen when viewing the video footage taken by the Mansal 18 team, and in most cases we had even been able to supply the makers' names as well.

Once again I had spoken the truth and I believe that it went some way towards reducing the scepticism of those who thought that we should not be making the trip.

From here onwards the process of preparing for the trip went smoothly. Some of the Gaul Families Association members were invited up to Aberdeen to see at first hand some of the equipment that would be used during the survey, while others, myself included, were invited to view it on video in Hull a few weeks before the trip got underway in June 2002.

On the 24th of June 2002 the long awaited

The Seisranger, photo: J & D Dodds

return trip to the wreck of the Gaul finally began. George Petty and I had once again teamed up for a trip to sea to assist the MAIB team as fishery experts on the multi-support vessel Seisranger that we were due to join in Aberdeen after our short flight north from Humberside.

We had both been retired for some years and had met many times in the intervening years. We still had plenty to talk about and we share much the same views as to how the Gaul came to be lost.

With the flights due to arrive at Aberdeen within minutes of each other, we were able to meet the five members of the MAIB team working under principal inspector Keith Dixon, and within minutes of claiming our luggage we were on our way to board the Seisranger.

First impressions can often be deceptive, but this was certainly not the case with the Seisranger, a spacious and well laid out vessel, and ideal for spending any amount of time on location inside the Arctic Circle at any time of the year. With everyone allocated a single cabin, it was easy to see that the Seisranger had been a wise choice for the job that lay ahead.

After settling in and being shown round the ship we became more and more impressed with what we saw. After a 36 hour delay, Seisranger made her way out of Aberdeen harbour at 1650 hours on 26th of June and proceeded across the North Sea to Bergen to take on fuel, stores and some additional crew members who would swell the ship's complement to almost 60 people.

Overnight the weather had freshened to a NW force 6 and this could well be the reason why not many people appeared at breakfast the following morning. Both George and I found this strange, especially after sampling what was on offer.

Much had changed since my last trip to sea. The ship's position at midday was posted on the notice board along with the distance to travel and our estimated time of arrival in Bergen. We docked in Bergen on time at 2030 hours, and tied up a short way from the city itself.

Although I had visited Bergen just once before, I had mixed thoughts and memories of my one and only visit. Steaming home from the Barents Sea as mate of the oil burning trawler Lord Lovat and fully expecting to be home for Christmas, we had the misfortune to break down with a serious engine problem. With some very unfavourable weather forecast, things did not look too promising as the chief engineer and the rest of the engine room squad set about trying to complete repairs under some very difficult weather conditions.

With the wind now gusting to over force 10, we had already put out a call for assistance, and this had been answered by another Hull trawler, Arctic Corsair, who was also making her way home for Christmas with very little time to spare.

What followed was a nightmare for all of us on the Lord Lovat. Yet some great seamanship by the crew of the Arctic Corsair was justly rewarded when they eventually got a line across to us in what were by now atrocious weather conditions that were showing no sign of easing.

To get a tow rope on to us was little short of a miracle and with the Lord Lovat completely at the mercy of the weather it seemed that a few miracles were handed out that night as we managed to connect the tow to our own tow line on an open deck under such conditions and without injury to anyone. But an hour later it all had to be done again when the tow parted.

Retrieving the towing cable on the whaleback of the Lord Lovat was sheer hell, and must have been the same for the crew of the Arctic Corsair, yet eventually another line was fired across and once again the tow was connected, but again within half an hour of starting the tow, the line had parted once again, leaving Lord Lovat to fall broadside to the weather. To try again under those conditions would have been futile and far too dangerous. During the last attempt the Arctic Corsair had suffered some damage to her boat deck and one of her lifeboats, so it could only be a matter of time before someone was seriously injured or worse.

At about this time a tug arrived on the scene, allowing Arctic Corsair to resume her way home to Hull and when the good luck messages had been exchanged we were left to face what was sure to be another very uncomfortable night.

With very little change in the weather forecast the following day was spent very much as

Some of the array of equipment that was loaded onto the deck of the Seisranger for the survey of the Gaul. (MAIB)

Some of the underwater vehicles used to survey and gain entrance to the wreck. (MAIB)

The author with one of the undersea vehicles deployed by the Seisranger during the survey. (MAIB)

the previous one had been. Yet on Christmas Eve there was a small amount of cheer when the chief engineer announced that he had been able to make repairs and was now prepared to try it out, albeit at half speed or less.

The ringing of the engine room telegraph sounded like an orchestra to us and very slowly, with the ship's wheel hard over to give her every bit of assistance, the Lord Lovat at last started to make way through the water and with something of a struggle came up into the wind, much to the relief of everyone on board.

Under such conditions to get Lord Lovat moving again our old chief engineer and his squad had done a marvellous job. During the time we had been laid to we had been driven many miles back to the north east and most of Christmas Day was spent dodging head to wind and barely holding our own in weather that gradually started to show signs of easing and changing, giving us a chance to make our way into some sheltered waters and eventually into Bergen. Finally we were alongside just before midday on Boxing Day, and our big Christmas dinner was a choice of fried haddock or fried cod.

With orders from Hull not to risk bringing the ship across the North Sea in any severe weather conditions, we eventually managed to take on a few stores, although practically everything in Bergen was closed. After some small adjustments to the engine we eventually left Bergen to remain in sheltered waters of

the fjords until a change in the weather would allow us to take the Lord Lovat back across the North Sea to Hull.

There was a slight moderation in the weather and also because we were all so fed up with how the trip had finished, we finally left the shelter of the south fjords and crossed the North Sea at half speed without any problems at all, arriving in Hull in the early hours of New Year's day. This meant that we all had to walk home as there was not a taxi to be found on the entire fish dock, a fitting end to what had been one hell of a trip and a great way to start the New Year.

Sitting at home with things getting back to normal after all the festivities had finished, a small piece in the evening paper caught my eye. This described what had happened to the Lord Lovat, and said that with a minor engine room defect the Lord Lovat had arrived safely on New Year's Day. One of the morning papers also covered the story in a few lines, but both forgot to mention that because of our delay our fish had failed to attract any buyers and after a month at sea in the middle of winter and being away over Christmas and New Year, most of the crew had walked off the dock with nothing to show for a full winter trip to Arctic fishing grounds.

This had been my only previous visit to Bergen and although it had been many years ago, it came back vividly to me as we made our way into the port. Our stay this time was only a few hours as we took on stores , bunkers and some more of the crew before departing in the early hours into some very familiar waters. We sailed form Bergen on the 28th of June into what could hardly be described as a summer's day. This was a good stiff breeze of force six or seven, which was enough to keep those on board who were not familiar with life at sea away from the dining room until they had found their sea legs.

However, with not a lot to do, it was time to get to know those who would be with us for the next month, or maybe even longer. Representing the Gaul families was Norman Fenton who, with a Channel 4 team, had been responsible for identifying the wreck of the Gaul. Also on board were marine consultant

My old friend George Petty in pensive mood on board the Seisranger at the Gaul wreck site.
(MAIB)

Graham McCombie, a likeable Scot, and another maritime consultant, Jeremy Colman, based in the Isle of Man, who was there to represent the families of the skipper and mate of the Gaul. The MAIB team was made up of principal inspector Keith Dixon, Cliff Brand, Tony Lewis, Alan Rushton and Graham Wilson. The forensic team was made up of detective inspector Andy Kirby and Chris Macguire. Also there making up the formidable array of expertise were Crawford Logan and Will Handley, while George Petty and myself were there to assist in any fishing matters that could arise and to assist with our knowledge of the inside layout and our all-round knowledge of the Gaul.

The first of many daily meetings was held on the 29th of June to discuss the plan of action for when we arrived at the wreck site. This also gave everyone the chance to air their views and express any thoughts they had on the matter in hand or to bring up any further points.

For those who had not passed this way before there was a chance to focus their cameras on the Lofoten Islands as we made our way past the Arctic Circle and for most of those on board this was their first time.

Sunday the 30th of June was a little on the cold side, overcast with a northerly wind. At this point our position was 69° 40'N, 016° 39'E. The further north we sailed, the better the weather became and some late evening sunshine was a welcome sight as we contin-

Captain Bjorn Johannessen on the Seisranger's bridge. (MAIB)

ued to close the distance to the wreck site of the Gaul. I had been invited by the captain of the Seisranger to visit the bridge at any time and readily accepted this invitation. Captain Bjorn Johannessen was a very likeable man with an excellent command of English and I always looked forward to my visits to the Seisranger's bridge to see for myself the vast changes that had taken place in a few years with the range of electronic equipment that was fitted in Seisranger's spacious and well fitted out bridge that impressed both George and myself a great deal.

On the morning of the first of July I was taking a shower when the tell-tale sign of the ship reducing speed told me that we were close to the position of the wreck. This was confirmed by the mate over breakfast when he told me that we were almost at the position that would be our location for the next few weeks.

The wreck site was located in a short time and soon pictures of the wreck of the Gaul were being transmitted to the many screens and monitors that seemed to be everywhere you looked in Seisranger's bridge and operations room.

Since the wreck of the Gaul had been first located, her position had become well documented. The ROVs were in the water quickly and soon sending back pictures of the Gaul and at first sight it seemed that the large amount of netting that festooned the wreck had been added to since the previous survey had taken place. So thick was the amount of netting lost on the ship that this would be a mammoth task to remove and something that was high on the list of priorities.

The daily rota of work to be carried out each day had been issued to everyone of us who had attended the first of our daily meetings and it was not difficult to figure out that the task ahead was not going to be an easy one. I had stated at our first meeting that I would not expect to lose much, if any, time at this time of the year, although bad weather could not be ruled out even in July at these high latitudes.

I had seen a video in Hull at one of the meetings I had attended there a month before we sailed, and although the cutting procedure to open the side of the Gaul seemed very impressive when carried out in tanks, I had no idea how well the equipment to gain entrance to the interior of the Gaul would perform when it came to the real thing.

Compared to some of the wrecks that have been located in recent years, the Gaul is not in exceptionally deep waters. But most of these ships that have attracted so much public interest were lost during the war and all had suffered structural damage of some sort. But in the case of the Gaul, although doors had been found to be open on the previous survey of the wreck, and apart from some hull damage at the bow, the Gaul remained virtually intact to the best of our knowledge, unless we were to reveal anything in the next few days close to the wreck on the sea bed that was covered with lost nets and fishing gear. So much net was laid over the wreck that George Petty and myself were under no illusion of the size of the task ahead and the time it would take to clear it. This was clearly a job that would take more than a day or two. But once positioned over the wreck one of the first tasks was to have a general look around the area and even this turned up a surprise or two.

When the wreck of the Gaul had been first located, and despite all the evidence that showed otherwise, many people still believed that the Gaul had been fishing at the time of the loss, simply because only one of the Gaul's trawl doors could be located in its normal position on the port quarter. This had a fair amount of net over it, but was still easy to identify. Yet as the camera closed in, it was a surprise to see that the port trawl door was not in its usual position but had been lifted up and dropped neatly inboard as if properly stowed. It was only the tell-tale sign of a full set of trawl gear wrapped around the stern of the Gaul that showed that some trawler had come fast on the stern of the Gaul and in unsuccessfully trying to free his gear had lifted the Gaul's port trawl door inboard.

We had still not located the starboard trawl door, the last piece of this particular puzzle, which would put an end to the speculation once and for all by accounting for all of the Gaul's fishing gear.

Everything was being recorded on this sur-

The author, in hard hat and high-visibility coat, as the Seisranger sailed from Bergen. (MAIB)

vey, with a continuous watch night and day that kept all of the observers well and truly occupied, glued to the monitors and missing nothing for the entire trip.

Since the previous visit to the wreck of the Gaul there had been a great deal of speculation about the mysterious cables on the sea bed in the vicinity of the wreck. Time and time again I had watched the television programmes that had gone to great lengths to highlight these findings, but never had I felt that these were anything other than trawl warps that had been lost when unfortunate trawlers had lost their gear after coming fast

George Petty and the author (in Hull FC cap) with Captain Bjorn Johannessen on the Seisranger's bridge. (MAIB)

on the wreck of the Gaul. There was plenty of evidence of this to be seen.

Most of these cables had been on the sea bed for twenty-five years and in that time had accumulated a certain amount of marine growth, but this did not stop people jumping to the conclusion that these were something to do with sinister acts of espionage. There had been speculation that one of these cable was leading to Sorøy Island sixty miles away to the south west. However, after having followed this cable that was supposed to lead to Sorøy Island, and without losing sight of it, we soon came to a mark of the kind that was commonly inserted into trawl warps to mark twenty-five fathom lengths. A further twenty-five fathoms along the cable, the camera came to another distinctive mark of the same kind. Moments later the cable was found to be heading north and then back towards the direction of the Gaul, giving every indication of a side trawler having come fast on the wreck, trying to come back to the fastening and trying to retrieve his warps, doors and trawl.

This mysterious cable failed to reach the military air base on Sorøy Island by about fifty-nine miles. Before the cameras were switched elsewhere, a piece of this cable about two fathoms long was cut out and brought back on board the Seisranger where I was asked by the forensic team to give my opinion on what had been found. This was just a formality as once the sand had been cleaned off it, a normal six stranded warp was revealed, of the type used by trawlers from Hull, Grimsby and many other places, and certainly not the type of cable that would be associated with espionage or submarines.

It seemed that at last the allegations that had linked the Gaul to all the acts of spying were now, and quite rightly, beginning to lose all credibility, and within the next few days there was more to follow.

The next day or two actually revealed very little as cutting away the nets covering the ship and breaking almost all the portholes was taking a lot of time. The main reason for this was the sheer thickness of the portholes and bridge windows. But these jobs had to be done if we were to gain access to the radio room and some of the berths, however time consuming this work was.

It was not until the following Saturday the sixth of July, that another significant discovery was made. On previous visits to the Gaul both doors leading to the factory were found to be open, yet it came as a surprise to find that while trying to trace the starboard trawl warp through the sheave that the net store on the starboard quarter was wide open. With no apparent damage to the clamps this was the last thing we had expected to see. This net store would lead through a door into the steering flat, but there was no evidence that this door was open. But with the cameras in the net store it was quite easy to identify some spare new nets and a certain amount of spare warps, all standard gear that trawlers would take to sea.

The area around the starboard quarter was certainly giving us some problems. Cutting through netting and a large amount of chain had once again taken up much of the day, but it was in this area that another significant find was made.

With everything now removed from around the starboard sheave except the warp running though it, the cameras were once again able to follow the warp and without once losing sight of it, leading us straight to the starboard trawl door, still shackled securely to the warp end and with all the links clearly showing, but not clipped to the Gaul's trawl, which was still on the deck.

Once this had been photographed, the last piece in this part of the puzzle had been found.

One of the daily meetings held on board the Seisranger during the survey. (MAIB)

For all the speculation that the Gaul had been fishing when she was lost the bubble had well and truly burst.

I had always strenuously denied that the Gaul was ever at any time involved in any acts of spying, or "information gathering," as it appears to be called now. Many times when I had been interviewed regarding the loss of the Gaul it was always a matter of time before the subject was brought up and although my answer was always the same that we had never been involved in anything of the kind, this answer never failed to raise a few eyebrows with many people still convinced of the Gaul's involvement in espionage.

High on the list of work still to be carried out was a full scale search of the radio room situated on the port side of the bridge. We had already made access to the bridge area much easier by cutting a much larger hole in the front of the bridge. This was already showing signs of starting to break up, which made the task that much easier.

Once inside the bridge the search for any additional transmitters or receivers would not be too difficult. Although the starboard side of the bridge showed signs of damage, the port side had escaped the worst of any damage and it was not too difficult to photograph the entire contents of the radio room.

Watching this on the monitors in the control room gave me a great deal of personal satisfaction when after a very extensive search it became plain that there was nothing in there that was not part of the usual radio and telecommunications equipment that had been installed when the Gaul had been built. Although we visited the radio room again for a second extensive search, as this was high on the priority list, nothing was found that could not be accounted for.

Possibly the most disappointing thing about the visits to the bridge was that it was not possible with any degree of certainty to establish what time was showing on any of the clocks that we had so far located. This had been high on my own list of priorities and there was even more disappointment when after locating the bridge telegraph it was not possible to read the settings because of the large amount of salt and debris that had accumulated on that side of the bridge.

By this time we had also gained entry through the door on the foredeck to the interior of the Gaul. We were half expecting a struggle to open these doors and it came as a surprise when the clamps had been set to the open position that we were able to open the doors without exerting much pressure at all.

Not knowing what to expect, there was an eerie silence from those who were on duty and sat watching the monitors, when after twenty-eight years this door that would lead to the Gaul's accommodation was finally opened.

If everything appeared to be going well at this critical stage of the proceedings, then this was certainly not the case and at this stage I felt that far too much time was being spent on jobs that were not important.

On gaining entry to the bridge, the clocks and barometer were located but it was not possible to get an accurate reading from these instruments. But we managed successfully to locate the rudder indicator and possibly because it was located at a higher position on the deckhead and had not been badly silted up, it was possible to see clearly that the rudder was set at an angle of 25° to port.

Knowing this I could not understand why so much time was spent clearing the rudder and in another area why so much time was spent measuring the indentations on the funnel, both of which tasks I believe took up a great deal of time that I feel would have been better used in other departments.

It was also at this point that we first began to witness problems with the cutting gear and this slowed down our progress to the extent that it was decided at one of our meetings to fly out an explosive expert, as this had been taken into consideration before we sailed from Aberdeen.

After losing so much vital time over the cutting equipment, it seemed that we would have to rely on explosives to gain entry to certain vital parts of the Gaul, but even at this critical stage we were not rushing into things if it could be avoided.

Although the problems with the cutting equipment had put us back a couple of days, not everything had come to a complete stop. But with so much netting still in evidence it was only to be expected that the ROV would occasionally come foul of the many obstructions that seemed to be laid in wait on and around the wreck. Yet I have nothing but praise for the young men who operated these machines and ensured that they were never out of commission for a minute longer than necessary. Their commitment to helping each other out of a tight corner was a pleasure to see.

On opening the door on the foredeck it was not possible to enter the accommodation on account of what appeared to be fuel oil. This was allowed to clear, and this was also the case when one of the hatches on the foredeck was opened. Not a great deal of fuel oil was released and it is possible that this came from the forward tanks that had been empty or almost empty and had also been damaged when the Gaul settled on the sea bed. With these doors and hatches so well fastened, this could be the reason why no oil slick was found during the extensive search for the Gaul when she was lost or in the years since.

My reason for thinking that the forward tanks would be empty was based simply on my own experience, as when I had been skipper of the Gaul, we had always used the forward tanks first. Taking into consideration the time the Gaul had been at sea and the time spent steaming to the fishing grounds, these fuel tanks would have been almost expended, leaving only a small residue in them that had clearly found its way out of the tanks after they had been ruptured.

On the 14th of July we entered a number of cabins and also gained entry to the sick bay. A number of bottles could be identified still in the racks. The sick bay was hardly the most likely place where human remains could be expected to be found, yet it was given full scrutiny by the cameras.

During the early morning of the 15th of July we recovered a pair of trousers from one of the cabins and later in the morning we recovered a thigh boot. Soon after this we were able to enter the skipper's cabin. This was of special importance to me, once again because of all the spying allegations that were claimed to be centred around the skipper's cabin. This area had been singled out for special attention to establish if there could be anything there that could link the Gaul to any kind of espionage activity. I had already mentioned that it might be possible to find the Gaul's log tin in the skipper's cabin, but unfortunately this was not the case.

Because we knew where to look it was not difficult to locate the clock and barometer in the skipper's dayroom, but after scrutinising the clock for some considerable time it was again not possible to say with any accuracy what time it was showing. What we did see clearly was that the ship's safe and all the filing cabinets had broken away from their fittings and were laid to the starboard side of the dayroom. As was to be expected, the skipper's cabin came in for some extra scrutiny, but just as in the radio room, nothing was found there that could remotely associate the Gaul with any acts of spying that she had been wrongly linked with for so many years.

During the early hours of the morning we paid a return visit to the bridge and radio room and once again every effort was made to see what was showing on the bridge telegraph and the clock, and despite this only a guess could be made.

I had just arrived on watch and taken my seat in the operations room when the first pictures started coming back from the factory deck, and very good pictures they were. There appeared to be very little silt in the factory deck and it was not a problem to pick out a number of items and to identify some of the machinery and conveyor belts. Other items such as aprons that were used by the men on the factory deck were also visible, as well as a duffle coat that was used when stowing frozen blocks in the hold.

With so much of the machinery in the factory deck being made of stainless steel, everything seemed to be in remarkably good condition and some of the markings on the pipes could be clearly seen. Despite all this, one could not miss the gratings that had formed the factory floor. These would normally have been laid out horizontally, but were now stood vertically, again suggesting that the Gaul had laid over on her starboard beam, reinforcing the evidence that we had already seen to support this theory.

If there were any areas of the Gaul where I thought there would be the best chance of recovering any human remains, these would be the crew's mess, the officers' mess and the galley. I had stated this repeatedly at many meetings over the previous year, and on the 17th of July we started to get back pictures of this area of the Gaul.

However, we were also having very little success with efforts to cut into the Gaul's side to gain access to crucial areas and it must be said that time was not on our side. As would be expected, the usual things that would be found on the mess deck were identified as the cameras picked up individual items such as knives and forks and some broken crockery and once again a number of chairs that had finished up on the starboard side of the mess deck. The galley was the same with many items that were expected, including a bread-making bowl and other things that were quite easily recognised.

Remaining in these areas throughout the following day we had the misfortune to get one of the ROVs tied up again, but it must be remembered that we were now reaching areas of the ship that had not been entered before. I feel sure that this trip presented some of the most exacting demands ever made on the Seisranger's equipment.

On Friday 19th of July a hole was finally cut into the side of the Gaul that allowed entry to the engine room. This was an achievement in itself although this was not high on my own list of priorities, as I felt sure that more time should have been centred on areas such as the mess deck. Although the team had been successful in cutting a hole in the Gaul's side to gain access to the engine room, once the steel plate was removed, the many pipes inside made access difficult and in my opinion, too much time was spent on this. It seemed appropriate that at 1900 that evening,

A Norwegian Coast Guard vessel brought out to us from Hammerfest an explosives expert who would remain with us for the rest of the trip, in case he was needed. At this point it was not possible to rule out that explosives would be needed.

Later that day we were able to enter another cabin and identified a sweater and a boot. We could also see other items such as wash basins, shaving cabinets and fire extinguishers still in their brackets, all of which indicated that a fire on board was not the cause of the Gaul's loss. Although these findings may seem quite insignificant to many people, it did enable us to eliminate several theories on the Gaul's loss.

On Sunday the 21st of July the cameras were again focused on the crew's mess area, where we located what we thought were clearly the first signs of human remains. We had already identified a shoe, and for some time the cameras had been focused on what did appear to be human remains. Our forensic experts were now called upon to bring all their knowledge to bear on these first finds.

Among the equipment brought out to us by the Coast Guard cutter were some magnets and with the arrival of these it was believed that there would be an improvement in the performance of the cutting equipment.

Although this equipment had been up and down for most of the day, it was not until 2330 that day that another hole was cut into the side of the Gaul into the officers' mess. From this area we finally recovered the first of what were later positively identified as human remains. Despite all that had gone on before, an eerie silence descended on the Seisranger with the confirmation that we had finally retrieved human remains. This had been the main aim of the voyage and this was carried out in complete silence.

Shortly after this first find, a second sighting was confirmed in this area along with a boot and a sock, and these were brought aboard the Seisranger into the custody of the forensic team.

On this day the ROVs had spent a great deal of time inside the wreck of the Gaul and as we had located no more confirmed sightings of human remains, the equipment was brought back aboard for some adjustments to be made before returning it to the wreck of the Gaul.

At times we often returned for a second look to different places that had already been visited. One of these was the trawl deck where we had spent so much time already and gained so much information, not only on this visit but on the survey carried out four years previously.

Although we had seen almost every part of the trawl deck that it was possible to see, there was one area that had not been examined and this was behind the winch. This particular area had a lot of net hanging over it from the back of the bridge, and in front of the winch were the Gaul's own bobbins and working trawl, plus a spare trawl. But now that we had partially removed these nets, it gave us the chance to get behind the trawl winch for the first time.

Once again I had a particular reason for wanting to see the ROV in this area. At meetings in London and Hull I had pointed out that the door behind the winch would possibly be the best place to gain entry to the inside of the Gaul as it would give us easier access to the mess deck area.

This was the one door that everyone passed through when going out to the deck to haul the trawl and when leaving the deck once the trawl had been shot. This door simply lead straight from the deck to the Gaul's accommodation areas.

With a great deal of the nets now cleared away from the area in front of the winch we now had the chance to kill two birds with one stone. Looking at the two warp drums on the winch it was clear that both drums had the same amount of warp on them. Not that there was anything left to prove over whether or not the Gaul had been fishing, but once this was established, it was possible now to go over the top of the winch where we found the door leading in from the deck open.

Once again finding a door open was greeted with a period of silence, and although we had gained another entry into the Gaul, we had not expected it to be in such a manner as this.

Some years ago George Petty and I on our first visit to the MAIB had discarded the order in which we were to view the tapes of the previous survey, principally because we thought that the deck area would give us a lot of the answers as to what had happened to the Gaul. Here we were once again coming up against something that was sure to raise a lot of eyebrows and certainly some more questions.

The trawl deck of the Gaul had certainly supplied us with a few surprises since the wreck had first been located. The doors leading to the factory deck had been found hooked back and leading to the engine room. On this trip we had found the doors to the net store open and now this door leading to the accommodation was also fully opened, yet all the doors and hatches on the foredeck had been found clamped and fastened down in the position we had found them in.

I have always thought that the Gaul was lost at around the time of the midday meal or just after when there were still a few of the crew still in or around the mess deck. If this was the case, then we can not rule out the possibility that this door was open because it offered the nearest escape route to those who would have been in the galley, crew mess or the officers' mess. However, it is anyone's guess if any of the crew managed to get off the Gaul and unfortunately we will never know.

Monday the 22 of July was regarded by many as the day that we would be heading home. In fact this was the day that we were granted a forty-eight hour extension. I certainly believe that this was a good decision and quite justified as we had lost a considerable amount of time. At this critical juncture of the trip , although we had located and retrieved some human remains, I am sure that everyone on board the Seisranger felt that it would only be a matter of time before we located more, and this turned out to be the case during this all-important two day extension. It was during this time that we located and recovered human remains from two more areas inside the Gaul.

In the early hours of the 24th of July it was time to bring the survey to an end and with the last of the few remaining jobs done, it was time for George Petty and myself to take a walk on deck to pay our respects as the Seisranger began to leave the position over the wreck of the Gaul that had been our location for 23 days.

Standing there on the deck with the midnight sun shining we were seeing this remote area in one of its better moods. Now the sea was almost flat calm, and although there was constant daylight and some weak sunshine, one could not help but think about how it had been when the Gaul was lost and how different it would have been in early February with constant snow and continuous gales, something familiar to some of the older fishermen. But now as we said our last goodbyes to those we had left behind us as we headed home, there would be ample time to look back over what had happened during the trip.

Now on our way back to Aberdeen, showered and rested, and with no watches to take, there was time to take stock and reflect on what had been required and what had been achieved during the survey of the Gaul. A list of requirements had been available to everyone who had attended the daily meetings, and these are as follows.

To establish if the remain of the crew are on board the Gaul.
This was done.

To help determine the most probable cause of the sinking.
We had uncovered a number of things that I believed would certainly help in determining how the Gaul was lost, and these were presented to the final enquiry.

To determine if any intelligence gathering equipment was to be found on the Gaul.
After a very extensive search of the radio room and the skipper's accommodation, nothing was found.

To recover human remains for DNA testing from the following areas: the crew mess, the crew recreation room, the officers' mess, the galley, the bridge, the chart room, the radio room, all accommodation spaces on the forecastle deck, the trawl deck, the main deck, and to recover samples of at least six crew members for DNA testing.

Access was gained to all of these places and also the electrical locker. Four separate sets of human remains were identified by DNA testing.

To examine the bridge control settings and other instruments.
As access to the bridge was not difficult, this area was visited on a number of occasions, but although all of the instruments were located, it was not always possible to read the settings. This was partly due to a large part of the bridge deckhead that had collapsed. The rudder indicator was found and showed a reading of 25° port rudder. The radars, sonar and sounders were all found in their original positions behind the skippers' console.

To examine the port funnel and the hatch at its base.
This was done.

To measure the controllable pitch propeller settings and the kort nozzle.
Both of these time consuming tasks were carried out.

To examine the fish loading hatches and the fastening lugs.
These jobs were done and no damage was found to any of the fastening lugs.

To locate the missing wheelhouse door.
This door was located quite early in the survey.

To examine the liferaft and ship's boat and securing release arrangements
These were all done.

To locate the missing starboard trawl door.
This was done.

139

Conclusions

It was when the survey was over and the Seisranger was making her way home along the Norwegian coast that I was asked to draw up a paper on my thoughts as to how the survey had gone, as well as my own views and opinions covering the time that we had spent over the wreck of the Gaul. I had no doubts whatever that the trip had been a success, yet I do not doubt that there will be those who would not agree with me on this.

Despite a number of setbacks, what was achieved during the survey can not be dismissed. We had gained access to many areas of the Gaul and a large amount of information had been collected by the cameras, as the entire survey had been filmed from start to finish, which had also included a large area of the sea bed around the Gaul. This was a mammoth task in itself and I doubt that this equipment will ever again be put through such a strenuous period as during the Gaul survey.

The list of tasks to be carried out had been long and a time-consuming and in my opinion some of these tasks were unnecessary and the time could have been more usefully used in other areas of the wreck. The validity of the decision not to use explosives to gain entry to the hull depended on your point of view. At a meeting in Hull it had been made plain that this was a possibility and no objection had been made. But when this was raised at one of our daily meetings on board the Seisranger, a number of people objected strongly.

It should not be forgotten that at this stage of the trip no human remains had been recovered. Although late in the trip some human remains were recovered, I have often wondered what the reaction would have been if no remains had been found. The decision not to use explosives was quite justified, but it was a close call. But I have little doubt that if the decision had been taken to use explosives earlier in the survey, I am sure that we would have recovered a far greater amount of human remains from the wreck, and this was, after all, the prime objective at the outset of the voyage.

With a little bit of luck and a lot of determination, we had gained access to almost every part of the Gaul and revealed many things that previous surveys had not been equipped to do, not only on the wreck, but over a large area of surrounding sea bed. Ideas that had been planted in peoples' minds and which had instilled a great deal of doubt and mistrust had been well and truly cleared up.

The trip in the Seisranger had been an experience in itself, seeing modern equipment working under these conditions deep inside the Arctic Circle and working with the young men and women who operated the equipment was a pleasure.

It was as I was in the operations room as the cameras entered the Gaul's factory deck for the first time that I had a total rethink of how the Gaul had been lost. The previous surveys had revealed that doors were open in different areas of the Gaul, but I don't think that anyone was ready for the shock when the cameras focused on the open offal chutes, leading from the factory deck to the open sea.

If I had learned anything during the Gaul investigation, it was to be wary of jumping to any conclusions. Yet seeing the offal chutes in the open position was food for thought. George and I are both familiar with how the offal chutes work and discussed this at length with the MAIB staff on board Seisranger. The offal chutes are designed to work so that waste can leave the ship without water being let in, and the Gaul's offal chutes had operated perfectly during previous trips. My feeling is that for any water to have made its way in through the offal chutes, then the Gaul would have had to have had her port side exposed to the weather for a considerable time, yet all the indications and reports are that the Gaul was dodging head to wind, as was every other ship on Cape Bank at the time. This leads me to believe that the offal chutes could have been opened by some force from inside the factory deck, or due to pressure building up inside the hull.

Taking into account all that I have seen and heard regarding the loss of the Gaul, I am convinced that she suffered a knockdown, caught broadside to the waves either through falling off her course or when turning at the end of her run. I am also still certain that many people have also continued to underestimate the severity of the weather at the time. Tank tests have shown that the Gaul could have laid over 60 to 70°, or possibly even more, and still righted herself. This may well be true under normal conditions, but taking into account the severity of the weather at the time, my view is that she would not have been able to right herself under these weather conditions, hit on the port side several times in succession by two or three very high and heavy seas.

I believe that the Gaul listed very heavily to starboard, and water could have entered the ship through any number of open hatches, including the offal chutes. However, I believe the main ingress of water would have been through the two large fish hatches leading to the factory deck that would have fallen open as the ship laid over to starboard. I had witnessed for myself how durable the model of the Gaul had been during tank tests and further tests had endorsed this.

Earlier on the day that we assume the Gaul was lost, she had been in touch with Wick radio with two messages sent at 1130 AM and earlier in the morning there had been VHF contact with other ships in the area. There is not the remotest chance that there was anything wrong with either of the Gaul's radios at this stage, yet the Gaul never managed to broadcast a mayday or any kind of distress message. This leads me to believe that whatever happened to the Gaul happened very quickly indeed.

There have been theories about water building up on the factory deck, resulting in the Gaul losing stability. These theories have been aired regularly, such as ideas about donkeys left running. I have always disputed these theories. It was standard practice for the men who worked on the filleting machines to turn the water off once the last few fish had been sent on their final journey to the skinning and packing benches. I also believe that as the filleting ships had more men working on their factory decks and as the processing of the fish took longer than on the ordinary block freezers, there is far less likelihood that water left running into the washing machine or to the spray jets on the filleting machine could have been overlooked, as by the time the processing had come to an end, these pieces of equipment would not have been in use for a considerable time.

It is believed that the Gaul ceased fishing in the early hours of the morning, yet I can not accept that from the time the last haul of fish was processed, nobody visited the factory deck for a period that has been proposed as being as long as ten or twelve hours. Factory hands, Baader mechanics and the ship's engineers would all have had reason to visit the factory deck regularly and the watch on the bridge would have expected the factory to be visited and checked regularly.

The damage to the port side funnel has been the subject of much speculation and this has been put down to pressure damage by some, although I believe, as there is no damage to the starboard funnel, that this is more in line with storm damage. Very close to the port funnel was the Gaul's workboat on its Schat davit, yet nothing of this workboat has been found, despite an extensive search over a wide area of sea bed. In addition, the port side bridge door was found on the bridge wing, while the starboard bridge door was found closed and undamaged. Many factors point to the Gaul having been struck very heavily on the port side, taking the full impact of one or more very heavy seas, while the starboard side appears to have suffered no apparent damage.

I have already described how I believe the Gaul came to have been lost and since my trip on the Seisranger when we found the offal chutes open and a hatch leading to the starboard quarter net store open, I see no reason to change my views as to how the Gaul came to be lost. In many ways, these findings have supported my view that the Gaul's loss can be attributed to bad luck - being in the wrong position in atrocious weather. But over the years I have been constantly surprised at the number of people who have ruled out or chosen to disregard the prime factor that brought about her loss - the weather. Many people have looked for other reasons and the long search for answers has explored many avenues but failed to come up with evidence to substantiate these numerous ideas, theories and accusations.

Once the wreck of the Gaul was located, many people jumped on the bandwagon and ideas abounded. This added a greater workload to the team on the Seisranger in July 2002, taking up valuable time during the survey that could have been more productively used elsewhere.

The Seisranger returned to Aberdeen in early August 2002 and after DNA testing it was confirmed in November 2002 that four sets of human remains had been identified, although with a lighter workload, this number could have been higher.

As the Seisranger steamed home from the three weeks we had spent on Cape Bank, there was time to take stock and assess what we had achieved during the survey - and to look forward to the formal inquiry that was expected to be held in Hull. There would undoubtedly be questions and answers, but I doubted that the answers would suit everyone.

Those That Got Away

Not all of the trawlers that were laid up in Hull and Grimsby ended up in the scrapyard. Many of the old side trawlers that remained eventually finished up as standby ships in the oil industry and for years provided a great service supporting the ever increasing number of oil and gas installations that appeared all over the North Sea.

Although there was no future for many of these fine ships here in Britain, a large number of British trawlers were sold to Spain, and ironically, have fished the waters around our own coasts for years, and still continue to do so.

While some of the more modern stern trawlers also moved into the offshore oil and gas industry as seismic survey vessels, others found lifelines as far away as Australia and New Zealand and others still have been seen in some of the world's remotest places.

One side trawler that escaped to take on a completely different role was Hamlings' St Giles. Renamed Sea Shepherd, she was engaged in a number of skirmishes in different parts of the world.

Across the river in Grimsby, Consolidated Fisheries' fine fleet of ships named after football teams made a number of short trips down the east coast to Lowestoft, as did a number of Ross Group's fleet of Cat boats, and gave years of service to the

Below: The Hull side trawler Arctic Corsair, seen here in some early spring sunshine and looking in tip-top condition, thanks to the many people who devoted so much time to restore and maintain the old trawler in such remarkable condition.
Now a museum and tied up in her home port of Hull, Arctic Corsair is a fitting tribute to the many fine trawlers that sailed form the city of Hull. Still looking like a working trawler, she attracts many visitors, interested to find out what life was like on board a trawler fishing in the Arctic.
It is almost hard to believe that she was built at Beverley in 1960, such has been the dedication of the many people who have fought to save her from being scrapped. As we enter a new millennium, we can hope that Hull's last side trawler is there for future generations to see the conditions that fishing crews worked under in some of the harshest and most remote places in the world.

oil industry while providing much needed employment both at sea and ashore.

It was always pleasant, at sea or ashore, to recognise a ship from the past, whether from Hull or from Grimsby, and on our arrival in the Falklands it came as no surprise to see that the two fishery patrol vessels turned out to be former Hull stern trawlers.

During the conflict with Argentina over the Falkland Islands, a number of stern trawlers were taken over by the Royal Navy. One of these, the Pict, was later sold to Spanish interests and was fishing very well in those unfamiliar waters.

Wherever these fine trawlers were sold, either to the northern or southern hemisphere, they went on to provide years of service for their new owners. Thirty years after the loss of the Gaul, the three sister ships are still in service and two of them are fishing in the North Atlantic. This speaks volumes about these fine ships, in spite of the bad publicity they received from some of the people who gave evidence at the reopened public enquiry in 2004 into the Gaul's loss.

While many of these former British fishing vessels have taken up new roles around the world, three of them have found very different parts to play. In Hull, Boyd Line's Arctic Corsair, now moored in the river Hull, has become a museum, while across the river the Ross Tiger does the same in Grimsby. In Fleetwood the stern trawler Jacinta has become a museum as well and all three ships attract thousands of visitors every year.

Seen here in the placid waters of Grimsby docks, the Ross Tiger, now open to the public as a museum, is a sad reminder of the once great fleet of Grimsby trawlers that fished all over the North Atlantic with great success.

The Freezers

In 1961 the Lord Nelson became the first freezer stern trawler to join the Hull fleet. Built in Germany, she was designed to freeze part of her catch, and land the latter part of her voyage fresh for sale on the market.

Although the Lord Nelson was a top earning ship, all the newly built stern trawlers that followed her into service both in Hull and Grimsby were designed to freeze the entire catch at sea.

The arrival of the Junella in 1962 opened the floodgates, and shortly after most large fishing companies placed orders with shipbuilders both at home and abroad as the trend towards stern trawling and freezing whole catches at sea signalled the start of a new era in deep sea fishing in both Humber ports.

Across the Humber in Grimsby the Ross Valiant, followed by the Conqueror and the Victory soon began to make their mark. Crews joining these new stern trawlers had to adapt to an entirely new way of life. Gone were the normal trips of three weeks' duration, as the freezers had to spend weeks and months on the fishing grounds in order to return home with a profitable trip.

The freezer fleet grew in size and trips to places like Newfoundland, Labrador and into the Gulf of Saint Lawrence became quite common, as the British freezer fleet joined the large and modern fleet of foreign trawlers already working these westerly grounds.

In the past a number of side trawlers had fished these banks, but the long steaming time across the Atlantic reduced fishing time and the quality of fish from these waters never matched the market price for the fish caught by ships working at Iceland and Bear Island.

Working and living conditions on these types of vessels soon made them favourites with the crews who soon adapted to the extra time that they spent at sea.

Hauling and shooting the trawl was done in far less time than on the old side trawlers, and offered more protection to the men working on the deck. Once the fish was hauled on board and tipped into the factory, the catch

Above: The Lord Nelson, the first ship of this kind when she joined the Hull fleet.
Photo: Hull Maritime Museum, Malcolm Fussey Collection

Below: J Marr's Junella looking very smart in Hull's Albert Dock.

Bottom: Hellyer Brothers' trawler Othello sustained severe damage when fire broke out on board while fishing off the Norwegian coast. Fortunately there was no loss of life and Othello returned to fishing after being refitted.

was then processed below decks. This was a far cry from the days when men had stood gutting on the open deck, often in rain, snow or frost, for days on end in some of the most inhospitable places in the world.

Apart from the deck, these ships offered more in the way of comfort for the crews. Better accommodation and leisure facilities were introduced as the freezers began to fish ever further away from their normal hunting grounds.

All appeared to be going well as the freezer fleet grew in size, and each new arrival offered more in the way of comfort and also safety. However, a fire on board Hamlings' St Finbarr during a trip to Newfoundland and Labrador resulted in loss of twelve of her crew.

News of the tragedy filtered through to Hull over Christmas, and once again brought home the dangers that can arise anywhere, and at any time, even in the finest of ships.

Despite efforts to tow the St Finbarr, she eventually sank, and the remaining survivors were picked up by another Hull freezer, the Orsino, which in later years also suffered a fire in accommodation spaces, resulting in the loss of a crew member and extensive damage.

Across the river in Grimsby, it was a fire on board that brought about the end of one of the port's most famous freezers, the Victory, a top earning ship. A fire in the engine room during a trip to the Barents Sea left the Victory dis-

Top: Hamling's trawler St. Finbarr suffered a fire on board that resulted in the deaths of twelve of her crew during a winter trip to Newfoundland. Efforts were made to tow the ship, but she sank on the way, with the crew taken off by the Orsino.

By 1966 all the major fishing companies had invested in stern trawling, and in 1967 the Coriolanus became the first Hull vessel that filleted and froze its catch at sea.

J Marr's Farnella was one of those fishing on Cape Bank on the day the Gaul was lost in February 1974.

Bottom: Hammond Innes, one of the most successful trawlers to fish from Hull.
All photos: Hull Maritime Museum, Malcolm Fussey Collection

abled, and she was eventually towed and beached on the Russian coast, where she remains. A sad end to a fine ship with such a famous name.

Although most of the freezers were comparatively newly built ships, the risk of fire on board gave some cause for alarm, and in 1978 on a trip to Bear Island, a fire on board the Grimsby freezer Roman resulted in three of her crew losing their lives and the vessel needing extensive repair on her return home.

The freezers were built in a number of different yards in different countries, but the problem of fire remained very much in evidence in these types of ships. A fire in 1972 on the Ranger Ajax, while on a trip to Greenland, resulted in the total loss of the vessel, fortunately without any loss of life, but it did not end there.

The following year the Norwegian built Seafridge Osprey had to be towed back to Hull to undergo repairs as a result of a fire that broke out in the vessel's accommodation. There had also been a number of lesser incidents where fire had broken out during the short period of time that these freezer trawlers operated out from Hull and Grimsby.

Unfortunately, we were never to see the full potential of these fine ships. Some of them were only recently new from their builders, yet they faced a very uncertain future. Politics once again played a major role in deciding the fate of these fine ships and the men who sailed in them.

These ships were landing the bulk of the fish that was at the time coming into the Humber ports, but time was fast running out for the modern fleet of freezers.

The westerly grounds across at Newfoundland and Labrador had for years been grossly overfished by vessels of all nations that, like our own fleet, spent months at a time on the fishing grounds and never gave the stocks of cod on the grounds a chance to recover. Consequently, these once prolific fishing grounds were lost, and a number of newly built freezer trawlers from Humberside found themselves facing a very uncertain future. Eventually there was to be no reprieve for any of them.

Top: Ross Valiant was one of the freezer trawlers that quickly made a mark with the Grimsby fleet when this class of ships was introduced.

Kirkella, another of J Marr's trawlers.

Bottom: St. Andrew's Dock in the 1970s, with a row of fine factory trawlers alongside.

All photos: Hull Maritime Museum, Malcolm Fussey Collection

Saving the Biggest Ones

An incident that rebounded somewhat occurred when I was the skipper of the Ranger Aurora, fishing at the time at Newfoundland, and not with a great deal of success. It seemed that the long trek across the Atlantic was going to have been a waste of time as we tried the area around Flemish Cap for only a few baskets of fish and then moved to the northeast corner of the Grand Banks, where we fared no better.

Some serious thinking was needed. There were only a few Hull ships in the area and after a talk with the skippers of the Coriolanus and the Cassio over the VHF, it was decided that we could venture further west into the Gulf of St. Lawrence, using the southerly route as there was still a lot of ice to the north of the Grand Banks.

To say that things looked bleak was certainly an understatement and I remember thinking that this was going to be the trip to end all trips for no other reason than we were fed up with steaming.

We came across some clear water off Cape Breton Island and we all decided to shoot there after picking up some marks on the sounder. Although this was nothing to get excited about, we all hauled ninety to a hundred baskets of reasonable sized cod. This was no great deal for the distance that we had travelled, it was still time to get down to some serious fishing with the hope that things would get better.

Through the next day things remained the same, with not a lot of ice to bother us. We managed a reasonable day's fishing, and as long as things got no worse, there seemed little point in leaving the area just yet.

The following day we were hauling just after midday when a small Canadian trawler came up close to our stern just as we were heaving a bag of fish up the ramp. But after taking a close look at what had been our best haul to date, he simply carried on steaming to the north-east, followed by two other small trawlers.

I thought this was a bit strange and checked to see where their course would take them. I talked it over with the skipper of the Cassio and between use we decided that it might be worth moving on after dark when the fishing started to slack off a bit, and this is just what we did.

Not encountering much ice on our overnight steam, we found ourselves the next morning in the Bay of Islands, and soon picked up about six trawlers fishing in the area. Yet after our first haul we only heaved on board a paltry thirty baskets of fish and I could see the looks of utter amazement on the faces of the crew, who I am sure thought I had gone off my head to steam overnight to thirty baskets from an area where we had been hauling a steady hundred baskets for each haul. After so much slack fishing, there was good reason to think this way, but all was not lost.

Shooting away again on shallower ground, it was obvious that we had been too deep on our first haul. As the indications on the sounder got better by the minute, it came as no surprise when we each hauled a good three hundred baskets each at the end of a tow of only two hours.

The fishing improved throughout the day and by nightfall there was enough in the factory to lay for the night and resume fishing at daybreak. With still a fair amount of ice in the area, this was ideal.

By now we had been away more than three weeks, with very little in the way of fish on board, and at last I had the chance to report to the office in North Shields that we had found some good fishing in the Bay of Islands. This good fishing was extremely welcome after travelling such a long distance and with slack fishing early in the trip. So the pressure was off slightly and I was surprised when coming up from a visit to the factory on our second day in the area when the Sparks read out a telegram to me from the office. This stated that we should understand that the fish we were catching in the area could contain worms, and was I aware of this?

I could hardly believe my ears and when

Sparks asked if there was a reply, I jokingly said: "Tell them that we are only saving and filleting the biggest and best worms."

I thought no more of it, until I went down to dinner, when Sparks mentioned that he had got the telegram away. To which I asked: "Which telegram?" Then I realised that he had sent the words I had intended as a joke, but which would be taken as a sarcastic remark at the offices in North Shields. But it had gone, with little that could be done about it.

Sat on the bridge thinking about this afterwards, certainly I had been aware that there could be some worms in the fish, but surely someone at the office must have seen our previous reports and realised just what a slack period of fishing we had been going through. The ice conditions had not helped at all and we were into our fourth week at sea, still with a lot of fish to catch. I was hardly going to leave the best fishing we had found so far or lose much sleep over a few bloody worms. There was no reply to the message to the office and I - wrongly, as it turned out - though that was the end of the matter.

The spell of good fishing held for the best part of two weeks and to get the most from it, we eventually called at St. John's in Newfoundland, very low on fuel, to take on bunkers, food and stores to see us through to the end of the trip.

With another round of good fishing, this time in the Wolfall area, followed by a steady spell on Flemish Cap, we eventually left for home with a full ship.

At the meeting of the various heads of departments that was always held when a ship arrived back, there was no mention of the telegram regarding the possibility of worms in the fish.

It was not until we returned to North Shields, a day before sailing, at the pre-sailing meeting to discuss where to spend the next trip, that I was informed that my reply to the office's telegram had been rather unusual.

I was momentarily lost for words and stumbled through a number of good reasons why if things had not improved, we would certainly have had to consider the possibility of saving the biggest and best worms. This raised a laugh and a nod of approval, showing that there is some humour to be found in trawler company offices.

Homeward Bound

Our journey from the equator to the Canary Islands was absolute bliss, flat calm, warm weather, and everyone made the most of it, with only light routine duties to be carried out during the day. It was a very relaxing time for everyone on board, as the younger crew members in particular became more and more excited as we neared the Canary Islands.

During one afternoon we passed through a large fleet of mostly Russian and Spanish trawlers fishing off the African coast. This vast fleet of mainly large factory trawlers stretched as far as the eye could see, but more important to us was that we had picked up the welcome sight of the Canary Islands on the radar.

It had been a remarkable journey home. We had not one poor day since leaving Port Stanley, and within three days of arriving in Spain we were still enjoying every minute of perfect weather.

Arriving on watch at 2000, we were passing through the Canary Islands with most of the crew either on deck or paying me a visit on the bridge. I was not short of company for the first two hours of the watch, but as the lights of Canaries dropped steadily astern, everyone gradually left the bridge to carry on either playing cards or dominoes to pass the time away.

The job of deciding who would stay with the ship and who would go home was made easier when a number of the older crew members volunteered to stay with the ship in Cadiz to allow some of the younger ones to return home on the bus that would be provided on our arrival. It had been decided that thirteen of us, myself included, would remain with the Fishing Explorer in Cadiz.

During the late evening watch, and forty-eight hours after passing the Canaries, we could make out the lights of Cadiz, and reduced speed as we would not be docking until the following morning at 0900. It was a clear, warm night as we slowly closed the land and more and more lights became visible along the coast.

At 0430 we stopped engines just outside Cadiz and waited for our docking pilot to arrive. It was a pleasant feeling.

All those who would be leaving us were ready with their gear packed, waiting for the arrival of the bus to take them home. Most of them had brought their suitcases on deck as we laid close to the entrance of Cadiz waiting for the launch to arrive with the harbour pilot.

I was not familiar with this part of Spain, but was assured on numerous occasions that I would find Cadiz a very interesting place during my stay.

At 0930 our pilot duly arrived on board, and on a fine Saturday morning late in October we berthed in Cadiz at 1000. As usual, the welcoming committee of customs officials, police and docking officials all descended on the ship at the same time, each waving some document or other that required my signature most urgently. It seemed that docking on a Saturday morning had not been written into the script, and we had spoiled everyone's weekend.

My Spanish was by now good enough for me to explain how long we had been at sea, and that had I known, I would have stayed out another two days: knowing how difficult it is working ashore and having to trudge home every night, and how I should have known better. My remark did at least break the ice and was taken in the spirit in which it was intended, raising a laugh and an enquiry as to where I had learned to speak Spanish.

Eventually, with all the paperwork behind us, everyone departed, but not before wishing us well during our stay in Cadiz, and assuring us that if we required anything, we had only to contact their various offices for everything to be taken care of.

My young colleague from Plymouth was on his way to Malaga to join a flight for London, while the crew members who were now preparing to leave us were gathering around the bus, and I felt that it was only fitting that I should spend a few minutes with them before they departed.

Shaking hands with the men who were leaving us was a moment I will never forget, happy to see them going, but a little sad that we were not all going together, and I am sure that they all felt the same way. They had been a first-class crew, and when one of them boarding the bus told me that he could now swear in perfect English, I told him I didn't know who could have taught him to use language like that, and there were laughs all round.

My last few moments were spent with Oscar the bosun, on whom so much had depended during the trip. I could only thank him and hope that I would see him again when we arrived with the ship back in La Coruña.

With the bus on its way, back on the Fishing Explorer, the ship seemed deserted with only thirteen of us remaining on board.

Money was available to those who required it, and fresh bread would be delivered to the vessel every morning. We had already taken on some fresh food, and things looked quite easy for those who stayed with the ship.

There would always be someone on board, but each night a different watch keeper would take over, so nobody would do more than one night on watch unless they chose to do so.

To make things easier for the cook who had remained behind with us, everyone arranged to have a meal ashore on our first night in Cadiz, while in the meantime, most of those who stayed behind were busy ringing home from a nearby call box.

The mate and I decided to have a meal ashore, but after being up all night prior to docking, it seemed a good idea to catch up on a few hours' sleep.

Waking up a few hours later, there was an eerie silence for the first time in months. It was a strange feeling indeed that there was no sound of engines running.

Most of the crew were on board, and after coffee, the mate, who was familiar with Cadiz after his years in the Spanish merchant navy, told me of a nice little restaurant where we would both go for a good meal and show me some of the night life of Cadiz.

I explained to those staying with the ship that we would not start discharging the fish until Monday morning, so we had at least a relaxing weekend to make the most of.

Taking a leisurely walk ashore off the dock on a lovely warm night was a welcome treat, and arriving at the restaurant that the mate had suggested, we were warmly greeted by the owner, his family and staff, and sat down to a lovely meal and excellent wine in beautiful surroundings - a perfect start to our first night ashore in Cadiz.

Cadiz

Our first night ashore in Cadiz was one of the best nights that anyone could have wished for after a long trip to sea. To sit and unwind, with no thought of fishing was the ideal way to relax.

I don't know why, but people seem to recognise seamen who have been away for some time, and a number of people came across and spoke to us, telling us how much they appreciated these freezer trawlers landing their catches in Cadiz for the amount of work that they provided for so many people.

After an excellent meal we had a stroll and a drink or two in a number of different bars, eventually meeting some of the crew and finishing up in a small bar in the early hours of Sunday morning before returning to the Fishing Explorer. Later that day I managed to buy some English newspapers, and spent the remainder of the day catching up on all the latest news.

On the Monday morning our hatches were removed and we started landing our fish into the factory and cold stores close to where we were tied up. Inside the factory all the work was done by young women, who repackaged all our fish into new cartons before it was again returned to the deep freeze part of the factory.

For the crew of the Fishing Explorer, there was very little to do, just light duties keeping the ship clean and a stroll for the papers, but most of us chose to have a walk ashore in the evening and a drink in one of the small bars that we had adopted as our local.

The amount of fish landed on the first day was 200 tonnes, and it seemed that we would not be leaving Cadiz until Saturday at the earliest. It seemed as if 200 tonnes a day was the maximum the factory could handle, as by Wednesday we had put ashore a little over 600 tonnes of fish.

Aboard the ship, things went on with little change in the routine, and little to do during the day and a visit to our local for a beer before returning to the ship in the early hours.

I had enjoyed the days in Cadiz, but return-ing to the Fishing Explorer on Friday, I was a little disappointed when work was finished for the day, leaving a small amount of fish to be landed. I was assured that this would all be finished by midday on Saturday.

It had been an enjoyable stay. The autumn weather had been perfect, and our nights ashore had been very enjoyable. Little wonder that our last night ashore was tinged with a lit-tle sadness as we spent most of it in the bar where we had been made most welcome dur-ing our stay.

Even some of the people who worked in the fish factory enjoyed a drink with us on the Friday night, and through until the early hours of Saturday morning, and although I had enjoyed every minute of our week in Cadiz, I was now ready to be moving on and heading north to La Coruña.

We had already taken on water, and as promised all the fish and the landing equip-ment had been removed from the Fishing Explorer by midday. We were ready to leave Cadiz and complete the last leg of our journey.

After the midday meal the gangway was taken on board and slowly we made our way out of Cadiz. Clearing the harbour, we headed towards Cape Saint Vincent. The weather forecast was quite good, and it appeared that it would remain fine until we expected to arrive in La Coruña sometime on the Monday after-noon.

On board the Fishing Explorer those who had stayed behind were now eager to get home, myself included. Through the night we passed a number of ships, and this made something of a change, and throughout Sunday we were constantly passing a ship of some description as we continued northwards.

The night passed without incident, and dur-ing the following morning watch we rounded Cape Finisterre, and it was almost over. At 1530 on a rather overcast Monday afternoon, the harbour tug edged us gently alongside in La Coruña, where a large crowd of people were eagerly awaiting our arrival.

All the crew who had left us in Cadiz were

there to greet us and collect the blocks of fish that they were allowed to take home to their families and friends. It was great to see them all again looking well and none the worse after our trip.

Once again it was time to say farewell to those of the crew who had volunteered to stay behind in Cadiz, and within an hour of tying up in La Coruña I was alone on the Fishing Explorer, apart from the small number of people attending to items on deck or in the engine room.

All the crew had left for their homes, and half an hour later I was taken by taxi to the hotel where I stayed until my flight home could be arranged.

After a meal in the hotel and a walk around La Coruña, followed by the first night's sleep in a bed for months, all my hopes of being back in England for the weekend were dashed, when after visiting the office I was told that it was proving extremely difficult to get me a flight to London.

I wanted for nothing during my stay in the hotel, and after cursing bad luck, I was eventually booked on a flight on the Sunday morning after five days in La Coruña.

It was good to be going home, and after the short flight to Gatwick, it was a great feeling to be back once again in England and back in Plymouth where it had all started.

Nothing had changed much and after a meal and a few drinks with friends down at the Barbican that went on a little longer than I had anticipated, I was eventually able to retire to my hotel. The next morning I was up to face the press who wanted to know about our trip to the Falklands, and the inevitable question of whether or not there was a future for British trawlers to fish in the South Atlantic?

It would have been nice to have been able to say: yes, there could be something of a future for British fishing in those waters. But in all honesty I had to admit that I felt the chance had already been missed. We were years too late and other countries had benefited while we hesitated. Britain's chance had been lost while other countries had been able to send fishing vessels there to a highly profitable fishery.

Poland, Spain, Russia, Korea and certainly Taiwan had made the most of these fishing grounds and were well established in those waters, leaving us to reflect on what could have been and that we had maybe been too hasty in selling off our own freezer fleet.

For myself, I had certainly enjoyed the experience throughout. It had been very different and I had no regrets about taking on the job. Having crossed the equator twice, I felt myself to be no better or worse a sailor, although I felt more at ease with myself.

Nothing had pleased me more during the trip than the way the crew had faced up to a month of inactivity in Montevideo at a crucial time in the trip. The work that had to be done on our winch motor was one of those things and nobody's fault.

Although we had encountered a few stoppages during the trip, the Fishing Explorer had certainly been up to the job of handling the weather we encountered during fishing in the Falklands at the height of winter.

I remained in Plymouth for ten days before travelling home to Hull and had already had discussions about returning with the Fishing Explorer to the Falklands. This I duly did, but not before taking the well-deserved holiday in the Canaries that I had promised myself when we had called there to take on fuel for the long voyage south.

Regrets

During the first week of the Ranger Castor's first trip, we were with a group of ships in the Cape Bank area. The fishing had been reasonable, and as it was still early days, this was giving me a chance to get adjusted to the new ship. But towards the end of the second week, a message from our agent in Honningsvåg asked for one of my crew to be flown home, as his father was dangerously ill and not expected to live long.

We hauled immediately and set course for Honningsvåg at full speed, arriving with minutes to spare. The man was put on the mail boat to Tromsø to catch a flight home. With the crewman on his way, I enquired about some spare parts, including spare blades for one of our filleting machines, but was told that they would not arrive until the following morning. There seemed little point in steaming to Cape Bank, so I decided to have a few hauls in the area of North Cape itself, to tow along the limit line and return to Honningsvåg in the morning for our spares, which would then leave us free to go where we wanted.

However, the best of plans do not always work out that way. Our tow close to the line was nothing special and the next one was no better, so as dusk approached, we again shot away the gear. We were still close to the line, but this time on Helsnes Bank. It may have been due to the time of the day, but things were very different this time. There were some very heavy marks of fish on the sounder and not another ship in sight, so things looked very promising indeed.

When we hauled after the evening meal, we had an exceptionally large haul of fish on the deck. Although the majority of it was coley, this was still a welcome sight in a new ship with a big fishroom to fill. After this first tow, the following three tows during the night were all very large hauls of mostly coley.

At daybreak, with the factory deck so full that it would not have been possible to get another fish on board, we made our way back into Honningsvåg. It had been a very good night's fishing and I make no excuses for not reporting it, but worse was to follow. In Honningsvåg I was told that the spares had arrived in three very large boxes. It would be easier if we were to tie up alongside the oil jetty so that the spares and a number of items for other ships could be brought round to us, as these would be difficult to handle from the deck of the pilot cutter onto our deck.

Once alongside I ventured aft for my breakfast, although it was getting late in the morning. Then, with all the crew at work in the factory, I returned to the bridge to find one of our sister ships almost within arms' reach, with the crew on deck looking for someone on board the Ranger Castor to take their ropes.

Tied up alongside with the fish hatches open, it was easy to see the amount of fish still waiting to be processed, and once alongside of us, some of their crew jumped aboard to talk to their friends. Word soon got around about our heavy night's fishing.

To put it mildly, I had been caught with my trousers down and I could offer no excuses for my actions - nor did I try to do so. My foolish actions had cost me a good friend, for the skipper of our sister ship and I did not speak again for many years. This was something that I regretted to the point where I never again failed to report good fishing.

It was after I had been retired for some years that I had to attend to some business in Hessle and went into a pub on a summer's day. With it being quite early in the day, the only other customer in the pub was my old friend.

We spoke for the first time in many years and the ice was broken as I bought him a drink. It had taken a long time, which had not been worth the loss of friendship, and I finally had the chance to apologise.

We had a great deal to talk about, and as one drink led to another, we spoke about how events had taken us both to fishing from Spain and how our lives had changed. Quite a bit later in the afternoon, with both of us a little unsteady on our feet, we shook hands before leaving the pub, but not before he was able to tell me jokingly that I should never try to pull a trick like that again. Not that there was likely to be a chance of that happening.

Many Questions, and Some Answers

The second inquiry into the loss of the Gaul opened in Hull on the 13th of January 2004, almost thirty years to the day after she had sailed from her home port for the last time. This was announced to those attending the inquiry, and it seemed appropriate that a minute's silence was observed for those who lost their lives on the Gaul on the 8th of February 1974.

With George Petty due to be called as the first witness, we had arranged to meet beforehand and duly arrived together at Europa House shortly before proceedings were due to begin. This gave us a chance to meet again some of the people who had sailed with us on the Seisranger survey in 2002. Much of the information gained during that survey, including the fact that remains of four members of the Gaul's crew had been retrieved, were to be made public for the first time at the inquiry.

Once the introductions were over, the proceedings were underway and George Petty was called to the witness box, a little later than scheduled. Throughout his evidence, which took up part of that first morning and part of the afternoon, followed by a second round of questioning the next morning that was brought to a close by a power failure, he performed with flying colours. During that second morning's questioning, he was asked to explain why he had been put ashore at Lodingen in Norway after sustaining an injury while the Gaul was steaming along the Norwegian coast to the fishing grounds. He was asked to explain in detail working procedures both on the trawl deck and the factory deck, including explaining at great length the workings of the offal chutes. He was asked what method he would use to slip a cable from the trawl doors if he had been unlucky enough to pick on up, and this seemed to indicate that there were still people who believed that the Gaul had been fishing and had come to grief after catching her gear on a submarine cable.

In all, George spent two long sessions in the witness box and must have breathed a sigh of relief as the questioning came to an end. At seventy-five years of age and with fifty years of experience at sea, George was being expected to recall things that had happened thirty years before.

My own turn in the witness box came on the 15th of January at the start of the afternoon session. As George Petty had done, I immediately chose to give evidence under oath, giving my name and stating my age as seventy-two.

It was not long before the inevitable questions relating to the Gaul's supposed spying and intelligence gathering activities were brought up, as there had been many years of speculation about this over the intervening thirty years. Being well used to this, I could only answer as I had done in the past, that although I had been aware that some ships sailing from Hull had assisted in these activities, the Gaul had certainly not been one of them.

I was asked if I remembered being buzzed by a Soviet aircraft during the last twenty-four hours of the Gaul's last trip in December 1973 when we were fishing close to the Soviet limit line in an area where we had been fishing very well on plaice.

As I had already given this information during the first inquiry into the Gaul's loss thirty years before, I could only agree that I did remember the incident, which was nothing out of the ordinary, and was quick to point out that we had not been fishing inside the Soviet 12 mile limit. With close to two hundred and fifty tonnes of what was mostly fillets on board, it would have been foolhardy in the extreme to jeopardise the catch by poaching inside the limit on the last few days of a trip.

I was also asked to give an account of the time that I had spent showing Peter Nellist around the Gaul, which had taken roughly an hour and half a few days before the Gaul sailed from Hull in January 1974. We had spoken on the bridge for some time, mostly about fishing, before going to the factory deck to complete the tour of the ship. Peter Nellist made some notes in a small notebook during our conversation and when he dropped me off at the dock that day, we said our goodbyes and I never saw Peter Nellist again after that day.

The inquiry also questioned me about water on the factory deck. I made my comments to the effect that there has to be water on a trawler's factory deck as the fish has to be washed, but with a crew as experienced as the Gaul's, there should be no reason why any buildup of water should occur while they were at work in the factory.

I also had to account for my reasons for not being on board during that final trip, and as I have already made plain, there was nothing sinister about my expecting a trip ashore after spending so much time at sea. I had spent almost a year on board the ship as the Ranger Castor before she was renamed the Gaul and felt by that time that I had earned a trip off, especially as the last trip I had completed shortly before Christmas had been a difficult one with long periods of bad weather. I had felt quite justified in taking a trip off after a year with only the normal time in dock between trips at home.

I was questioned as to whether or not I thought it unfortunate that the Gaul's three senior officers were all making their first trips in the Gaul. Skipper Peter Nellist, mate Maurice Spurgeon and chief engineer John O'Brien were all new to the vessel, although it was pointed out that John O'Brien had previously served as the Gaul's second engineer. But I could only agree that these were unusual circumstances, only brought about as George Petty had unfortunately been taken ill and had to be put ashore on the way to the fishing grounds.

My questioning took up much of that afternoon's session, but after a few more questions, I was allowed to stand down. The following morning, Mr. D Oswald, who had been in charge of the British United Trawlers' fleet of freezers was in the witness box and was soon explaining the workings of the company system for the freezer trawlers to report in to the office during their time on the fishing grounds. He explained the reasons for the delay in reporting to the authorities that the Gaul had failed to report, failing to respond to calls from other ships in the Cape Bank area. Mr. Oswald occupied the witness box for most of the day, eventually standing down for his place to be taken by Stanley Waterman, a well-known and much respected radio officer who had spent many years on trawlers. He gave a very good description of his duties and the role played by a radio officer on a ship such as the Gaul.

I had known Stanley Waterman from boyhood. Like many lads brought up in the Hessle Road area, he had decided early to go to sea and took the decision early to train as a radio officer and spent time in some of Hull's top-earning fishing vessels. When fishing had become all but finished in Hull, he later served as radio officer in some of the fishery patrol vessels operating in Falkland Island waters. With his many years of experience, he was able to answer questions put to him clearly and precisely, and was duly thanked for his contribution to the inquiry.

The bombshells that came from the next witness, Malcolm Scott, were something that I was not quite prepared for. Early in his evidence, Mr. Scott was quick to point out that he was a marine surveyor, not a seaman. He had been based in Hull at the time of the Gaul's loss. It soon became clear that Mr. Scott had a very poor opinion of anything connected to the fishing industry and to those attending the hearing, it would have been easy to come to the opinion that Mr. Scott had an axe to grind towards the new owners of the Gaul and her sister ships.

The inquiry heard repeated reports of poor maintenance on these C Class trawlers and I was left wondering if British United Trawlers had purchased these practically new trawlers simply for their scrap value, such was the poor picture of their conditions that was painted for the inquiry.

After telling the inquiry that he had inspected the Gaul's three sister ships, now renamed Kelt, Kurd and Arab, and finding them in a generally poor condition, Mr. Scott said that he assumed the Gaul to have been in a similar condition. This was something I found hard to accept. There had been two years between the launch of the Ranger Cadmus, first of the quartet, and the delivery of the Ranger Castor. Mr. Scott remarked that he had visited the Kurd in dock between trips and found her in a very untidy state, with nets, bobbins, spare parts and tins strewn across the deck. Try as I might, I find it hard to imagine what Mr. Scott expected to find on the deck of a stern trawler being prepared for a winter trip north of the Arctic Circle.

The tins would certainly have been the heavy grease that was in widespread use on trawlers to lubricate the running gear on deck and what Mr. Scott found on the Kurd's deck would have been a perfectly normal state of affairs, with a large amount of gear in the process of being stowed away while shore crews would have been at work in many parts of the ship.

But the Gaul's maintenance problems remained a subject to which the inquiry returned several times. A statement made by a former engineer on the Gaul in 1974 suggested that the ship had been plagued with engine trouble and losing large amounts of lube oil. Yet there were no papers or receipts available to show where any repairs had been carried out - simply because the only Norwegian port visited by the Ranger Castor had been Honningsvaag, for the sole purpose of taking on bunkers. Prior to that we had called at St. John's in Newfoundland for some repairs to the fish meal plant. This had been done because we were in the early stages of a trip and not having the meal plant running would have meant a significant loss of income for the ship and its crew. If this had happened later in the trip, I doubt that I would have sacrificed fishing time for these relatively minor repairs.

These were the only occasions when the ship had been taken into foreign ports and the Gaul had never lost fishing time through any breakdowns.

Another marine surveyor, Captain Newbury, was next in the witness box and he added a touch of humour by commenting that a hammer is as good a way as any of freeing a rusted up door. Yet a remark that he made to the effect that the men who worked the Gaul's factory deck could hardly be classed as seamen raised a few eyebrows among the fisher-

men in the room. My own feelings were that the two marine surveyors were more than a little out of touch with how a stern trawler operates and the everyday work and maintenance that is carried out at sea. To my mind, the suggestion that the factory hands were not seamen could not be further from the truth, as many of the factory crew had spent years as deckhands fishing in some of the most remote and least hospitable places possible. As these men grew older, the arrival of freezer trawlers had offered them the opportunity of less physically demanding work on the factory deck, while their places were taken on deck by younger men who were keen to gain some experience.

The evidence of the two marine surveyors was followed by Dick Sabberton, who had been deputy marine superintendent at British United Trawlers. He explained how repairs were dealt with in the fishing industry, with work contracted out to certain companies around St. Andrew's Dock. Evidence given by Ron Dry, who had been foreman shipwright with many years' service with both Hellyer Brothers and British United Trawlers, also contrasted with the reports that the marine surveyors had given.

I had known both Ron Dry and Dick Sabberton very well, having spent many years myself with Hellyer Brothers. I knew from personal experience that both men ran their departments with exceptional efficiency and their having been taken aback by the reports of the poor condition of the trawlers came as no surprise to me.

On the fourth day, I received a surprise when skipper Laurence Wileman gave his evidence, claiming that he had been offered the post as skipper of the Gaul, but had turned this down because a former mate on the vessel had told him that the Gaul was always breaking down, telling him that the ship was a handcart.

Before the inquiry's proceedings were brought to a close for the weekend, Philip McCarthy, who had been mate of the Grimsby trawler Victory on Cape Bank in February 1974, told the inquiry that in a conversation with Maurice Spurgeon over the VHF as the weather worsened, he had made the remark that the Gaul was a 'f***ing cow and a half to steer in hand.'

From this we can assume that the Gaul had been steering by hand for some reason. This could have been due to a problem with the autopilot that had been reported faulty, or on account of the worsening weather the decision had been made to switch to hand steering simply to ease the load on the autopilot in the increasingly difficult conditions.

I find it hard to believe that there could have been a fault with the autopilot after the ship left Hull, simply because we must remember that the Gaul had entered Westfjord to put George Petty ashore at Lodingen and then proceeded through the narrowest part of the fjords to pick up Maurice Spurgeon at Tromsø. It is hardly likely that the Norwegian pilots would have consented to take the ship through the fjords if there had been the least trouble with the steering.

The second week of the inquiry opened with an audio link. An officer with a rank equivalent to a first secretary in HM Diplomatic Service was to give evidence, but nobody in the room had any idea where the evidence was being given from.

Once contact had been established, the man from the Secret Intelligence Service, or SIS, as MI6 is officially known, stated that there was nothing in official records to suggest that the Gaul or the Ranger Castor, to use her former name, had used for any purpose other than fishing. In addition, he confirmed that neither Peter Nellist nor Maurice Spurgeon, nor any of the Gaul's crew, had been engaged in any intelligence tasks on behalf of SIS.

However, it was mentioned that Peter Nellist had been mate of the stern trawler Cassio some years previously when she had been sent to a fisheries exhibition in Leningrad in the old Soviet Union.

Once the mystery man had finished his evidence, it was the turn of Royal Navy Commander Adam Peters. From him the inquiry heard that two Hull trawlers, the Invincible and the Lord Nelson, had been used in an unsuccessful attempt to locate and recover a stray Soviet missile, although skipper Roy Waller of the Invincible later told the inquiry that he had been under the impression at the time that they were trying to recover a camera that had been towed astern of an American submarine. The question was put to Commander Peters whether or not after the failure of these two trawlers to recover the missile, the Gaul had been used for the same task. But he pointed out that the two trawlers had been specifically chartered for this operation by the Ministry of Defence, and after they had failed to locate it, no further attempts were made.

Two more Hull skippers gave evidence. The first was Roy Waller of the Invincible, who described how he had been asked by the trawler's owner Graham Hellyer to carry a Royal Naval Commander on a trip in the Invincible to try to recover what he believed at the time to be a camera. In this trip he went to an area known to fishermen as the Duck's Back, some fifty miles off the Russian coast, but after five days in the area, he had been forced to move elsewhere as the weather deteriorated. Roy Waller said in his evidence that although he believed he was searching for a camera, it was not until much later that he learned he had been searching for a lost Soviet missile.

He was followed into the witness box by Ken Madden, who had been skipper of the Gaul's sister ship Kelt. I had known both Roy Waller and Ken Madden for many years, in fact since we had all been teenagers serving as deckhands.

In his evidence, Ken Madden stated how on the 7th of February 1974, he had passed very close to the Gaul, just a day before it has been assumed the Gaul was lost. At 1800 on that day he held a VHF conversation with Peter Nellist, in which he said that his intentions were to try deeper waters to the north where he thought there might be better fishing.

Ken Madden also went on to refute the opinion given by marine surveyor Malcolm Scott that the Kelt's standard of maintenance had been poor. He told the inquiry that he had never heard such a load of cock and bull, but he stated that the Kelt's lube oil pipes were susceptible to fracture about three times a year. He would stop engines to carry out repairs at sea, but stated that at no time had the Kelt's engine stopped without warning and commented that the Kelt had been a well-found, efficient and well maintained trawler.

It was during one of the breaks that gave many of those attending the opportunity to step outside for a quick smoke that I was told it would be likely that I would be recalled to give further evidence. I readily agreed, but hardly expected this to happen that same day.

On Wednesday 28th of January, I was recalled for the afternoon session and the questions were about the supposed regular breakdowns that the Gaul suffered. Throughout the first eleven days of the inquiry, we had listened to so much criticism of the state of repair of the four C class trawlers, that I commented that it seemed British United Trawlers had bought the four practically new ships for their scrap value, which did at least raise a few eyebrows.

I again made my points, refuting the suggestion that the Gaul had needed repair s abroad, as my only calls to port were to take on bunkers and to have the fish meal plant repaired on one occasion. At times, the questions and answers became a little heated. These allegations of breakdowns came from a diary and scribbled notes, not from the ship's requisition log books. While bills had been produced for work carried out in Hull, there were no bills or receipts for work carried out abroad - and this was simply because they had never existed.

However, I did manage to inject a lighter note with the remark that with so many breakdowns, I was beginning to wonder how we had ever managed to get the ship out of the River Humber, never mind to the fishing grounds.

With so many negative comments about the state of repair of the ships, I felt that I had to speak out about the regular work done by the crew, which included either a morning or an afternoon on the way to the fishing grounds that was always spent greasing anything that turned. This included the main winch, all of the blocks and sheaves, the five ton winch and all of the storm doors. This was routine work

and was carried out in the same way on all of the Hull and Grimsby trawlers.

With so many questions about burst pipes, it came as no great surprise when one of the inquiry assessors asked me if I knew what Thistlebond was. It was something of a surprise when he asked if I could describe it, and I replied that it was used in a way similar to a sticking plaster, laid over a fracture and covered with a compound that would set solid. This was used mainly to repair fractured pipes and I made the comment that I would not be surprised if many ships did not have more Thistlebond on their pipework than original piping.

Of course there had been breakdowns on board, but none of these had ever been serious enough to warrant taking the ship into port. Apart from the usual minor repairs, the Ranger Castor had never had a major engine defect of any description, despite all the allegations that had been made during the inquiry.

Shortly before the inquiry came to a close that day, the last witness was Terry Thresh, a local lad from Hessle Road and one of four brothers, all of whom had obtained their skipper's certificates at a comparatively early age. Terry had spent much of his career with Boyd Line, coming ashore after thirty years at sea to take over as the company's general manager before he retired.

Despite all the evidence that had been presented, there was still a hard core of people who were convinced that the Gaul had been fishing at the time of her loss, but it has to be said that most of these people had spent little, if any, time fishing.

Terry Thresh explained how he would have gone about clearing a sea-bed cable caught over a trawl door, something that I and doubtless many of the fishermen present were familiar with, but which I am sure many people in the room had not the slightest understanding of. Terry was also asked about the doors usually used across the top at the ramp of most stern trawlers. He explained that on one occasion, he had experienced a large following sea had struck the closed gates, resulting in some damage to them that resulted in them being difficult to open when the time came to resume fishing. Terry told the inquiry that after that incident, he had made a habit of leaving the doors open. This was a habit that I had also adopted after a similar experience during heavy weather on a winter trip to Bear Island.

The theory that the Gaul could have snagged a cable while fishing was brought to everyone's attention by Mr. Eric Long. For myself, I could never accept that anyone could be so stupid as to lay an uncovered cable of any kind on Cape Bank, an area fished heavily by trawlers on practically every day of the year.

I could also not accept the method proposed by Mr. Long to clear a cable in a gale of wind. This involved using a gilson wire to heave the cable almost to the top of the stern gantry, thus transferring the weight of the cable from the comparatively low point of the towing sheave to another point high above the deck. This proposal was not well received by the many skippers and mates at the inquiry.

From an early stage of the proceedings, the duff and offal chutes on the Gaul's factory deck were never out of the firing line for long. Whatever line of questioning opened up, it was never long before it was brought round to these two chutes that were located on the starboard side, leading out from the factory deck to the sea.

The inquiry heard form the marine surveyors that these could have rusted up, but this was something that I could not accept, as the Gaul had been fishing and these chutes would have been in use right up to the last haul.

The Gaul and several other trawlers fishing on Cape Bank at the time had reported on the freezer schedule as catching sizable amounts of duffs in each haul, so the chutes would have been in constant use. Even in moderate weather, there was always movement and water splashing into them, which would have prevented them from seizing up. These chutes had a simple flap mechanism and were located not far above the waterline, so any defect would have been noticed immediately and repaired as a priority.

The duff and offal chutes were an important part of the factory deck, as it was through these that any waste left the ship from the processing area. Any problem with the chutes would have meant a lot of waste material such as duffs and pieces of whalebone building up in the factory and this was a situation that would never have been allowed to develop.

Once opened, the chutes needed no operating, with whatever waste there was to be disposed of being thrown into the chutes, after which the waste's own weight was enough to open the flap, letting it slide into the sea, while as soon as the waste had gone, the flaps closed again under their own counterbalance weight. In his evidence, George Petty has described the duff and offal chutes and told the inquiry that as far as he knew, by the time he left the ship there were no defects in the Gaul's chutes

On the many occasions that I had visited the factory decks of the many ships I served on, I had frequently needed to use the chutes myself to dispose of waste and I had never once been aware of a chute that had seized up through rust or any other reason. The flaps were so efficient that even when the sea had passed right down the side of the ship, they closed up as intended and there was no ingress of water at all, only the sound of air being forced into the factory deck from around what seemed to be perfectly watertight flaps.

Yet the inquiry was being asked to consider a hundred tonnes of water making its way into the Gaul's factory deck in a very short time indeed through chutes that had never malfunctioned. This seemed to be the direction that the inquiry was taking, with the idea that the duff and offal chutes on the factory deck had failed to allow the factory deck to flood being seen as the most likely reason for the Gaul's loss. In my own mind I was far from convinced that there had been any ingress of water in this way. I also found it hard to pay too much attention to reports that the Gaul had been seen laid broadside to the wind, as I knew from my own experience that no skipper of a high-sided freezer trawler would want his ship in this position as very quickly the ship would find itself stern to wind, which was not a very healthy position to be in, certainly not in deteriorating weather for any length of time.

Throughout the inquiry, a number of people

who were unable to attend in person made available statements regarding their positions at the time. One of these was Ben Ashcroft, the son of one of the most successful skippers in Hull and a successful fisherman in his own right, Ben Ashcroft had sailed as skipper at the early age of only 21, working for many years for Hellyer Brothers as had his father Arthur Ambrose Ashcroft, who in the Benvolio had completed a string of short trips with excellent grossings that are still talked about today. Ben had skippered a number of the company's trawlers and by the time of the loss of the Gaul had come ashore to take over the post of ship's husband for British United Trawlers. He had been the ideal choice to take over the role of managing a 30-strong workforce responsible for all of the maintenance on company trawlers between trips.

In his statement, Ben Ashcroft stated that he had visited the Gaul several times prior to her sailing in January 1974, and that these had been nothing untoward when he had visited her for the last time just prior to sailing, with no sign of any unusual equipment. Further to his statement, he mentioned that it was a quite normal situation for there to be water on the factory deck of a trawler while fish was being washed and processed. He commented that skipper Peter Nellist as a fully competent seaman who had in fact sailed with him as mate of the Cassio, and Ben went so far as to praise him as a first class mate and seaman and added that he had no doubts whatsoever about Peter Nellist's qualities as an experienced trawler skipper.

This was only one of the many tributes to Peter Nellist in the emotion-charged room, and of course there were many others form every skipper called to give evidence.

In May 1974 the Norwegian whaler Rover had recovered a life buoy close into the land that was later identified as having belonged to the Gaul by the team who had painted the ship in its new colours during the handover from the Ranger Fishing Company to British United Trawlers and the change of name from Ranger Castor to the Gaul.

Although I have never seen this life buoy as a great mystery, it was another topic that was highlighted by the Wreck Commissioner Mr. Justice Steele who was chairing the inquiry. Speaking to the courtroom, he said that he recognised that this was a cause of concern to the families of the crew and that he would assist with solving any oddities that he could.

At the time of the life buoy's recovery, it added to the speculation that the Gaul had been sunk by a foreign power, which at that time during the Cold War could only mean the Soviet Union. I had heard it mentioned that the life buoy could have been planted to put anyone off searching for the Gaul, although I never met anyone who could explain how a life buoy floating with wind and current for three months could achieve this.

But after all the speculation about duff chutes and floating life buoys, it was a change to hear an account by Jeremy Coleman of a weather hindcast carried out by a certain Dr. Cardone, using information on wind fields, sea states and local observations to build up a picture of how wind and weather conditions had developed. Dr. Cardone's hindcast covered the period from 1st to the 9th of February 1974, during which the Gaul arrived on the grounds and began fishing, up to the time that we assume she was lost. A slide was shown to the inquiry of the weather state on the 7th of February, showing the Gaul in the northern part of a large depression that was centred on the Baltic and moving east, with the weather conditions in the Barents Sea no more than a force six at midday on that day.

By 1800 that day, the wind had freshened to a force seven, and at midnight it is estimated that the Gaul was still fishing in wind speeds of in the region of 25 knots. Around midnight the weather appears to have taken a turn for the worse, steadily deteriorating overnight to a wind speed of 40 knots and considerable seas by 0600 on the 8th of February, by which time most of the trawlers had stopped fishing.

According to the hindcast, by midday on the 8th of February, the wind was a force 9, an estimated 40 knots, with reports of heavy snow and by 1800 that day, there had been no moderation in the weather. The estimated maximum wave height on Cape Bank at the time has been put at 12.50 metres, or 41 feet, but in view of the known damage sustained by a number of trawlers fishing there, I am certain that the reports from some very experienced skippers in the area of some much larger waves have not been exaggerated. Also to be taken into consideration was that the current runs in an easterly direction, opposite to the direction of wind and sea with the Gaul at a less than ideal position on almost the shoalest part of Cape Bank.

The weather was a factor that was returned to several times and every skipper and mate who gave evidence did not fail to comment on how severe it had been. Fishermen are down to earth people who do not habitually exaggerate anything, yet every one made the point that the conditions were unusually harsh on the day we assume the Gaul to have been lost.

Evidence from skipper Michael Keillor, who at the time had been junior bosun of the Farnella, told how the ship had been hit by a huge wave while dodging on Cape Bank. He commented that while a force ten gale presents severe weather conditions, the weather at the time had been more extreme than would be expected in any gale.

Mr. Keillor described how, when the weather had eased, he and the crew were able to assess the damage. This included how a derrick between forty and fifty feet above deck level had been lost during the storm. The skipper of the Farnella at the time had said that the weather had been so bad that the ship's bows had been stoved in. I felt that Mr. Keillor had given a good and accurate account of the conditions and left nobody in any doubt as to how bad the weather can be on those fishing grounds in the middle of winter.

Skipper Alf Eagle of the Farnella described the same incident and his comments were that the weather was a s bad as he had ever seen in the Barents Sea, adding that with continuous snow and poor visibility, it was practically impossible to see these huge seas coming until they had almost hit the ship.

Skipper Peter Abbey, who had served in a number of the Ranger ships and was skipper of the Arab in February 1974, described the weather as south-easterly force 8/9, gusting force 10, with heavy seas and continuous snow. He added that he had seen worse weather, but I do not doubt this, taking into account his considerable experience.

Skipper Ken Madden of the Kelt - another of the C class trawlers - described the weather as force 9 to 10, while skipper Ernie McCoid on the Pict, another modern freezer owned by British United Trawlers, explained how his ship had sustained damage when she hit a terrific sea head on that actually stopped the ship dead in its tracks. This also caused damage to the Pict's plating in front of the bridge and swept away some gear from the deck.

The Orsino, another British United Trawlers freezer was also in the area, skippered by Dick Spencer who described that the seas were as high as the bridge, which in a vessel of this size is a considerable height.

Mick Patterson, who had been mate of the Criscilla, told the inquiry that the only way you would want a ship heading would be head to wind under those conditions, describing the wind as being force 9 to 10.

Yet we cannot overlook the fact that there were a number of other trawlers, some of them more vulnerable side trawlers, within a few miles of the position at the time we presume the Gaul was lost. The wind was from something of an unusual direction for the time of year, as many skippers will point out that as trawlers assemble on the Norwegian coast in the areas of Malangen Bank and Norwest Bank, and up to Bear Island, the gales tend to be from the north-west, as so many skippers have found to their cost when shooting a lot of warp as they ventured into the deeper water off the edges of the banks.

Like so many others who have dodged through these waters in coal and oil burning side trawlers as well as in modern larger stern trawlers, through storm force winds, we normally came through them shaken but fully intact. Yet in this case it seems that even with winds short of full storm force and from the unusual direction of ESE had produced such high seas that many trawlers suffered an unusual amount of damage.

As the inquiry progressed and concerned itself with the results of tank tests and the volume of water that would be needed to sink the

Gaul, I began to get the distinct impression that many people had already made up their minds as to the causes of her loss. Water entering the factory deck through the duff and offal chutes while the Gaul had the wind on her port quarter seemed to be the favoured explanation, yet I am still not convinced.

It may be my advancing years, but it seemed to me as well that most of the film we were shown of the tank tests with the model of the Gaul showed her with the wind aft of the beam, a position that could support the duff and offal chute theory.

During the inquiry, we had heard from many experienced skippers just how severe the weather at the time had been, bad enough for trawlers to sustain damage even when dodging head to wind, If we are to believe the British and Norwegian skippers who reported storm damage, and I see no reason not to, then I find it very hard to believe that Peter Nellist - who everyone, myself included, had spoken so highly of - could have had the Gaul steaming on a course with the wind on the port quarter, especially as the safer and more comfortable option would have been simply to reduce speed and head into the wind.

Even back at the 1974 inquiry, I remember experienced skippers describing the weather at the time on Cape Bank as simply atrocious, remarking that under those conditions, the only way you would want a ship heading would be into the wind and I still find it inconceivable that Peter Nellist would have done anything other than just that.

There had been suggestions that the Gaul had been on a south-westerly course towards Malangen Bank, as Peter Nellist had been reported at one point before the weather had worsened to its full extent as saying that he intended to steam in towards the land, while mate Maurice Spurgeon was reported as having said in a conversation over the VHF that the skipper had said they would be in for a long dodge this time.

The Gaul would have had a considerable distance to travel before picking up any kind of a lee, and after having only been on Cape Bank for two days, it seems unlikely that Peter Nellist would have wanted to move from the area where he had so far seen the best fishing of the trip to make the substantial move to Malangen Bank.

These were my thoughts as we came to the end of the four week inquiry, but there was still time to hear from another of the experts who had accompanied us on the Seisranger survey.

A marine engineer, Graham McCombie was called to give evidence at the end of the final week. He explained that there was no evidence to suggest that the Gaul had suffered an engine failure prior to her sinking. He told the inquiry that the position that the propeller had been found in indicated that she had not lost power until after she had begun to sink. He explained that the pitch of the propeller would have returned automatically to zero if the engine had failed while the ship was afloat.

Asked by Counsel Nigel Meeson QC if it would be safe to infer that the full ahead pitch found on the Gaul's propeller proved that the Gaul had not suffered a breakdown, Graham McCombie replied readily that this was his interpretation.

Under further questioning by Timothy Saloman, the Gaul families' counsel, he was commented that British United Trawlers had not seemed to have carried out the same level of maintenance on the Gaul and her sister ships as the previous owners had. All in all, I found all the talk of maintenance somewhat harsh on the new owners, who had taken over the Ranger fleet with the Gaul midway through a trip at Newfoundland. The Ranger ships had spent hardly any time in dock since the takeover by British United Trawlers, leaving little time for maintenance and it was only on the last full trip in late 1973 that the Gaul had sailed from the port of Hull for her new owners.

One of the final exchanges of the inquiry took place when Barry Peck, a master mariner with experience in laying underwater cables, took the stand. He told the inquiry that he was sure that the cable seen on underwater footage near the wreck of the Gaul was a telecommunications cable, although this was definitely not the opinion of Nigel Meeson QC, who questioned him at length. After comments about the Gaul having snagged a cable, Mr. Justice Steel also questioned Mr. Peck's expertise on a number of the answers that he gave.

As any fisherman knows, trawl warps have for years been marked at twenty-five fathoms intervals. Although I could splice a wire at a young age, I lay no claim to being an expert, but I say without a doubt that the wire close to the wreck of the Gaul was certainly a trawl warp. I would go so far as to say that the two wires running parallel to each other on the sea-bed were most likely from the same trawler that had been unfortunate enough to lose an entire set of gear after coming fast on the wreck of the Gaul. Apart from a section of combination wire rope that was almost rotted through, there was nothing that had been seen in any of the surveys that remotely resembled a communications cable.

Nigel Meeson's questioning of Mr. Peck had certainly been interesting and livened up the proceedings. Referring to a length of cable that appeared to be going in a straight line, Mr. Peck said that it seemed to have a slight curve to it, at which Mr. Meeson replied that he needed to see his optician if that were the case. These hostile exchanges continued throughout this evidence, but to anyone in the room with even a passing knowledge of fishing gear, the cable in question could not have been anything other than a trawl warp with thirty years of marine growth around it, as the marks on the wire made very clear. After Mr. Peck's evidence, I do not think that many people in the room were convinced that there were any communication cables in the vicinity of the Gaul or that she had been lost after picking up such a cable on her fishing gear.

Before the inquiry closed for the weekend, Tony Bowman, who runs a marine casualty investigation business in Hampshire and who also sat as the chairman of a panel of experts advising the inquiry, spoke to say that in the opinion of the panel of experts, the most likely cause of the loss of the Gaul had been through flooding of the factory deck through the duff and offal chutes. I don't think that this came as a surprise to anyone.

Mr. Bowman went on to explain that in his opinion, the crew would have been unable to send a distress signal owing to the ship's angle of list, describing how a climbing a staircase with an angle of 45° becomes similar scaling a mountain when there is an additional list. He added that it would be impossible to rule out that some of the crew may have been injured and would have had no time to take effective action.

Although I agreed with practically everything that Tony Bowman had to say, I still regard the theory of the duff and offal chutes as being the reason for the factory deck flooding as being unconvincing.

Before bringing the proceedings to a close for a two week break, Mr. Justice Steel announced that when the court was reconvened, there would be an opportunity for the families of the 36 men lost with the Gaul to have their say. He added that he wanted them to have an opportunity to raise any matter they thought relevant and to throw any further light that they could on what had happened to the Gaul.

He also said that the families would have the opportunity to draw to his attention any matters they felt had not been addressed and to voice any concern they felt at evidence that had been presented to the inquiry. With these words, the inquiry was closed.

After sitting there for a month, George Petty and I had both had a chance to look back and reflect on the many changes that had taken place in the few years since we had both retired. The courtroom resembled the bridge of a spaceship, scattered with computers and screens. There is no doubt that it had been an interesting month, with the inquiry well organised and with people from all walks of life coming from miles away to give their evidence. It had been a pleasure to meet some old friends and faces from the past, each one with his own views of what the inquiry's conclusions would be when the court reopened for its final few days.

Closing the Inquiry

The inquiry into the loss of the Gaul reconvened on the 23rd of February 2004, but not before a few other matters had come to light. During the two week recess, several letters had arrived and these were read out to the court. But the one that was of the most interest to me was from Charles Powell, who had been mate of the Ranger Castor on her maiden voyage. He had made the remark that she had always been breaking down, but to clarify his comments,he stated that he had been referring only to the teething problems that occurred during the first few weeks - something that many people, the press included, had latched onto and interpreted in the wrong light. Charlie went on to state that to the best of his knowledge, the following two trips had been trouble-free.

I felt that Charlie's comments vindicated my own position, when I had told the court, during some intense questioning from Mr. Salomon during the early stages of the inquiry, that I had never had to take the ship in for any repairs.

The Gaul's factory deck and the duff and offal chutes were once again brought to the fore when Mr. Meeson commented that it was common practice for water to be left running on the factory deck with the water systems rarely turned off, then suggesting that the factory deck could have been left unmanned for as long as six hours. This suggestion amazed me and a number of other people who had spent long periods in factory trawlers.

Journalist Graham Smith dropped the cat among the pigeons, stating that an anonymous source, a former chief petty officer on a nuclear submarine, had claimed to have overheard a conversation between two officers in which one of the two men remarked that a submarine in the Barents Sea in 1974 had snagged a trawler's nets and dragged it along until it sank. The allegation was that the submarine had not been permitted to search for survivors, being under orders to remain undetected.

Not surprisingly, with all the accumulated evidence to show that the Gaul had not been fishing at the time of her loss, Mr. Meeson dismissed the allegations as absurd, commenting that he had spoken to Graham Smith, who was not able to provide any further information.

In his closing speech, Mr. Meeson entirely ruled out that the Gaul had been lost after snagging a sea-bed cable, or through fire, ice, explosion, collision or grounding and went on to squash the long-held theory that the Gaul had been boarded by the Soviets and deliberately sunk.

His final comment was that the Gaul's loss could most likely be attributed to accumulated water on the factory deck, which had caused her to list heavily to starboard, also preventing the crew from taking any effective measures or sending a distress signal.

The second Gaul inquiry came to a finish on the 27th of February 2004, thirty years after the events under review had taken place.

Throughout that day those of us attending listened to the summing up speeches, before which Mr. Justice Steel had invited anyone present who wished to stand and air their views.

Ray Smith, who had campaigned for so long for redundancy payments for fishermen, gave his own personal view of what it was like working on the factory deck of a ship like the Gaul, as he had sailed in one of the three other C class trawlers. He gave a totally different picture to the ones presented earlier in the hearing, telling the court that the factory decks of these ships were so dry that it was often possible to walk about in a pair of slippers.

My own opportunity to speak came shortly before the end of the morning session, as there were a number of points that I wanted to raise that I felt had not been brought to the court's notice.

My comments were to make plain that I did not feel that the ideas that had been put before the court about the Gaul being lost through water entering the factory deck through the duff and offal chutes, with a build-up of water on the deck aided by water being left running was a credible theory. It had been claimed that this situation had been brought about with the Gaul steaming with the wind on the port quarter and it had been suggested that the chutes could have rusted up.

I took the opportunity to remind the court that the very experienced fishermen who had given evidence had described the weather conditions at the time as 'appalling' and 'atrocious', and another had made the comment that the only way you would want a ship heading under those conditions would be head to wind. I do not for one moment see any reason to doubt the words of these men.

Although human error can not be ruled out, I believe the idea that water could have built up gradually on the factory deck is not a possibility. There were enough people who would have had reason to visit the factory deck of the ship even when the Gaul was not fishing that something of this nature would have been noticed. The engineers used the factory deck as their normal route to and from the engine room and the Baader mechanics would certainly have had reason to be there, as would the men who carried out the fire rounds that were taken seriously on these ships after the losses of life that had occurred due to fires on several British freezer trawlers in the previous few years.

I have always maintained that head to wind in severe weather conditions, the Gaul was as good a ship as you could wish to have under you and that she was not lost in this way, for all of the reasons that have already been explained.

As well as Ray Smith and myself, many relatives of men lost on the Gaul took the opportunity to speak and I am sure that there could have been nobody in the room who was not moved as they listened to the memories read out to the court, describing loved ones who were still as fresh in their minds as they had been thirty years before.

It was an emotional time for those of us who had attended the inquiry, some of us having been there every day. For some it ended in tears, but for others I am sure there was simply relief that this long inquiry had finally come to a close. It had certainly been an eventful and memorable time, and the strain showed on many faces as people mingled, paying their tributes and expressing their thanks and goodbyes.

The Inquiry's Findings - At Last

The findings of the inquiry into the loss of the Gaul were due to be made public on Friday the 17th of December 2004 at the Guildhall in city of Hull. As George Petty and I had both sailed in the Gaul, and had also attended every day of the inquiry and given evidence, we decided that it would be fitting if we were both there to hear the findings of a long and exhausting inquiry.

Since the close of the hearing in February, we had met several times and speculated on the witnesses who had given evidence, many of them under oath, and the inquiry's eventual findings that we were about to hear read out by Mr. Justice Steel, who had been assisted throughout by assessors Dr. David Aldwinkle, Peter Craven and Alan Hopper.

It had been widely anticipated that the inquiry's findings would point towards the duff and offal chutes being responsible for an ingress of water that built up and caused the Gaul to capsize, so quickly that there was no time for a distress call to be transmitted. Once proceedings had got underway, this is what was duly announced and it did not surprise me the least little bit.

What did surprise me was the findings that the reason for the duff and offal chutes being found in the open position by the survey was down to poor maintenance and that they had rusted up in that position. Yet it was the opinion of those who had sailed in these C class trawlers that if the chutes had rusted up, then it would certainly have been in the closed position, and this is an opinion that I would agree with entirely.

I am of the belief that it is too much of a coincidence that both of these chutes should rust up in the same position. I believe firmly that both chutes were in perfect working order right up to the time that the Gaul was lost, and they were forced open by pressure from within the factory deck, as they had been designed to do.

Based on the evidence that the freezer schedule had showed of the Gaul and other ships catching duffs during their time on Cape Bank, but there is no report of the Gaul's crew having trouble dumping the duffs back. With the Gaul at an early stage of the trip that could not have been completed without these chutes working properly , the spell of bad weather that the Gaul was dodging through presented an ideal opportunity to steam to Honningsvåg to have them repaired. But unlike the steering problems that had been reported, there had been no mention of a problem with the duff and offal chutes.

A year after the loss of the Gaul, I sailed as skipper of her sister ship Kelt, taking the ship form Milford Haven with a skeleton crew before bringing her back to Hull to prepare for a voyage to the Norwegian coast, leaving on the 1st of February 1975.

Part of this trip was spent on Cape Bank and apart from the usual gales and conditions that go hand-in-hand with fishing in the Arctic in winter, there was nothing at all unusual about the trip - no breakdowns, no engine problems and certainly not anything wrong with the duff and offal chutes. In fact, I served in four of the Ranger trawlers and was never aware of a problem with any of their chutes. I am convinced that they were never put down for maintenance by the shore crews simply because they were of simple, robust construction and never went wrong.

I was also concerned that with the time and expense that went into the inquiry, I could never understand why a replica of the duff and offal chutes was not built to demonstrate their operation to the court. This would have been relatively straightforward, but as it was, a photocopied diagram of the chute mechanism was used, and this showed very little.

Let us not forget that thirty years on, two of the Gaul's sister ships are still fishing in the North Atlantic, something that may come as a surprise to the people who were so keen to condemn these ships, even though they were practically new at the time of the Gaul's loss, the Gaul being the newest of the four.

Reading through the overview of the findings, there were several items that took me by surprise, but none more than the entry stating that it was believed that after 0915 on the day that the Gaul is believed to have been lost, there would have been no reason for any of the crew to enter the factory deck, even though the inquiry had been informed that the factory deck was regularly visited even when the ship was not actively fishing.

Experienced skippers and mates from Fleetwood, Hull and Grimsby, who had all been fishing on Cape Bank, had given evidence and all expressed their accounts of how harsh the weather conditions had been on that day, yet it appears that the knowledge and experience of these men counted very little to the inquiry.

I am certain that the Gaul was dodging like every other vessel at the time, and the assumption that she was on a southerly course to reach shelter appears to rest entirely on a single remark during a VHF conversation. I believe that this may have been the skipper's original intention, but as the weather deteriorated still further and from what people who were on those fishing grounds at the time have told me, like every other trawler on Cape Bank that day, the Gaul was dodging head to wind for a considerable period before she was lost.

Evidence from men with years of experience who had seen it all time and again seems to have been largely disregarded. I find it very hard to believe that the Gaul was on a southerly course in these conditions with the wind two to four points fore side of her port beam. In earlier conversation, an experienced skipper recalled hearing the mate of the Gaul mentioning the skipper telling him that they were in for a long dodge, yet in spite of this evidence, the inquiry found the Gaul to be on a southerly heading, which undoubtedly suits the duff and offal chutes scenario that the Gaul's loss has been attributed to.

My own feeling is that the Gaul was dodging head to wind in the vicinity of J Marr's trawler Southella. Whether the Gaul was at the end of her run and turning to run back before the wind, or whether she was knocked off course is open to endless peculation, but I believe that she was caught broadside to the weather at the critical moment that she was hit by the three successive and exceptionally large seas that shortly after broke over the Southella, where they caused damage. The open doors on the Gaul's deck would certainly have contributed to her flooding, but the critical point would have been when the fish hatches that had not been clamped shut fell open as she listed past 90°, allowing water to flood into the factory deck and from this point there was no hope that the Gaul could have righted herself.

But in spite of everything, much good had come from the inquiry, although, as could have been expected, a number of people could not accept the inquiry's findings. Although I myself am not able to agree with the findings of the inquiry on how the Gaul was lost, I could only fully support the inquiry's findings on the spyship theories and the far-fetched tales of Soviet involvement in the Gaul's loss. The survey and the inquiry went to some considerable lengths to allow the theories of communications cables being around the wreck to be dismissed and to make it plain that there was no equipment related to intelligence gathering in the Gaul's bridge. I now feel that for the most part those people who had been influenced by a sensationalist media that had time and again tried to grab headlines with tales of spying in the far North have now widely accepted that this was not the case.

Maybe the final words should be those of Mr. Justice David Steel, who in his summing up said that: "We also hope that the crew of the Gaul can now continue to rest in peace, memories of them no longer disturbed by the sort of speculation that was perhaps inevitably caused by their dramatic and apparently inexplicable disappearance."

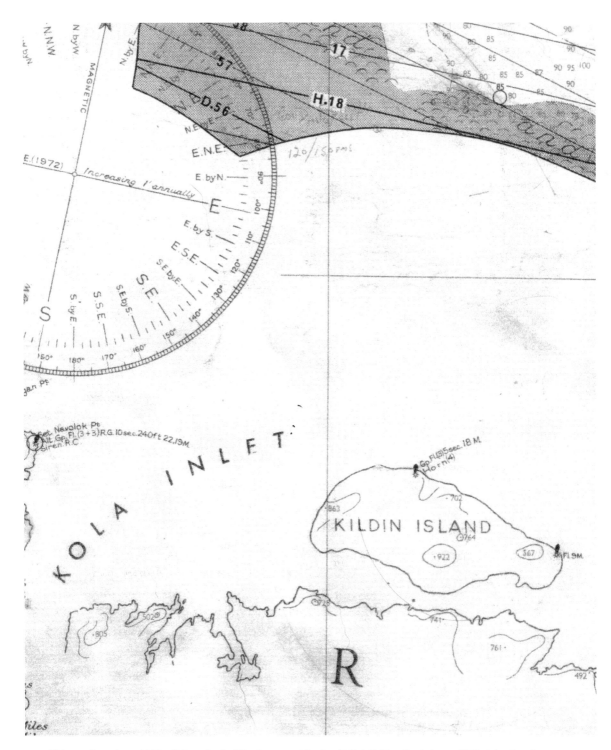

This section of an old Kingfisher chart of the type used by the British fishing fleet shows Kildin Island and the eastern side of the Kola Peninsula, as well as fishing grounds to the north. Kildin Island was the home of the mighty Soviet Northern Fleet, just twelve miles from where British trawlers were routinely able to fish quite legally. Needless to say, sightings of warships and submarines were nothing unusual along this stretch of the coast near Murmansk.

Appendix – The Freezer Schedule

This is the freezer schedule from the day of the Gaul's arrival on Cape Bank.
The Gaul failed to report on the 1630 or the 2330 freezer scheds on the 8th of February.
It has been generally assumed that she was lost on 8th of February 1974.

Tuesday 05/02/74, 1030

Dane	2 Hauls 70, 90 Baskets
Swanella	Steaming
A Freebooter	48 blox. 70 baskets
Cassio	Steaming
Victory	40 baskets, now steaming westerly
Pict	150, 80 baskets. Just hauling. Yesterday 3 tons
Kirkella	Shooting soon North Cape Bank
Orsino	Blank night, steaming
Skua	60, 100 baskets
Arab	100, 20 baskets
Criscilla	30, 45 blox, steaming
Cordella	39 blox, steaming
L Parkes	slack night changing grounds
Northella	70, 40 baskets
Gaul	40 baskets, steaming west
A Raider	100 baskets, Malangen
Farnella	Steaming
Sir Fred	Left yesterday AM.
Skipper B Wharham. BND, NNE	

1630

Dane	1 haul, 40 baskets, paralysed, changed trawl
Swanella	36 blox. Same position
A Freebooter	80 baskets
Cassio	Shooting soon
Victory	1st tow. Same position as Arab
Pict	160, 160 baskets
Kirkella	First tow Cape Bank
Orsino	Just shot, Cape Bank
Skua	80 baskets
Arab	100 baskets, parted headline leg
Criscilla	First tow Cape Bank

Cordella	Just shot, Northella position
L Parkes	Just shot, North Cape Bank
Northella	120 baskets
Gaul	First tow. North Cape Bank Group
A Raider	80 baskets
Farnella	Steaming

2330

Dane	60 Baskets 24 hrs 2. 18 tons fillets Malangen
Swanella	72 blox. Total blox 192
A Freebooter	80 baskets. Total blox 220
Cassio	50 baskets
Victory	85 blox including fish from yesterday Total blox16
Pict	100 baskets
Kirkella	78 blox 80 baskets
Orsino	Blank day Northella position
Skua	80 baskets. 24 hrs 5 tons fillets
Arab	70 baskets. 24 hrs 5 tons fillets
Criscilla	50 baskets
Cordella	70, 70 baskets
L Parkes	22 blox North Cape Bank. Just hauling
Northella	100 baskets. No block tally. Conveyor broken in factory
Gaul	100 baskets, including 10 baskets of duff
A Raider	Malangen, laid with freezer trouble
Farnella	Steaming

Wednesday 06/02/74, 1030

Dane	80 Baskets, cod ends out, 20 baskets
Swanella	47 blox. 120 baskets. North Cape Bank
A Freebooter	40, 90 baskets

Cassio	Bound Honningsvag
Victory	90, 40 baskets, same position as Northella
Pict	60, 60 baskets 72,00N 25,10E. Y'day, 7 ton fillets
Kirkella	60 blox, 70 baskets. group position
Orsino	54,48 blox
Skua	200, 40 baskets
Arab	100, 100 baskets
Criscilla	25, 19 blox, 80 baskets
Cordella	70 baskets
L Parkes	71 blox. 100 baskets
Northella	40, 50 baskets
Gaul	90, 100 baskets
A Raider	69 blox
Farnella	Steaming
Sir Fred Parkes	Steaming

1630

Dane	Not hauled yet
Swanella	40 blox
A Freebooter	Steamed back. Just hauling
Cassio	Alongside in Honningsvag
Victory	50 baskets, just hauling
Pict	60 baskets
Kirkella	90 baskets
Orsino	36 blox, just hauling
Skua	30 baskets, paralysed
Arab	70 baskets
Criscilla	27 blox
Cordella	50 baskets
L Parkes	36 blox
Northella	50, 100 baskets
Gaul	40 baskets, parted warp link in sheave
A Raider	75 blox
Farnella	1st haul, North Cape Bank
Sir Fred Parkes	Steaming

2330

Dane	130 baskets. 24 hours 3 tons fillets
Swanella	17, 24 blox. Total blox 216
A Freebooter	80, 70 baskets. Total blox 205
Cassio	In Honningsvag
Victory	40, 100 baskets. Total blox 216
Pict	Just shooting pelagic

Kirkella	70 blox. Total blox 230
Orsino	55, 43 blox. Total blox 236
Skua	40 baskets. 24 hrs 4 tons fillets
Arab	100 baskets
Criscilla	100 baskets. Total blox 192. Just hauling
Cordella	64 blox
L Parkes	41 blox Total blox 271
Gaul	Not heard
A Raider	92 blox. CEO since shooting 373 blox
Northella	120 baskets 71.50N, 25.00E Total blox 273
Farnella	97 blox. Just hauled 20 baskets
Sir Fred Parkes	Steaming

Thursday 07/02/74
1030

Dane	120, 50 Baskets
Swanella	267, 65 blox. North Cape Bank
A Freebooter	48, 41 blox
Cassio	1st Tow. North Cape Bank
Victory	40, 120 baskets. 6 hours tow winch trouble
Pict	On first tow bottom trawl. Yesterday 2 tons fillets
Kirkella	60, 90 baskets. Some duff each haul. North Cape Bank
Orsino	34, 34 blox
Skua	120, 60 baskets
Arab	Blank night. Steamed Shot yesterday 4-5 tons
Criscilla	40, 40 blox, 70 baskets
Cordella	28, 49 blox
L Parkes	28, 27 blox, 70 baskets
Northella	33, 54 blox, 80 baskets. Some duffs
Gaul	70, 70, 70 baskets, lat 72.15N, 25.50E, lot of duff
A Raider	39 blox
Sir Fred Parkes	Steaming
Kelt	4 tons fillets. North Cape Bank

1630

Dane	50 Baskets
Swanella	26 blox
A Freebooter	58 blox
Cassio	5 blox
Victory	Just hauling
Pict	60 baskets
Kirkella	60 baskets
Orsino	23 blox. Just hauling
Skua	120 baskets
Arab	40 baskets. Steamed Shot North Cape Bank
Criscilla	40 baskets
Cordella	77 blox
L Parkes	13 blox
Northella	40 baskets
Gaul	60 baskets
A Raider	35 blox. Cod ends out
Farnella	40 baskets
Sir Fred Parkes	Bound Andenes to drop man off

2330

Dane	Parted back strop Nil. 24 hours 2-13 tons fillets
Swanella	33 blox. Total blox 191
A Freebooter	29 blox. Total blox 170. Malangen Bank
Cassio	80baskets
Victory	Bound Honningsvag. Winch job
Pict	70 baskets
Kirkella	1st tow Hjelmsoy
Orsino	30 blox. Total blox 128 72.25N 22.40E
Skua	30 baskets. 24 hrs 4 tons fillets 70.20N 17.20E
Arab	80 baskets. 24 hrs 2 tons fillets
Criscilla	20 baskets. Total blox 167. Cape Bank Just hauling
Cordella	2 Hauls, 60 baskets. Nil
L Parkes	69 blox Total blox 221
Northella	36 blox
Gaul	1 haul paralysed/ Laid mending
A Raider	77 blox. Just hauled 150. NW corner of N.West Bank
Farnella	Since shooting 290 blox
Sir Fred Parkes	

Friday 08/02/74, 1030

Dane	120, 100 Baskets. Tiesten ground
Swanella	49 blox. North Cape Bank
A Freebooter	50, 60 baskets
Cassio	Laid weather
Victory	In Honningsvag
Pict	Dodging North Cape Bank area. Y'day 1-5 tons
Kirkella	Laid/ Dodging
Orsino	1 haul Nil. Now laid/ Dodging
Skua	50, 40 baskets
Arab	Laid for weather
Criscilla	Laid for weather
Cordella	L/Dodging
L Parkes	L/Dodging
Northella	L/Dodging
Gaul	Laid for weather North Cape Bank
A Raider	39 blox78, 35 blox
Farnella	L/ Dodging North Cape Bank
Sir Fred Parkes	First haul North-West Bank 30 baskets

1630

Dane	110 Baskets
Swanella	L/D
A Freebooter	85 blox
Cassio	L/D
Victory	Honningsvag
Pict	L/D
Kirkella	L/D
Orsino	L/D
Skua	80 baskets
Arab	L/D
Criscilla	L/D
Cordella	L/D
L Parkes	L/D
Northella	Dodging down Porsanger fjord to put man ashore
Gaul	Not heard
A Raider	41 blox. 50 baskets. Belly out
Farnella	L/D
Sir Fred Parkes	60, 60 baskets